The Imbalance of Power

THE IMBALANCE OF POWER

Leadership, Masculinity and Wealth in the Amazon

Marc Brightman

berghahn
NEW YORK · OXFORD
www.berghahnbooks.com

First published in 2016 by
Berghahn Books
www.berghahnbooks.com

© 2016, 2020 Marc Brightman
First paperback edition published in 2020

Library of Congress Cataloging-in-Publication Data

Names: Brightman, Marc, author.
Title: The imbalance of power : leadership, masculinity and wealth in the Amazon / Marc
   Brightman.
Description: New York : Berghahn Books, [2017] | Includes bibliographical references and
   index.
Identifiers: LCCN 2016022366| ISBN 9781785333095 (hardback : alk. paper) |
   ISBN 9781785333101 (ebook)
Subjects: LCSH: Trio Indians. | Wayana Indians. | Akuriyo Indians. | Power (Social sci-
   ences)—Guiana. | Group identity—Guiana. | Leadership—Guiana. |
   Masculinity—Political aspects—Guiana. | Guiana—Ethnic relations.
Classification: LCC F2420.1.T7 B75 2017 | DDC 305.800988—dc23
LC record available at https://lccn.loc.gov/2016022366

British Library Cataloguing in Publication Data

A catalogue record for this book is available from the British Library

ISBN 978-1-78533-309-5 hardback
ISBN 978-1-78920-842-9 paperback
ISBN 978-1-78533-310-1 ebook

Dedicated to Kïsi

The Guiana Indians are a perfectly free people, having no division of land, and being without any government.
    —John Gabriel Stedman, *Narrative of a Five Years' Expedition against the Revolted Negroes of Surinam in Guiana*

What does a chief without power do?
    —Pierre Clastres, *Archaeology of Violence*

CONTENTS

FIGURES, ILLUSTRATIONS AND TABLES

TABLES

ACKNOWLEDGEMENTS

I was lucky enough to be introduced to lowland South American ethnology through the teaching of Peter Rivière, who has continued to help me with advice and rare material on the Trio. Stephen Hugh-Jones prepared me for the bewildering experience of fieldwork and I could not have had a better guide as I struggled to craft it into ethnography.

Many scholars and friends in England, France and Brazil have given their support: Audrey Butt Colson, Eithne Carlin, Jean-Pierre and Bonnie Chaumeil, Gérard Collomb, Damien Davy, Carlos Fausto, German Freire, Casey High, Mette High, Christine Hugh-Jones, José Antonio Kelly, James Leach, George and Laura Mentore, Henry Stobart, Marilyn Strathern, Olga Ulturgasheva, Piers Vitebsky, Eduardo Viveiros de Castro, members of the Nucléo de História Indígena e do Indigenismo of the University of São Paolo (especially Dominique Gallois, Gabriel Barbosa and Denise Grupioni). Earlier versions of the text have benefited from the suggestions of Vanessa Grotti, Stephen Hugh-Jones, Sian Lazar, George Mentore, Peter Rivière and Marilyn Strathern. Needless to say, all of its shortcomings are still my own fault.

In Suriname, I wish to thank Gilbert Luitjes for vital introductions and logistical help; Otto Dunker, for flying beyond the call of duty, green vegetables and tales of the frontier; Cees and Ineke Koelewijn, for their generous hospitality and their unique insights and anecdotes; Hillary de Bruin and the staff of Cultuurstudies in Paramaribo. In Guyana, I am grateful to Suraiya Ismail for opening her house to me and Vanessa in Georgetown; Jennifer Wishart and the members of the Amerindian Research Unit for help and advice; Adrian Gomes and his family, Ekupa and the people of Erepoimo, and the James family for their hospitality in the Rupununi. In French Guiana, the Tiouka family were warm hosts in Awala.

The collaboration of those who participated in my research was invaluable. These include Brigitte Wyngaarde (Lokono *chef coutumière*, Balaté), Jean-Auberic Charles (Kali'na *chef coutumier*, Kourou), Philippe Aquila and Guillaume Kouyouri (editors of *Oka Mag*), Beverley de Vries and Bruce Hoffman of ACT, and Annette Tjon Sie Fat of Conservation International.

I am above all grateful to all of the people who welcomed me in Tëpu and Antecume Pata, my friends and especially my host family. To protect their identities, I have used pseudonyms in the text, and I therefore list all in alphabetical order: Aiku, Aina, Airi, Antecume, Api, Demas, Deny, Ercilio, Ësoro, Itapë, Jan, Josipa, Kamenio, Kïsi, Kosani, Kulitaïkë, Kuritune, Marcel, Manase, Mati, Mimisiku, Mosesi, Nauku, Nowa, Nupi, Pakëri, Pesoro, Peti, Pikumi, Pirou, Pitu, Rïime, Rora, Rosi, Rosina, Sara, Sarakë, Sintia, Suntu, Supipi, Tapinkili, Tapiro, Thomas, Tiki, Tiwimo, Tompouce, Tumali, Tupi, Tupiro, Wakëimai. Those to whom I was closest know who they are and my warmest thanks go to them. I also thank my family for trying to understand why I needed to spend so many years in the depths of the Amazon and in the dusty corridors of the University Library. Finally, my wife Vanessa has been my constant muse and shrewdest critic since even before we became anthropologists together. This book will not really be complete – and a certain 'imbalance' will remain – until it sits next to her accompanying volume, which will offer an alternative perspective on the experiences that we shared, and whose completion has been happily delayed to nurture our two wonderful sons, Ettore and Dario.

I conducted this research thanks to funding from the ESRC, and to smaller grants from St. John's College (Cambridge), the Ling Roth Fund, the Smuts Memorial Fund and the Crowther Beynon Fund.

A Note on Trio and Wayana
Language and Orthography

Trio and Wayana are both Carib languages, and I use the orthography first introduced by missionaries from the Summer Institute of Linguistics in the 1950s, and adapted by various parties thereafter; my usage corresponds to the most current conventions taught in primary schools.[1]

Both languages have a seven vowel system:

i   ï   u   e   ë   o   a

Ï is a high-central vowel pronounced with the tongue high in the mouth and with spread lips. *Ë* is a mid-central vowel and pronounced like *a* in 'about', but with spread rather than rounded lips (Carlin 2002). The other vowels are pronounced roughly as /i:/, /u:/, /e/, /o/, /a:/.

The principal differences between Trio and Wayana orthography are with the palatal glide phoneme /j/, which is written *j* in Trio and *y* in Wayana, and the flap /r/, written *r* in Trio and *l* in Wayana (ibid. 2004). A number of proper names have their own conventional spellings independent of these orthographic conventions, e.g. 'Akuriyo'. When it is not clear from context which language is being used, terms in the text are marked 'T', 'W' or 'A' to indicate whether they are Trio, Wayana or Akuriyo. Except for proper names, non-English words are italicized.

Notes

1. Based on Carlin 2004.

ABBREVIATIONS

ACT Amazon Conservation Team

COICA *Coordenadora de las Organizaciones Indigenas de la Cuenca Amazonica*

DRC Dutch Reformed Church

DTL Door To Life Mission

FUNAI *Fundação Nacional do Índio*

MAF Mission Aviation Fellowship

T Trio

TI *Terra Indígena*

UFM Unevangelised Fields Mission

VIDS Vereniging van Inheemse Dorpshoofden in Suriname

W Wayana

WIM West Indies Mission

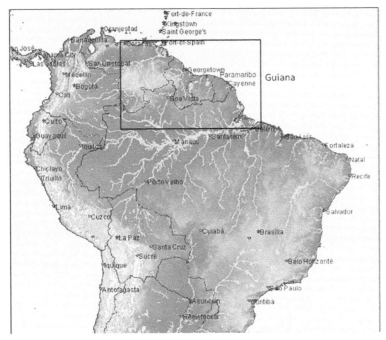

Map 1. Guiana

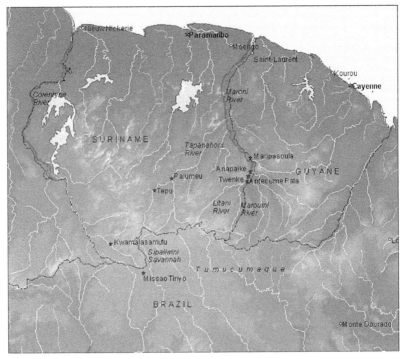

Map 2. The upper Tapanahoni

INTRODUCTION

The philosophers who have examined the foundations of society have all felt the need to go back to the
state of nature, but none of them has succeeded.
　—Jean-Jacques Rousseau *Discourse on Inequality*[1]

When I returned to Suriname in November 2011, I learned of a scandal
that was causing turmoil among the Trio. It was a case of adultery, in
which one man, Luuk, had been carrying on an affair with the wife of
another man, Sam.[2] One day Sam caught them in the act. He reacted
furiously. He waited for an opportunity, then, together with some of his
kinsmen, attacked Luuk and beat him up. Soon, rumours circulated that
Luuk wanted to demand a cash payment as compensation for the inju-
ries he had received. Sam's anger rose again. He went, again with some
kinsmen, to Luuk's house at night, armed with guns and machetes. He
seemed intent on killing him. Some men intervened, but it was clear that
the matter would have to be settled by independent parties. This was
complicated by the fact that Sam was the brother of Silvijn, a village
leader, and Luuk was married to the daughter of Douwe, the other village
leader. The dispute risked turning into a factional crisis that could tear
the whole village apart. Gossip spread like wildfire, and thanks to mobile
telephone and shortwave radio, this conflict was soon the talk of all the
Trio villages and those living in the city of Paramaribo. The church elders
held concerned discussions with their mentors in the city. At last, it was
decided that this was a matter for the church to resolve, and an American missionary who had spent his life ministering to the neighbouring

Wayana, together with the Trio Granman, Vigo, flew to Tëpu in a specially chartered light aircraft. After long consultations and deliberations, it was decided that Sam should leave the village with his family, at least for a while. The last I heard, he was to go to live in Kwamalasamutu, a large Trio village nearer the Brazilian border.

This story illustrates how a petty dispute can quickly turn into a political crisis in a small-scale society. The events were underpinned by a wide array of circumstances, which hinged upon the interplay between gender relations, kinship ties and leadership roles. They took place against the historical background of the concentration of the population around mission stations, which brought distant affines (who would previously have avoided one another) into everyday contact. The coresidence of affines brings new tensions into play, and in this case these in turn called for the intervention of a hierarchy of leadership extending beyond the specific village concerned, and even beyond the Trio themselves to some non-Amerindian organizations that have played a historic role in the demographic and material changes in Trio life over the past half-century. And yet the solution that was found at the end of this episode was perhaps surprisingly traditional: the most serious disputes among Trio people have always been resolved through the physical separation of the parties concerned. This can have implications that go beyond the interventions of existing leaders. In such cases, when a man leaves his village to allow the social harmony to be restored, his exile often marks the beginning of a new political formation: as we shall see, he may found his own village and become a leader in his own right.

This recourse to longstanding solutions to what may seem to be relatively new problems raises questions about the extent to which the dramatic social and economic changes that the Trio and their neighbours have experienced in recent decades have impinged upon long-term patterns of political action. This book is concerned accordingly with the question of cultural continuity in the face of historical change, and shows how a type of political leadership deeply grounded in specific, collectively held ideals and practices of kinship and masculinity can provide a powerful form of cultural resilience. At the same time, the book addresses the ways in which political leadership itself shapes society through space and time. On another level, it is about how a cultural ideal of masculinity is played out and realized through leadership. Leadership and masculinity are intertwined in many ways, but perhaps the most important activity common to both is the manipulation (though not necessarily the accumulation) of wealth – that is, objects and persons of value. It is through the manipulation of wealth that masculine capacities are brought to bear upon the life of the community.

Political theory, gender studies and economics converge in their shared concern with equality and inequality. In classical political theory, 'primitive' societies are assumed to be egalitarian, and property is assumed to be absent. Property and inequality are understood to be in causal relationships with each other: Thomas Hobbes (1996) takes the establishment of sovereign power and monopoly over violence to be the necessary condition for the accumulation of wealth, while Rousseau (1992) understands the emergence of private-property rights to be the cause of inequality, exploitation and subjugation. Meanwhile, gender inequality and male domination of women have been associated with the treatment of women as property since Aristotle.

Arguments about inequality rely heavily upon the assumption that culture and society exist on a separate plane of existence from nature, and place them in a separate field of analysis. Certain feminist scholars have challenged the conflation and subjection of women and nature, arguing that women are 'no more "part of nature" or "closer to nature" than men are', but few political thinkers have gone a step further to 'contest the idea that real human life proceeds in a hyperseparated sphere of culture, for which nature is inessential' (Plumwood 2006: 55). In the anthropology of indigenous Amazonia, however, it is now widely agreed that nature and culture are at best mutually constituted and context-dependent, if they are valid categories at all (Descola 2005; Seeger 1981; Viveiros de Castro 1998). This has significant implications for understanding indigenous political thought.

Guianan Leadership

The Trio word for 'thumb' is *jeinja itamu*, which literally means 'leader (or grandfather) of the hand'. This illustrates the fact that leadership, masculinity and kinship are implicated in Trio ways of classifying the world, and how they are replicated on different scales, from below that of the individual (as parts of the body) through the nuclear family to the village and, perhaps, beyond.[3] Three kinds of hierarchical differentiation are at play here, in the fields of gender, age and space, illustrating how symmetry and differentiation are taken for granted by Guianan Amerindians[4] as fundamental aspects of social and cosmological order. However, asymmetrical relationships in Guiana are not usually absolute; they shift with time and are perspective and scale-dependent. This gives rise to an aggregate impression of overall equality, and it is this serendipitous result of multiple asymmetries that gives the illusion, and arguably an aggregate effect, of equality.

According to Peter Rivière, a Trio leader is expected to lead by example and to be a competent organizer, a good speaker, generous and knowledgeable (1984: 73). In a 'political economy of people not of goods', a leader 'lacks any formal means of control other than his personal influence and competence' (ibid.: 93, 94). The roles of a head of family and leader of a village are 'identical' (Rivière 1969: 234). His duty, although he can be seen as standing between or mediating the inside and the outside of the community, 'if anything ... is to strengthen the inside which he owns and symbolizes.' (ibid.: 268). As a symbol of the community, he is the social incarnation of the network of relations he represents. I would add to Rivière's characterization that the asymmetrical relationship between a man and his dependents (wife, daughters, sons-in-law) is one node in a network of such miniature hierarchical formations, composing what may be termed a 'heterarchy', which is further differentiated by the prominence of some men and their families over others.

Rivière's characterization of leadership is largely based upon a reconstruction of Trio society with the elements and effects of contact with missionaries removed. To acquire a fuller understanding of Trio leadership and Guianan society in general it is necessary to see how they function in relation to contemporary circumstances and to consider this in the light of earlier situations. For example, Rivière's distinction between people and goods may benefit from taking into account the ways in which things may represent or even 'embody' persons (Grotti 2007; Van Velthem 2003). Missionization has also had important effects on political economy, allowing accumulation of material wealth and creating greater needs for other scarce resources – fuel, salt, metal goods, etc. Because of the ways in which these goods are obtained, that is to say, through the control of networks of people, they remain implicated in those networks through their 'biographies' (Hoskins 1998). The point to retain here is that things can take on greater importance as a result of their associations with persons. This will not surprise students of exchange theory. But the objects in question do not necessarily have the quality of gifts in what is primarily a sharing economy.

Guiana[5]

The Guiana Shield forms a continental island bordered by the Amazon, Negro and Orinoco rivers, and by the Atlantic. The urban centres (Paramaribo, Cayenne, Macapá, Belém, Manaus, Ciudad Bolívar, Ciudad Guayana, Georgetown) are to be found at the edge of the region (with the exception of Boa Vista), and the sparse Amerindian populations live in the interior. The large population centres are all situated on the coast or riverbanks. Control of goods and state political power are concentrated on the physical periphery of the 'island', the inhabitants of which see the 'hinterland' as both the location of natural resources to be exploited, and as dangerously wild. Legal ownership of land is correspondingly more secure and less disputed in the more populous edges of the island.[6] This view is echoed on the level of national sovereignty: the borders near the coastline between countries are generally agreed, whereas those in the interior are still disputed. These include the area between the Tapanahoni and the upper Maroni in the case of French Guiana and Suriname, and that between the Sipaliwini and the New River in the case of Guyana and Suriname; meanwhile Venezuela claims all of Guyana west of the Essequibo.

On this great scale of inter-state relations, and regarding space in these terms defined by zones or boundaries, the political geography of the region is a reversal of that of the Amerindian village. Nature is at the centre of the region, with culture at its periphery. However, this apparent reversal of the conventional view only exists from a cartographic perspective; if we look at the political geography of the region more closely from the point of view of coastal dwellers, a more complex picture emerges. In Paramaribo, for example, coastal French Guiana is often regarded as a beacon of civilization because of its greater wealth and relative lack of political corruption. Meanwhile political power follows economic lines. The most sought-after resources are concentrated in the urban centres on the region's periphery (even if, like gold, they are brought there from the interior), and those who control these resources have a monopoly on political power.

Things appear quite differently from the point of view of Amerindian people, particularly the relatively autonomous groups living in the interior. The Trio, Wayana and Akuriyo live in remote locations, far beyond any roads, where even river travel is difficult because of the shallow water and numerous dangerous rapids. Until the 1950s, when air travel became possible, access from the coast was only possible by river, and Trio continued to travel to the coast by river in the 1960s (P. Rivière pers. comm. 2008). Their villages are surrounded by forest, which they see as a rich but treacherous resource, and they regard the city in similar terms.

The Trio, Wayana and Akuriyo

The Trio, Wayana and Akuriyo are each composed of a number of previously distinct groups that amalgamated through the process of population concentration resulting from the creation of mission stations. As the Trio and Wayana, and, to a lesser extent, the Akuriyo, have become officially recognized as 'tribes' or 'ethnic groups' by nation states, they have become increasingly real as categories of identity, and the traceability of their historical construction (see chapter 1) makes them no less significant. Those who speak Trio (*Tarëno ijomi*) call themselves *Tirio* when addressing outsiders, but further layers of identity appear under other circumstances. Bearing in mind these qualifications as to their identity, the Trio comprise about 2,300 people.[7] In Suriname, they live on the upper Tapanahoni and the Sipaliwini rivers, and in Brazil they live on the Paru de Oeste and Cuxaré, in the Terra Indígena (TI) Parque de Tumucumaque. The Wayana are about 1,600 in number.[8] In Suriname and French Guiana, they live on the upper Tapanahoni and on the Maroni and its tributaries the Tampok, the Marouini and the Litani. In Brazil, they live on the Paru d'Este river in TI Parque de Tumucumaque and TI Rio Paru d'Este. The Trio and Wayana alike live primarily from swidden horticulture, their principal crop being bitter manioc, and hunting and fishing. They have a Dravidianate relationship terminology (Henley 1996), an important feature of which is the practical emphasis on the distinction between kin and affines from the point of view of ego, rather than from that of a descent group.

Most of the fieldwork on which this book is based was carried out in the village of Tëpu on the upper Tapanahoni river in Suriname. I spent a further period in the village of Antecume Pata at the confluence of the Litani and Marouini rivers in French Guiana. Tëpu, like all of the officially recognized Surinamese and Brazilian Trio villages, was created as a mission station. The Protestant evangelical mission 'Door to Life', which was soon taken over by West Indies Mission (WIM),[9] created the first missions among the Trio of Suriname from 1960 following 'Operation Grasshopper', a military operation to cut airstrips. This was initiated by the government as a step towards the 'opening up' of the 'interior' to economic exploitation, and largely seems to have been motivated by the desire to secure the southern part of the frontiers in the disputed headwater region discussed above. The missionaries' main role was in the next stage of the process: concentrating and 'civilizing' the Amerindians. The first important Trio mission station on the Tapanahoni was Palumeu, situated at the mouth of the Palumeu river, a major affluent of the Tapanahoni, and in the late 1960s a faction of Trio who were discontent with life there founded the village of Tëpu several hours upstream by motorized canoe. This move was organized by Claude Leavitt of Unevangelised Fields Mission (UFM),[10] who was on loan to WIM because of his field skills (Conley 2000: 389), and who is said by some elderly residents to have been the 'real' founder of Tëpu. The foundation of the village appears to be linked to Leavitt's leadership around the same time of the expeditions to concentrate the Akuriyo, whose eventual settlement took place in Tëpu itself.

The airstrip was cut in 1971, and a health post was created by the Christian medical mission Medische Zending and run by missionary nurses from the Dutch Reformed Church (DRC). Education was at first also provided by volunteers from the DRC, Cees and Ineke Koelewijn, who continue to visit the village regularly and who were present some of the time while I conducted fieldwork. A state school was later created using funding from the Margreet Kauffman Foundation. Another important actor in the village is the US-based conservation NGO Amazon Conservation Team (ACT), which supports the local apprenticeship of plant medicine and has sponsored cultural mapping projects among the Trio and Wayana in Suriname and in Brazil (Brightman 2008b, 2012).

Tëpu has a population of about 330 people, comprising a slight majority of Trio, many Wayana, and most of the surviving Akuriyo. The population has remained roughly stable since the 1970s except for the period during and immediately after the civil war. President Desi Bouterse, who came to power following a coup d'état in 1980 (who returned to the presidency in 2010, this time following democratic election) violently suppressed the 1986 uprising of the Jungle Commando,[11] leading to the 'war of the interior', which brought fighting even to the remote Sipaliwini district where the Trio live. Government recruiting agents tried to attract Amerindians as soldiers, possibly by force, causing many Trio to flee to Brazil, especially to the Catholic mission station village of Missão Tiriós on the Paru de Oeste. This led to several marriages, as a result of which, when people began to go back to Tëpu after the war, some stayed in Missão and others returned with their local spouses. This migration to Missão followed existing paths – people had moved around and across the region for as long as memories and records can attest, and visitors still frequently make the journey (see chapter 3). Today, although people travel long distances by river (with outboard motors) and by air, it is more difficult than in the past to travel on foot because there are fewer villages along the way due to the concentration of populations around mission stations.

Antecume Pata was founded by André Cognat (known in Wayana as Antecume), a Frenchman from near Lyon who was adopted by a Wayana family in the early 1960s after they saved him from drowning in rapids during a solitary expedition up the Maroni. The village is situated on an island among the rapids at the confluence of the Litani and Marouini rivers on the border between Suriname and French Guiana. As well as Wayana from Litani, its inhabitants include families of Wayana and Apalai who fled gold miners and pelt hunters on the Jari and Paru d'Este river in

Brazil during the late 1960s and 70s. Antecume Pata is located in an area that was protected under the *arrêté préfectoral* of 1970 which covers the southern section of French Guiana until the creation of the Parc Amazonien de Guyane in 2007. Both the *arrêté préfectoral* and the park have theoretically provided protection from placer mining,[12] missionaries and disease, although the village's proximity to the Surinamese border (which the river itself constitutes) greatly reduces the regulation's effect. It is highly significant that this village was not created by missionaries, but by a local leader, and that this leader is a white Frenchman who adopted Wayana culture and married a Wayana woman.[13]

Fieldwork and its Limitations

When I arrived in Suriname, Jacob, a medical mission nurse with extensive experience of working among the Trio, encouraged me to go to Tëpu because it was not getting its fair share of 'projects' compared to the other Trio villages. He arranged for me to meet Douwe, the Hoofdkapitein ('head captain') of Tëpu, who happened to be in Paramaribo, to ask for his permission to go the village. This was a matter of courtesy and respect rather than regulation, for Amerindian villages in Suriname are not protected by official access restrictions, unlike in neighbouring countries. The only practical way to get to Tëpu is by light aircraft. While I waited for a chance to share a charter flight, I spent my time meeting visiting Trio people and conservation workers in Paramaribo. The flight was repeatedly postponed, as Adam, a man from Tëpu who has a government post as a Trio representative in Paramaribo, awaited his long overdue salary.

In Tëpu, the Kapitein, Silvijn, at first allocated a cook and a work helper, saying in broken English, 'I give you these women.' Although this gave the appearance of a manifestation of his authority, I later found it had been the product of much persuasion and negotiation on his part. It was immediately clear that the 'cook' (a teenage girl who lived next door) found this arrangement as awkward as I did, and my unusual desire to share family meals soon made her help unnecessary. However, the 'translator', Emma, gradually became my most important interlocutor and a good friend. She obviously relished her duties, which gave her a welcome escape from the daily tasks of processing cassava and childcare.

Emma's father, Gabriel, though the son of Waiãpi parents, had been adopted at a young age by Wayana people in Antecume Pata, and his wife is a Trio from Tëpu. This has led the family to migrate several times between the two villages. As a result of her upbringing and several years of school in Antecume Pata, Emma speaks fluent Wayana and good French,

as well as Trio. This was important in an extremely multilingual environment. There were a handful of Portuguese speakers, but their knowledge
of Portuguese was much less extensive than Emma's knowledge of French;
communication in Dutch or Sranan Tongo with those who knew either
language was problematic because the level of knowledge was limited on
both sides. Emma's French education also gave her a level of literacy considerably higher than most of her contemporaries in Tëpu, which aided
in the translation of concepts as well as giving her unparalleled skills as a
field assistant. I was fortunate to be able to benefit from her abilities: her
gender would have been an obstacle to our interaction had it not been
for the fact that I was accompanied by my partner, Vanessa Grotti. Due
to Emma's conventional female modesty, for some time I could scarcely
communicate directly with her, and had to do so through Vanessa. Even
after Emma began to address Vanessa as her elder sister, this placed me in
the position of affine to her and her family, and it was only the intimacy
of sharing a household and food that led to my also being treated by them
as kin. This brought corresponding obligations: my lack of skill in hunting and fishing meant that I had to provide for the family in other ways,
by bringing objects and cash. I came to depend on Emma and her family –
particularly her father, Gabriel, and her Trio grandfather, Boasz – for food
as well as information, and I spent most of my days with them, although
as I grew more confident and knowledgeable I gradually became able to
interact with people from other households, and went about on visits of
my own.

A few months after I began my fieldwork, Gabriel told me of his intention to bring his wife and his unmarried daughters to Antecume Pata,
although it was some time before the move was finally organized. The
main reason he gave for wanting to go there was that he missed his relatives, and this was especially acute because his sister (by adoption) was
seriously ill.[14] Gabriel gave less emphasis to other motivations: by returning to Antecume Pata, he hoped to get better schooling for his children.
He would also secure French nationality for his next child, and try to
obtain French papers for himself, in order to have access to social security
and quality healthcare. Following her father's suggestion, Emma travelled
separately with Vanessa and me via Paramaribo, which gave her, on what
was her first visit there, the opportunity to obtain a Surinamese identity
card, allowing her access to various Surinamese benefits (she was born in
Tëpu). This also allowed her to take a scheduled flight to Benzdorp, next
to Maripasoula, which helped to reduce the overall cost of migration.

These mundane practicalities helped to illuminate some of the themes
of my research: the importance and advantages of travel in the contemporary world; the tensions between state benefits and brideservice; men's

control over their daughters; the consumerist elation of going to the city for the first time: all these things and many more became apparent through ordinary events as well as through ceremonial activities or the daily round. The way in which I conducted my research brought some disadvantages, however: working with Trio and Wayana made it more difficult to master either language; the extensive travel put a strain on my budget and personal relationships; relying on local food meant suffering cycles of abundance and scarcity to which my body never became accustomed; I was not tied to any Surinamese or French institutions, and therefore had no infrastructure to support me; even being part of a couple in the field had the disadvantage of encouraging the assumption that we were self-sufficient and thus making it seem less natural for us to eat with others, let alone be 'adopted'. But all of these problems were balanced by advantages: working in several sites enabled me to study how kinship, trade and various forms of communication link people across space, state borders and identity groups. Through my reliance on local food, I shared substance with local people and reinforced our relationships. Because of my independence from any institutions, I avoided inviting prejudice because of any associations that these institutions have for local people.

Structure and Scope of the Book

The first chapter introduces the Trio, Wayana and Akuriyo as distinct groups by juxtaposing life histories, myths and historical sources. It shows the role of leaders in creating groups and group identity in given locations, and how this underpins Guianan patterns of ethnic identity that form as a network of continual change, a network of transformations, as contingent events are transposed through political agency to fit the conventional structures of imagined social organization.

In chapter 2 I focus on housebuilding as analogous to village foundation and as a crystallization of kinship networks. The foundation of a village begins with the clearing of land and building of a house. When more houses are built in an existing village, the mobilization of people involved in housebuilding involves the exercise of male capacities to influence collective action. The house as an expression of kinship is used in this context to frame a discussion of spatial dimensions of the structural conditions for leadership.

Chapter 3 explores the relationships between male capacities and networks of influence in the realm of affinity. It focuses on speech and movement, oratory and mediation with outsiders, including trade, these being important forms of action expected of a leader. In this chapter I make the case for the essentially mediatory role of the leader, and it is shown that the role can be played out in different ways. The exploration of the various forms of communication also shows how they create, articulate and perpetuate social difference, and thus demonstrates that the asymmetrical relationships of which leadership is the primary manifestation exist on different scales.

In chapter 4 I return to the collectivity, to show how the exchange of persons occurs ritually and symbolically on a group level, and I consider the importance of leadership in achieving this. I show that ritual and musical celebration, which are used to manipulate affinal relations, are a way of incorporating outside influence, in the form of persons, things and knowledge, recalling the discussion of communication in the first chapter: with leaders taking the role of protagonists, society is constantly renewed by the repetition of various forms of this process, whether the 'outside' is represented by the worlds of other Amerindians, Maroons, white people, animals or spirits. However, I argue that gender roles are inverted during ritual acts of incorporation, and the act of incorporation is an enactment of feminine agency.

The movement of persons and objects raises questions about the relationships between them. In chapter 5 I consider these as a form of property relations: relationships between persons can be seen in terms of property and belonging, and, following Marilyn Strathern (1996) I explore how property articulates networks of relationships. I argue that relationships of belonging between persons are more important than those between persons and objects, and that the latter are regarded in terms of the former. These questions are considered in terms of relationships with land, and territoriality and kinship are brought together in a discussion of the importance of village foundation for the establishment of leadership.

In the concluding chapter I discuss the wider implications of the argument presented throughout the book, and consider its implications for matters such as native Amazonians' relationships with the state, and native perspectives on historical change.

Notes

1. 'Les philosophes qui ont examiné les fondements de la société ont tous senti la nécessité de remonter jusqu'à l'état de nature, mais aucun d'eux n'y est arrivé.' All translations are by the author.

2. I have used pseudonyms throughout, with the exception of certain locally well-known figures whose identity, even if their names were changed, would remain clear to many readers.

3. This should not be mistaken for an organic model for society. If anything, the Guianan body is a reflection of society rather than the reverse. For a similar use of scale, see Strathern 2000 and Viveiros de Castro 2001.

4. Throughout the text (except in quotations), native Amazonian people are referred to as 'Amerindian', to distinguish them from the coastal 'Indians' or 'East Indians' who descend from indentured labourers from India.

5. When referring to the region as a whole, I have chosen to maintain the established geographical (and geological) appellation, 'Guiana', rather than 'Guayana' (the Venezuelan Spanish usage adopted by Whitehead and Aleman 2009) or 'the Guianas', a slightly ambiguous term that may be taken as referring only to Guyana, Suriname (as former Dutch Guiana) and French Guiana.

6. There are important exceptions such as coastal Kali'na and Lokono Amerindian land claims.

7. This includes 1,400 in Suriname and 939 in Brazil (http://www.socioambiental.org/pib/epi/tiriyo/tiriyo.shtm); the latter figure includes the Kaxuyana, who continue to identify themselves as distinct despite much intermarriage.

8. This includes 400 in Suriname, 800 in French Guiana and 415 in Brazil (http://www.socioambiental.org/ pib/epi/aparai/aparai.shtm); these figures include the Apalai, with whom the Wayana have intermarried extensively. The Akuriyo case, which is discussed here, bears superficial resemblances, but belongs to a different order because although they coreside with the Trio, they scarcely intermarry, a fact that I attribute to the Akuriyo's former status as nomadic foragers who lacked knowledge of bitter manioc cultivation.

9. Now known as World Team.

10. Recently renamed as CrossWorld Foundation.

11. Launched from Maroon villages, led by Ronnie Brunswijk and backed by the Netherlands and France.

12. Goldmining is an important issue with political dimensions beyond the scope of this book. For Suriname, see Heemskerk 2001 and Veiga 1997; for the Wayana of French Guiana, see Meunier 2004: 71ff.; for the Amazon region as a whole see Cleary 1990 and MacMillan 1995; for general discussion of extractive industry in Amazonia, see Brightman et al. 2006/7.

13. These points are discussed in chapters 2 and 5.

14. She quickly recovered after his arrival, which appeared quite normal; for Trio and Wayana people, separation from relatives can lead to illness.

Chapter 1

MAKING TRIO AND OTHER PEOPLES

(Pulls off several layers [of the onion] together)

There's a most surprising lot of layers! / Are we never coming to the kernel?

(Pulls all that is left to pieces)

There isn't one! To the innermost bit / It's nothing but layers, smaller and smaller. / Nature's a joker!

—Henrik Ibsen, *Peer Gynt*

Wealth, for the peoples of Guiana, consists of persons rather than things (Rivière 1984). Leadership involves the manipulation of persons, and this occurs primarily through the kinship system. The leader exercises his capacity and influence to become a magnified person, the embodiment of the group. What, then, is a group? How is it composed and defined? How has this been changing since concentration in mission stations, and what is the effect on leadership? In order to answer these questions, I must begin by outlining some formal changes that have occurred through missionization and engagement with the state.

Over the last five decades, missionaries and the state have sought to appropriate Trio leadership as a mechanism of official political representation. With the moral support of the state, the Baptist missionaries used their influence in the 1960s to impose an authority structure that they could understand and control upon the seemingly amorphous Trio society. They introduced the officially recognized traditional authority system of the Maroons, descendents of rebel African slaves living in semi-autonomous tribal societies along the large rivers between Trio and Wayana territory and the coastal plain.[1] This system operates through a hierarchical scheme of Granman (paramount chief), Hoofdkapitein (headcaptain), Kapitein (captain) and Basja (overseer). The Granman is appointed by the 'tribe', but subject to approval by the state, in a system that has developed on an ad hoc basis since the 1760 treaty between the Ndjuka and the Dutch state – which also included the 'free Indians' as beneficiaries (Kambel and MacKay 1999: 58). Among the Maroons the office of Granman is in principle inherited matrilineally, and the missionaries and the state have promoted a system of patrilineal inheritance of authority among the Trio and Wayana. In practice, a Granman will be a well-established leader who already has longstanding relations with state officials. There is no formal system for choosing a Granman among the Amerindians, but the choice will be made following discussion between leaders at a communal meeting called a *krutu*, modelled upon the Maroon institution of the same name. It is thus, as far as possible, a collective decision, which favours men with strong networks of kin and trading partners, and with strong personal qualities, especially oratorical skills.

The reasons why the missionaries introduced the Maroon system are twofold. The first is that the system was recognized by the state already, and constituted a way of formally subordinating the Amerindians to the state while acknowledging the very considerable degree of autonomy that they enjoyed in practice. The Granman is not subordinate to the regional authority, but governs a technically parallel system, the autonomy of which is, however, limited by a relationship of clientelism: holders of 'traditional authority' positions receive stipends from the state (which were originally gifts of prestige objects). The second attraction for the missionaries, although it is likely to stem from the fact of the Granman's relative autonomy from the state, rather than from the missionaries' knowledge of Maroon society, is a religious one. The Maroon Granman derives his authority directly from Gaan Gadu (God) (Pakosie 1996). Although it has non-Christian origins, this idea of direct political subservience to God without the intervention of a secular or priestly authority agrees with evangelical Christian political theology, and justifies the missionaries' continued intervention as mentors to Amerindian leaders.

Granman Vigo is thus the official representative of all the Trio in Suriname; Douwe is Hoofdkapitein in Tëpu, and Silvijn is Kapitein. There are several Basjas, among whom the most active are Storm and Jonathan. In practice, this seemingly clear hierarchical system of organization masks something much more intricate. Vigo rarely has anything to do with the affairs of the people of Tëpu, and his authority is scarcely recognized there. Silvijn and Douwe divide their activities not according to function, but according to their personal connections. The Basjas tend to operate as miniature local leaders in their own right. They act on their own initiative rather than following the orders of the Kapitein or Hoofdkapitein, and sometimes, as in the case of Jonathan, emerge as rivals to the Kapitein for local preeminence. Nevertheless, the system operates as a channel for the influence of the Church, and the Baptist missionaries have from the beginning succeeded in appointing their favourite converts and pastors to official leadership roles. This gives the latter a significant monopoly on both trade and the control of prestigious knowledge, which I describe in chapter 3.

Once a Kapitein or Granman has been recognized as such by the state, he[2] is 'leader' for the rest of his life. Organs of development, whether governmental or nongovernmental (Amazon Conservation Team 2010), together with the principal indigenous organization, VIDS (Vereniging van Inheemse Dorpshoofden in Suriname), all agree that reinforcing these 'traditional authorities' is a priority.[3] The official recognition of the village ensures that it is the focus for 'development' and infrastructure, and the consequent presence of schools, clinics and airstrips helps to preserve the leader's position by maintaining the integrity of his constituency. It is now in the interest of all Trio, for instance, to be represented at the highest possible level, as 'the Trio tribe' and Trio people are well aware. An array of factors thus converge to promote permanence and stability, in opposition to the shifting pattern of traditional Guianan social reproduction.

Relationships with white people and the state highlight the dual nature of change and continuity in leadership. Two examples illustrate this: One of the 'official', uniformed leaders in Palumeu in 1963 was a thoroughly uncharismatic individual, who was skilled neither at speaking nor at ordinary men's activities. When Dutch officials first arrived in the area to organize cutting the airstrip, and asked to speak to the leader, he had been pushed to the front because nobody wanted to have to do the job (P. Rivière pers. comm. 2008). The other example is that of André Cognat, the white Wayana leader, who is sometimes accused of not being a real Wayana by those who wish to contest his authority. These examples both seem to evoke the scenario described by Pierre Clastres (1974) of the power of the group over the leader. However, the role of mediator does give these leaders a certain power. In both cases, unwilling individuals fell almost by chance into the role of mediator with the outside, in this case urban society (Cognat never intended or sought to become a leader). A continuity can be seen with older patterns in these forms of leadership, to the extent that they can be seen as transformations, in Lévi-Strauss's sense, of their predecessors. Cognat illustrates this best, for he embodies a proliferation of transformations. Most obviously, he is a white man transformed into a Wayana, but as such it is not merely his bodily attributes that were transformed (by adornment, *marake* ritual passage, commensality, etc.). Because he performed these bodily transformations, and because he learned to behave like a Wayana more generally, his ontological perspective appeared to become that of a Wayana. Meanwhile, like a shaman, he seems to be able to oscillate between Wayana and white people's perspectives, as he can still 'see' like a white person, and can still transform himself into a white man, putting on white people's clothes to go into their world, the city. His powerful transformability, which is the very essence of his capacity, and the reason others want him as a leader, causes him to share the ambivalent status of the shaman, who it is feared may change into the Other and lose his real humanity (cf. Brightman and Grotti 2012). It is in this sense that people challenge his authority when they draw attention to his whiteness,[4] and paradoxically this is exactly how leadership worked before white people became such an important source of influence.

Ethnogenesis

The question of change and continuity, of stability and impermanence, is the key element in the relationship between leadership and social organization that, it will become increasingly clear, is a problematic one. It raises the problem of ethnicity and group identity, and reveals the danger of equating 'groups with social structure and … politics with society' (Strathern 1991a: 2). Today, it is relatively easy to point to a Trio or Wayana village on a map, and to say that another is a mixed village inhabited by Trio, Wayana and Akuriyo. However, such images and labels mask a more complex picture. By looking at how group identities emerge, we can begin to see how a leader's capacity to maintain his sphere of influence is what constitutes collectivities over time. The history of the emergence of a collectivity defining itself in terms of shared language and culture is known as ethnogenesis, and this is sometimes understood as a reactive process, especially in the case of domination by states or colonial powers (Hill 1996). As Neil Whitehead has argued, 'the ethnic character of the peoples of modern Surinam [and Guiana in general] have emerged from earlier ethnic formations, and for this reason it is not possible to simply project these modern ethnographic paradigms back into the past' (1996: 21).

Group identity is about more than just shared language and 'culture', however, and anthropologists have often shown how it is underpinned by kinship. But there are no corporate groups or lineages in Guianan society (Rivière 1969, 1984; Overing 1975) and, like other Amerindians, 'a group of kinsmen is not a circumscribed group, as a clan or village community would be. It shades out in all directions, and integrates into innumerable others' (Kroeber, in Lévi-Strauss 1983: 172). Here, identity is rhetorically constituted through the iteration of narratives. These narratives must be understood in terms of indigenous cosmology, characterized by shifting social relations between human and nonhuman; it is in the shape of these relations that continuities in discourse and practice coincide. The logic of the transformation of narratives of identity into historical groups and vice versa, is the same as that of myth, which absorbs history and dissolves time (Lévi-Strauss 1964; Gow 2001). These narratives give an illusion of dia-chronic ethnic identity as they mythologize historical residence groups, while in fact continuity lies in the structure of the narratives themselves, rather than their content.

A Theory of Continuity

To understand Trio identity it is worth clarifying a number of concepts: *imoitï, jana, mono eka* and *wïtoto*. *Imoitï*, often translated locally as 'my family', refers to kin and coresident affines, and can have a more or less expansive field of reference depending on situation. *Jana* (cf. yana [W], *kare* [A]), often applied as a suffix to the names of groups, is a word for a collectivity that some ethnographers have understood as exogamous clans, within larger tribal indentity groups, although this is a problematic interpretation, as I will discuss below (it is true that a larger collective category exists, and it is known as *mono eka*, literally 'big name', but I suggest that this current usage is largely the result of concentration of smaller groups in large villages at mission stations). Finally, the Trio use the word *wïtoto* to refer to Amerindians in general, as opposed to urban people (*pananakiri*), Maroons (*mekoro*) and Brazilians (*karaiwa*). However, in a moral register, it can also distinguish human beings from nonhumans or those of uncertain status.

Trio people show little interest in tracing their ancestry to define group identity. This is not unusual: in Amazonia, 'theories of conception sel-dom are related to notions of descent in any clear-cut or consistent way, and even within a single community there often is little consensus about precisely what goes into making a baby' (Conklin 2001: 147). Yet, on the basis that Trio men regard themselves as passing on their blood through their semen (Grupioni n.d.; cf. Chapuis 1998), Denise Grupioni has concluded that the various *jana* or peoples, described in earlier ethnographies (e.g. Frikel 1960; Rivière 1969; Cortez 1977) as 'subgroups', are exogamous, predominantly patrilineal groups, identifying themselves with an ancestor (Grupioni n.d. 2002). Grupioni provides statistical evidence to show that people almost never marry within their own subgroup, and a requirement for exogamy would motivate group leaders to seek alliances with other groups. At the heart of the argument is the Trio word *itïpï*, or 'continuity', which Grupioni claims refers to a diachronic, temporal, masculine principle that is complementary to the synchronic, spatial, feminine principle of village foundation and housebuilding (2005).[5] Grupioni thus effectively presents *itïpï* as descent groups or lineages, and in so doing follows Protásio Frikel (1960; cf. Frikel and Cortez 1972; Cortez 1977).

Frikel was a Franciscan missionary who for many years was in charge of the Trio mission station in Brazil, Missão. He himself thought that the Trio subgroups' concentration in the mission station was causing them to disappear, and wrote that from the second generation they lost the notion of descent in terms of lineages and sibs, and forgot which groups they belonged to (1971: 34). If these 'sibs' had indeed been exogamous groups, it seems unlikely that missionization would dissolve their identity in this way; on the contrary, one would expect them to increase in importance as a result of permanent settlement. Neither I, nor Rivière (1969: 64), ever heard the word *itïpï* except as the root of verbs and adjectives (*itïpïhte*, 'to marry'; *itïpïme*, 'adjacent'), and although these can be associated with genealogy, they are also applicable to other fields. This appears also to have been Grupioni's experience, as she translates *itïpï* as 'continuity' rather than 'lineage', although the latter would correspond more closely to her interpretations.

The adjective *itïpïme* is a relative term, and the same person may be described as *itïpïme* in comparison with a more distant individual (genealogically or spatially), as well as *itïpïmeta* (neg.) in comparison with another, closer individual. I much more frequently heard the word *imoitï* used to describe genealogical relatives. This term is very similar to the Parakanã category, *te'ynia*, which 'can be glossed as "relative" and implies some level of identity shared between those who define themselves this way'. Among the Parakanã it is 'marked by mutuality and by sharing, with the exclusion of exchange, hostility and sex' (Fausto 1995: 63). Unlike the Parakanã, however, coresidence seems to have somewhat greater relative importance for the Trio than *imoitï/te'ynia*. This is clearly related to the fact that the Trio, like other Guianan groups, mask affinity among coresidents, and this does not occur among the Parakanã (Fausto 1995: 65; Rivière 1984). Both Rivière and Grupioni write that *imoitï* refers primarily to coresidents and coresident relatives; Rivière also finds that it includes individuals who have at some time in the past been coresidents. I did also hear *imoitï* used to refer to persons whose only relationship to the speaker was genealogical – that is, who were not coresident, including even cases of persons who had never been coresident – and I can therefore see very little difference in practice between *imoitï* and *itïpïme*.

There are technical differences: the former is a noun, and is primarily a spatial referent, whereas the latter is an adjective, and primarily refers to genealogical relationships and their analogues. But the fact that the words are otherwise almost interchangeable reflects the fact that space and genealogy are difficult to separate. Moreover, the fact that *itïpï-* (notwithstanding Grupioni's evidence) does not appear to be used as a noun, reflects the fact that for Trio people and their neighbours genealogy exists only as a practice (of little importance), and not as an entity; there are no corporate groups: other people are seen in terms of their relationship to ego, and ego does not see him- or herself as a member of an autonomous group such as a lineage. I suspect that one cause of confusion is the conflation of *itïpï-* with the term *jana* ('people'), which refers to 'ethnic' or identity groups. It is possible that this reflects a difference in the Trio language as spoken in Brazil and Suriname – Rivière describes a similar difference between his data and those of Frikel (Rivière 1969: 64n) – and if so it illustrates the perils of relying too heavily on linguistic data for sociological and cultural analysis.

Substance and Filiation

The association made by Grupioni between *jana* and *ïtïpï* suggests that she infers a folk theory of descent from folk theories of filiation; but this confusion of descent and filiation is only part of the problem. She emphasizes the transmission of the bloodline through the semen, but matters are actually more complex. Trio personhood is composed of bodies and souls. The *omore* is the embodied eye-soul or image-soul, also associated with the shadow. It is called omorenpë – 'former or defunct soul' – after its departure from the body through death. The eye-soul is drawn from a common reservoir created by the ancestor/culture hero Përëpërëwa; spirit and flesh are passed from the man to the woman during sexual intercourse, but the soul of the child is nourished by both parents, and the spiritual connection after birth is said to be strongest between child and mother, 'a spiritual counterpart to the umbilical cord' (Rivière 1969: 63). There are other kinds of soul that are less consistently mentioned by Trio, which reside in other parts of the body. These aspects of soul, or soul matter, seem to reside where there is a pulse, such as in the wrists, neck and below the knees, and in the heart. This is why Trio people adorn these parts of the body with bead ornaments, especially on children, whose souls are not yet considered to be firmly attached to their bodies, making them more vulnerable to spirit attack. Along with body and soul, there is a further constitutent element of the person for Trio people, which is name, eka. This has been interpreted as performing the role of binding the body and soul together (Rivière 1997). The name persists after death, although it is not uttered for a period, until body and soul are fully separated and the corporeal elements of the individual person have been forgotten. At this point the name of a deceased person, often a grandparent, can be given to a baby. Names seem to be elements or emanations of the self, and the living cannot share names. Moreover, each individual has several names, at least one of which is never uttered; the others are 'public' names, which have less powerful associations with the soul.

As this implies, Trio notions of personhood and filiation are complex, but they are also inconsistent. The degree to which male substance is emphasized appears to vary between peoples and circumstances. Wayana appear to have a greater tendency to give equal emphasis to male and female substance (Chapuis and Rivière 2003: 629n.) than the Trio, and the Akuriyo appear to give more emphasis to male substance than the Trio (Jara 1990). My own investigations suggested that all three groups tend to believe substance is transmitted from both father and mother, while giving marginally greater emphasis to the inheritance of the identity of the father, but there is no consensus of opinion on the matter even among coresidents of the same ethnic origins, and most people claim to have no knowledge of such an esoteric subject. These vague ideas of filiation are far from providing a clear basis for marriage rules based on exogamic clans.

It is very clear that the Trio do not have corporate groups, clans or lineages and the primary expression and framework for marriage is to be found in the relationship terminology and on the level of individual relationships – a fact that was convincingly established long ago (Hurault 1972; Rivière 1969; cf. Overing 1975; Seeger et al. 1979; Dumont 1983). It seems likely that the genealogical appearance of *jana* exogamy derives from the desirability of sister exchange, the point of which is to create alliances and increase the size of the local group. If marriage partners are chosen according to the principles that I will outline later, in chapter 2, of sister exchange, cross-cousin marriage and marriage with a sister's daughter, then men will end up marrying women from different genealogical lines of descent from themselves, even if such lines have no cultural significance whatsoever. *Jana* exogamy, if and when it occurs, does not constitute an ideology in its own right, but merely results from actual marriage practices and ideals. A comparable case is that of the Parakanã, who have a preference for avuncular-patrilateral marriage, many features of which would be worth comparing in a separate discussion. What is significant here is that, although their system might allow one to try to identify

> a transmission of alliance between 'patrilines', it does not on the other hand invest these 'patrilines' with a substantive status – they are not, and cannot be, formal units of exchange, since their register is minimalist (to avoid the ambiguous term 'individualistic') and rests more upon the relationship between full brothers or male first cousins [*germanos*] than upon the supposed solidarity between members of the same agnatic group.... The calculation of reciprocity ... does not depend on any supra-individual entity acting according to its own interests (Fausto 1991: 239–40).

This corresponds to the minimal generational depth among both the Parakanã and the Trio (cf. Fausto 1995: 98). The Parakanã, like the Trio, have what Carlos Fausto cautiously calls 'subgroups' but, as among the Trio, these groups are not themselves units of exchange: 'the marriage regime lacks ... any sociocentric logic, working in a minimal register of deferred symmetrical exchange without groups. The patrilines are the general effect of these exchanges, and their existence is an epiphenomenon of the terminological structure and of the alliance regime' (ibid.: 249). In other words, if we want to identify 'lines', they are *'defined by exchange, not by descent'* (ibid.: 101, original emphasis).

This is not to say that the genealogy is without significance, or that the relationship terminology and residence are the only frames of reference for Trio kinship. As I hope is already evident from the above discussion, biological relationships do have some significance for Trio people, who may refer even to biological relatives at two or three degrees of distance, who are living in other villages or in the city, as their family, *imoitï*. A comparison with the Parakanã again suggests itself: for them, while relationship terminology 'constitutes a privileged language for classifying, defining and establishing relations in the social field in its totality', the 'genealogical substrate' is still important, because, 'the more distant these [genealogical] links, the less consistent will be the classificatory grid. The category applied to a distant relative becomes "light", it is almost only a *name* for which it is necessary to provide content. The genealogy is the "anchor" of the meaning and that which allows its translation' (ibid.: 63).

Telling Stories, Making Groups

In my experience Trio people do not seem to consider their identity on the level of *itïpï* or *jana* to be very important. Many people are not sure which *jana* they belong to, and rather than signifying a line of descent from a particular ancestor, the *jana* appears to be associated more characteristically with a particular group of people who were living together in the past, and whose individual identities have been forgotten. The mythico-historical narratives in which different *jana* feature treat them as groups, and there is never any mention of a corresponding, eponymous individual who may have founded the group. Moreover, the stories tend to be exogenous (i.e. told from a point of view outside the group concerned), and people more readily speculate about the *jana* of others than they do about their own, suggesting that the *jana* can more plausibly be regarded as exogenous appellations.[6]

There is sometimes considerable disparity between the names given to groups by their own members and those given to them by other groups. The Akuriyo used to call the Trio the 'Lelejana' ('bat people') and the Wayana the 'Ëlukujana' ('caterpillar people'). During the early encounters before missionization, they called white people 'Në'reipotapë' ('transformed ones', *në're* referring to the Trio, suggesting that the white people were transformed Trio) (Yohner 1970a: 7). All three denominations associate the groups in question with spirits. Caterpillars are considered powerful and dangerous spirits, mainly because of their ability to metamorphose, which is in itself a fundamental attribute of spirits. Akuriyo in Tëpu invariably scowl and mutter *kureta, wïrïpë* ('bad, spirits'), when bats flit past in the evening.

Men who 'know', grandfathers, particularly those whose knowledge is widely acknowledged and respected, such as Bram and Levi, Douwe and Silvijn, can speak about the *jana* and other esoteric matters with confidence. They do so in terms of historical group entities rather than of groups descended from an ancestor. By contrast, culture heroes such as Jaraware are spoken of as creators/ancestors of '(real) people', not the creators of *jana*. Through time *jana* are constantly changing and reforming, and 'other' people who would once have been classified under one *jana* denomination or another can become 'real' people (Tarëno, Wayana, etc.). Marriage does not occur as an alliance between groups, but between persons, and group identities change merely as a result of the aggregate of individual marriages and other events such as wars and epidemics.

There is a constant interplay between an ideal of endogamy and a practice of exogamy, which is managed rhetorically to preserve group identity. Old men told me that intermarriage between different groups (in terms of both *mono eka* [Trio, Wayana, Waiwai, etc.], but also of *jana*) did not occur in the past. During a visit to a Waiwai village in Guyana in 2003, I learned that the marriages between Waiwai and Wapishana represented a new phenomenon. Wapishana households were separately situated on the periphery of the village. Intermarriage is not really new, but it is always described as exceptional.[7] Niels Fock was told the very same thing, when he asked his Waiwai informants how long the Waiwai had been intermarrying with the Mawayana and the Wapishana (1963: 202), and he noted that this information contrasted with what he had learned from earlier authors about intermarriage between the Waiwai, the Parukoto, the Taruma and the Mawayana (ibid.: 7).[8] It seems that continuity consists in *forgetting* past interethnic alliances, rather than institutionalizing them: this enables differences between groups to be maintained, making alliance a continual possibility. Intergroup relations thus operate according to the same logic as settlement endogamy (and indeed the two very often coexist): either difference or sameness is emphasized according to the desired outcome of any given situation (Overing 1975; Lepri 2005).

This picture of constancy in change is borne out by an examination of Frikel's interpretation (1960) of the various *janas*, as subdivisible in turn into lineages. According to him, the chief of a sib is called a *tamútupe*, and 'while the role of tamútupe is independent and supreme within the sibs, that of patá-entu [village leader] by its nature, is limited to its local group' (ibid.: 12). This interpretation of the *jana* as highly organized descent groups is based primarily on the preconceptions of 1950s kinship theory, derived from Africanist ethnography,[9] as various facts make clear: *Tamutupë*, in my experience, means 'old man', and is frequently used in contexts that could have no connotations whatsoever with descent groups, to refer to outsiders (of the ethnic group, although fictional kinship may exist), and even to total strangers. It connotes authority only insofar as it is an expression of generational or age hierarchy. It is true that the meaning of the term may have shifted, but even in Frikel's time matters were far from obvious, and his admission of this shows that he had plenty of room for speculation: after conjuring a picture of supreme sib chiefs presiding over local leaders in a 'sib council', he writes:

> But, due to the frequent schisms within sibs and local groups, there has been a certain disintegration of the governmental system.... As a cause of this phenomenon of incipient governmental dissolution, Trio people themselves indicate, generally, the death of the eldest generation and, depending on it, the lack of ancient discipline and of fidelity to the tradition of the ancestors, this lack being caused by the contact and influence of neighbours.... On the one hand one may interpret this as a symptom of disorganization, but on the other, also as a sort of emancipation of the new generation.... This growth of a 'modern spirit' among the youth, however, is regarded with mistrust and discontent by the older people still remaining in the tribe, who formulate their opinion in this way: 'Eh! Our old tamútupe have all died already. And these young people aren't good for anything any more!' (ibid.: 12).

It is, revealingly, only at this point in his account that Frikel begins to refer to local accounts and opinions, which appear to qualify rather than confirm his analysis. Like Fock's description of intertribal marriage, the local interpretations heard by Frikel are identical in spirit to those expressed by local Trio and Wayana today. The elderly lament the passing of the old ways of life, while the adolescents follow the fashions of Paramaribo and Maripasoula. Meanwhile, the middle generation of men in their prime copes with urban technology and trade, while also managing matters of family and subsistence in just the same manner as previous generations. The elderly of 2005 would have been the youth of Frikel's day. But this is more than the familiar story of teenage rebels and the nostalgia of old age. There is a broader pattern of constant regeneration, made possible by the *idea* of order rather than by order itself. What Frikel interpreted as a contemporary process of 'acculturation' (ibid.: 19) was in fact a manifestation of a constant pattern.

Although there are no formal lineages, Trio people consider the immediate and short-term continuation of the 'we' group ('real' people, kin) to be important. This is expressed concretely by the desire to have a large number of children and grandchildren. Leaders constantly exhort people to look after their children, to take proper care of them. Such emphasis may be due to the fact that place of residence during childhood, and social rather than biological parenthood, tend to be the key factors in determining ethnicity. Gabriel, for example, was born a Waiãpi, but adopted by Wayana. As an adult, he married a Trio woman. He still regards himself as a Wayana, showing that his metamorphosis of identity from Wayãpi to Wayana was completed at the onset of adulthood.

Time, History and Identity

According to the pre-missionization pattern of Guianan village life, local populations rarely grew larger than about thirty because conflict was avoided through migration: the settlement[10] would break up and disperse to form new settlements when serious tension developed (Rivière 1984). The avoidance of conflict also characterized relationships between different settlements. Because there were, under normal circumstances, no 'chieftains' uniting several settlements, and leadership roles were usually played by village founders, no clear distinction can be made between locality and ethnicity. The evidence from before missionization suggests a picture of regularly shifting settlement locations, with trade relationships and intermarriage between settlements waxing and waning (despite ideals of settlement endogamy, relationships between settlements appear often to have been sealed through the exchange of women) (Chapuis 2003; Koelewijn and Rivière 1987). We can add to this the numerous *janas* or 'peoples' that populate the accounts of early explorers,[11] maps of nineteenth-century explorers[12] and indigenous narratives (e.g. ibid.), and the contradictions between the different accounts of their names and the names given by Trio today of their *jana* (see below).

Indigenous Guianan notions of time appear to be based around the 'developmental cycle' (Goody 1958) referred to above, rather than a linear scale corresponding to genealogy. Temporal continuity, at least in terms of ordinary events, is perceived as cyclical rather than linear. Eithne Carlin shows that the Trio tense form used to describe events in the 'nonrecent past', as opposed to that used to describe those in the 'immediate past', is scarcely used except by older people. Past events not witnessed by the speaker are described using the 'nonfinite' form of the verb. The 'temporal adverbial', *pena*, meaning 'long ago', is used to refer to events that took place from a few hours or even minutes ago,[13] to the remote primordial or mythic past (Carlin 2004: 291); just how 'long ago' it refers to is indicated by context and emphasis (from *pena* to *pe-e-e-e-na*). Narratives of myth and history can be given a rough order of occurrence, but this order appears only on an ad hoc basis – when an order of events is elicited, it is drawn out logically by the interlocutor. Trio people regard myth and history as serving to explain the current order of things, and do not arrange them in a linear progression. Moreover, while historical events are often recalled with often surprising clarity, they tend to be described as very brief statements of fact, such as, 'there was a war against the Wayana', unless the events were personally experienced by the narrator. The introduction of Christianity, the Gregorian calendar and the teaching of history in schools are in the process of changing this. However, as the Trio's own history is not taught to them in schools, and since even the academic world has difficulty in reconstructing and dating their past, it is likely that their narratives will continue to collapse the passage of time to give meaning to historical events in mythical terms.

'The Trio' as a Group

How then do Trio people conceive of themselves as a group? Insofar as we can imagine the history of ethnogenesis in the central Guianas, all evidence points to the conclusion that there has been a pattern of constant but gradual change in group identity, whether in the form of exogenous appellations or of 'we' groups, and according to this pattern the idea of a fixed notion of 'tribe', frequently used to refer to Trio, Wayana and other

Guianan groups in nonspecialist (and some specialist) literature, is shown to be an illusion. It is true that such identities could far outlast the lifespan of premission villages, but they were looser and more short-lived than they would have been under the more concentrated conditions that are becoming established today.

'Trio' is a Dutchified term for *tirijo*, and is now used to refer to the people who call themselves 'Tarëno', or 'the people here'.[14] I follow convention in using the name 'Trio' to refer to all of the self-denominated Tarëno. This avoids confusion because in certain circumstances *tarëno*[15] is also locally used to refer to Akuriyo and Wayana coresidents. The name 'Trio' may derive from one of the group identities whose temporary nature I demonstrated above.[16] Carlin (2004: 14) quotes Tristan, a former Trio shaman, who claims that the 'Tïrïjo' were a subgroup of the *mono eka* (big/inclusive name) Pïrëujana.[17] The local distinction that Carlin (ibid.) has identified between *mono eka* and *jana*, roughly translatable as 'inclusive group' and 'subgroup' respectively, is very different from Frikel's 'sibs' and 'lineages' (1960: 2ff.). *Mono eka* tend to be auto-denominations of 'we' groups, whereas *jana* appear as exogenous appellations. For example, I learned from Tristan's sons Silvijn and Jack that they, and he, were Pïrëujana themselves.

The relationship between *mono eka* and *jana* is defined by their relative power and influence, and by the point of view of the speaker. In the past, according to Tristan, Silvijn and Jack, from the point of view of a Pïrëujana, Tïrïjo would be regarded as wife-takers and therefore inferior. It is probably due to colonial contact that this relationship has now been reversed and Trio/Tïrïjo has become a *mono eka*: some of the first groups to be missionized must have been Trio, leading Pïrëujana effectively to become one of its subgroups. This distinction between *mono eka* and *jana* clearly shows that hierarchical relationships between group designations are locally recognized. Despite this, such hierarchies, like those of villages and local groups, were neither permanent nor objective, and a *mono eka* at one time may have been an ordinary *jana* at another. However, the impact of missionization can be seen in the fact that the relationship between *mono eka* and *jana* has now apparently become fixed. This is proven by the fact that Silvijn and his father Tristan were both village leaders (Tristan was also a powerful shaman, a man of even greater capacity), and yet the identity of the village they led remained Trio rather than becoming Pïrëujana.

Looking at each group and tracing its history, as we go back in time we will find that it divides and redivides, fragmenting into a kaleidoscope of ethnicities. But going forwards in time, external influence, in the form not only of knowledge, but of identity itself, is constantly drawn upon to change the local group, while allowing it to reproduce. The fact that the next generation is genealogically different from the previous is always hidden by the fact that the process of integration, the primary form of which is marriage, makes consanguines. The politics of relations between the groups that exist at any one time are fundamentally influenced by this pattern.

Ethnogenesis and Alterity

In descriptions in narratives or informal conversation, *jana* may be differentiated by language, dialect or accent, by appearance, or by level of 'savagery' (*itupon*, 'forest people', are considered more barbaric and dangerous than river or village people, *patapon*). Meanwhile, their origins and their waxing and waning physical integrity are the product of the strategic location and relocation of individuals. Through the historical contingencies and changing patterns of migrations, alliance, trade, avoidance and warfare over long time periods, identities changed, appeared and disappeared. In times of war, 'subgroups' merge through intermarriage when they have been decimated – when they are tired of fighting, they arrange a marriage alliance, and in extreme cases this may mean that one group becomes incorporated into another (Kuliyaman, in Chapuis and Rivière 2003: 573).

The difficulty that people in Tëpu sometimes have in remembering their *jana* suggests that even in times of peace some identities become absorbed by others. Various individuals told me which *jana* they belonged to, but most were unable to do so, particularly younger people. The Aramajana ('sweat bee people') and the Aramiso ('Pigeon people') were together the most numerous *jana* in the village. There were also Pïrëujana ('Arrow[cane] people'), including Silvijn and his brothers and son, and one Okomojana ('Wasp people') – the latter are said to be the most numerous group in Kwamalasamutu. My interlocutors remembered stories of wars with the Wayana, the Tunajana, the Mawajana, the Apalai and the Kali'na. The Kali'na, they said, were sent by white people to fight the Trio.[18]

More charismatic and knowledgeable men have a clearer sense of *jana* identity (cf. Heckenberger 2005: 290). For instance, in Tëpu, as mentioned earlier, Kapitein Silvijn, like his father Tristan, is able clearly to name his *jana* (Pïrëujana); they are unusual in this respect, and represent the most influential family in Tëpu. Similarly, some of the most important and longstanding residents in Tëpu, such as Bram, Pesoro and Storm, claim to be Pïropï, or 'Chest', which is used as an auto-denomination by those Trio who consider themselves to be the 'real' Trio from the area around Ararapadu. These people claim to be the first to have accepted missionization, lending support to my argument above about how Trio became a *mono eka*. Bram, when asked about his *jana*, answered with obvious pride, and Storm claims his family was the first to come to the Tëpu area. Such men who were among the first converts have been able to build up more robust networks of influence than others, and most of the 'reliable' converted Trio men who took part in the Akuriyo contact expeditions (see below) were Pïropï, including Bram and Pesoro themselves.

The distinctions between *jana* can be so subtle that they are the subject of speculation among the Amerindians themselves. What may originally have been one *jana* may become two, one of which may be regarded as less human than the other. The best example of this is the Pianakoto or Pianokoto, about which there has been some ethnographic debate. Frikel betrays a glimmer of acknowledgement of the transformability of group names when he concludes that the Trio probably called either themselves or marginal groups 'Pianakotó' in the past (he is ambiguous as to which) (1964: 104). Robert Schomburgk, however, clearly distinguishes the 'Pianoghottos' from the 'Drios', noting that although they dressed similarly and both painted their bodies with *urucu* dye[19] leaving only the face, the 'Drio' was the only group he encountered whose members 'ornamented their bodies by incisions' (1845: 85). It has generally been assumed that Piana- and Piano-koto were simply spelling variations of the same name. The only exception to this is that Frikel (1960: 2–3), distinguishes the two, writing that the Pianokoto were synonymous with the Kukuyána,[20] a group hostile to intertribal contact. But he later contradicts himself, claiming that the expressions 'Piána' and 'Piáno' correspond to a dialectical difference between the Trio and the 'tribes of the Trombetas', respectively (1964: 97n). Rivière makes no distinction between Pianakoto and Pianokoto, and he found that Trio people had no memory of them (1969: 19). According to my interlocutors, however, the distinction was very clear, and they had to correct me on a number of occasions when I mistook one for another. They told me that the Pianakoto, the Eagle people, were indeed one of many ethnonyms now subsumed under the category of Tarëno. They had been enemies and friends of the Trio at different times, but they are clearly considered real 'people' (Wïtoto). The Pianokoto, on the other hand, are said to be hirsute forest-dwelling savages, dangerous and warlike, and more like spirits than humans.[21] Their condition is said to be similar to that once shared by the Wajiarikure and the Akuriyo (see below).

The subtlety with which *jana* identities change, splitting and merging, or becoming encompassed by or encompassing others, makes it difficult to find etic categories suitable to describe them. The many narratives that fill the cosmos with a proliferation of 'peoples', as I have tried to convey, are an expression of an animist cosmology in which the semi-human and nonhuman universe is organized in the same way as society itself (Brightman, Grotti and Ulturgasheva 2012). It is this quality of the universe that allows the all-important transformations of affines into kin: social relations exist even outside human society. What is remarkable in this context is the resilience of categories – of *jana* – in the face of change, and this in itself is enough to justify at least the hypothesis that they are, or were, exogamous clans as Frikel and Grupioni have claimed. My own suggestion, however – that the *jana* have persisted, in a less systematic way, at the conjuncture of history, myth and kinship – is the only one for which we have strong evidence.

Missionization and Ethnicity: The Contact of the Akuriyo

The influence of *pananakiri* (urban people [T]) of one sort or another upon Guianan ethnicities has been much greater than most ethnographic accounts allow (cf. Henley 1982). The *mono eka* of Tarëno/Trio, like that of the Waiwai (2001), as overarching categories incorporating various *jana* or 'subgroups', emerged with sustained and direct contact between Wïtoto (Amerindian [T]) and *pananakiri*. Wayana and Trio of all ages, from Tëpu, Antecume Pata and Missão, told me that in the past, the peoples used constantly to fight each other; they were fierce (*ëire*) and did not know how to live together, but the *pananakiri* brought peace, allowing different peoples to live together in large settlements instead of going to war with each other. Their commensality, in the form of collective visitors' feasts, allows the sharing of substance in a peaceful manner, and the incorporation of the group through nurture (Grotti 2009a). According to Clastres, the emergence of harmony and the end of war herald the beginning of social differentiation and the concentration of power in the hands of the chief; this constitutes the emergence of the state (2010). Without necessarily subscribing fully to his argument, it is useful to bear it in mind as we consider the case of the Akuriyo.

In Tëpu, there are a few men who are the very antithesis of the leader confident of his capacity and influence. Caitano, Ramon and Jaime are very rarely seen together. But all three have the same furtive glancing look, the slightly stooped walk, shoulders hunched, as though they expected children to throw missiles at them at any moment as they walked past. They lack confidence, never speak in public and are shy in conversation. When they ask for something, they put out their hands submissively like street beggars. They can be seen fetching and carrying objects, and now and again they emerge from the forest with the largest and most highly prized game animals. These are the Akuriyo, and their story is of an extraordinary emergence out of isolation, and into semi-slavery (Grotti 2010).

The Trio's shift to large, permanent villages involved the concentration of previously dispersed settlements in mission stations. Certain Trio men, with demonstrated capacity as hunters and influence acquired through their receptiveness to missionary teaching, were instrumental in another, more radical change undergone by the Akuriyo, a nomadic hunting and gathering people who lived in isolation near Trio territory until the late 1960s. The Trio and Wayana called them 'wild people' (*wajiarikure*), and contacted them in the late 1960s and early 1970s, in expeditions led by evangelical Protestant missionaries. At that time they numbered at least sixty-six (Yohner 1970a: 15). Before this occurred, the 'Akuriyo' avoided contact with other ethnic groups, and were feared by their neighbours.

In both historical sources and native accounts, the Akuriyo are often confused with other isolated peoples and mythical beings, particularly the Okomojana, the Wajiarikure and the Wama. The differences between these groups are unclear; although they have different names and some of the stories about them are distinct, often different narrators tell the same stories involving different groups as protagonists. My interlocutors in Tëpu were all clear that the Akuriyo, themselves made up of the Akuraekare and the Turaekare, were the same group as that known to Trio, Wayana and Kali'na as Wajiarikure/Wayalikule, and that they became known as Akuriyo through missionization and domestication.[22] The name Akuriyo comes from an auto-denomination used by one of the allied (intermarrying) groups into which the nomadic foragers had organized themselves: the Akuriekare ('Agouti[23] people'). Although these different *kare* (collectivities, cf. *jana*) used to be very numerous according to Fabiola Jara's informant, only one other was brought to Tëpu: the Turaekare ('Capuchin monkey[24] people') (1990: 23). My own main Akuriyo informant, Sil, told me that his father was 'Turajana', or 'Taribijana', these being a partial and full translation respectively into Trio of 'Turaekare'.

Just weeks before the first missionary expedition in 1968, the French-naturalized Wayana André Cognat visited a group of twenty-seven Akuriyo on the Ouaramapane creek, with two other Wayana, and found them in good health, and reasonably friendly (A. Cognat pers. comm.; Cognat and Massot 1977). Describing the same expedition, André's adopted brother Mimisiku told me, 'the Akuriyo also say *kule* [good] to people, because they are not bad.' Shortly afterwards, the first of a series of Trio and Wayana expeditions, led by American missionaries, located a group of Akuriyo. On subsequent expeditions, some Trio remained with the Akuriyo to gain their confidence and learn their language. After various other sedentarization schemes failed (planting fruit trees and manioc, starting a Maroon-run manioc 'farm' to encourage trade, etc.), and progressive contact had led to major health problems among the Akuriyo, the missionaries decided to cut their losses and bring the Akuriyo to settle in Tëpu with the Trio (Schoen n.d.; Schoen and Crocker n.d.; Yohner 1970a, b, c; Schoen 1971; Conley 2000: 393).

Primarily because they were nomadic hunter-gatherers, the Akuriyo were considered wild and inhuman by their captors – indeed, were it not for the influence of the missionaries, the Trio and Wayana would not have contacted them at all for the purposes of trade or alliance. If they had entered into a cycle of raids with each other then, because of their perceived wildness, the Trio and Wayana would have taken no prisoners – indeed, this is what occurs in the story of Aturai (Koelewijn and Rivière 1987: 253ff.; see below). Although the Akuriyo had deliberately and completely isolated themselves, hoping to exclude themselves from the Janus logic of war and trade, the result was a prolonged Hobbesian war – effectively a 'cold' war, with a constant threat of violence. The sudden transformation of the relationship between Trio and Wayana and Akuriyo from that of enemy strangers to coresidents has had far-reaching consequences, but here I shall look at the relationship in terms of historical inter-group relations and kinship.[25] The Akuriyo in Tëpu today are effectively servants or 'captive slaves' (Santos Granero 2009) of the Trio and Wayana. Akuriyo nuclear families live in different parts of the village, each attached to the household of a Trio family. Although they are spoken of as children, Akuriyo men are also often treated in some respects as though they were sons-in-law, as subservient a relationship as is possible between adults in traditional kinship terms, and implying indebtedness. However, it is rare to find an Akuriyo man actually married to a Trio or Wayana woman. The only cases are of young Akuriyo marrying old women. One Trio man in Kwamalasamutu gave his widowed mother-in-law in marriage to a young Akuriyo, who then performed all of the brideservice duties that her son-in-law owed to her (P. Rivière pers. comm. 2008). On the other hand, for a Trio man to be married to an Akuriyo woman is favourable in practical terms, because he can hardly be obliged to carry out brideservice for an Akuriyo father-in-law.[26] The only example of this in Tëpu involved a Trio man who was said to have murdered a young Akuriyo boy who had made himself unpopular by stealing things. The Trio man left the village for at least six months. He then returned and married the boy's mother.

In Guiana, coresidence usually leads to social absorption – structurally, through marriage, and affectively, through commensality. That this has not happened to the Akuriyo cannot simply be attributed to the influence of missionaries, because many other evangelized groups have been incorporated (cf. Howard 2001), and missionaries have been largely absent from the village since the outbreak of the war of the interior in the mid-1980s. Narratives of identity that have defined certain 'peoples' as fierce and cannibalistic play a role. These narratives differentiate 'superior', riverine, horticulturalist, trading people from 'inferior', forest-dwelling, foraging people. They lead the domestication of such peoples to take on a different character from the domestication of other horticulturalist peoples. Akuriyo are treated and addressed as nonkin, but they are fed, nurtured and educated as though in order to make them into kin. They are in a constant state of becoming, but are also, partly as a result of this, reduced socially. Their status recalls the Jivaroan process of shrinking heads: as enemy others, they must undergo a process of reduction that takes the form of social incorporation as children of the local group. But this process takes away their agency and renders them innocuous (Descola 1993: 302–7). The twist in the Trio and Wayana's relationship with the Akuriyo is that the Akuriyo can still be rendered their agency when they go into the forest, where they can become powerful hunters who can 'see' as no Trio or Wayana can (Grotti 2009b). The Trio and Wayana, with Akuriyo to hunt for them, are therefore able to concentrate on cultivating their familiarity with the more powerful knowledge of white people.

In terms of leadership, the case of the Akuriyo is both telling and exceptional. The contact expeditions gave an opportunity for men such as Bram and Pesoro to demonstrate their capacities and to extend their influence. Yet instead of incorporating the Akuriyo as kin following their domestication, they maintained a kernel of difference. The Akuriyo, after they were brought to Tëpu, were parcelled out among their captors, and became their wards. They are referred to as both 'children' (*jimuku*) and as subordinates/sons-in-law (*pëito*). What appears as a case of familiarizing predation (Fausto 2001) is carried out across the distinction between consanguinity and affinity, and the Akuriyo remain servants to this day, never fully familiarized. The reason for this, I suspect, has much to do with the fact that their custodians have taken on the Christian missionary role of teachers (*enpa*), teaching the Akuriyo both how to live as Trio, and about the gospel. These men of capacity and influence thus take on a nurturing role, favouring homogenization and domestication, which is usually associated with female agency. As Marilyn Strathern has argued, 'men and women alternate between orientation towards their own sex (which separates them from the other) and orientation to the other (which combines it with their own). In that framework, a person can act from either gender position' (2001a: 226). From this point of view, male leaders embody female agency when incorporating others, and this also occurs during rituals, as chapter 4 will show.

Slavery and Identity

Recalling Clastres's argument about the emergence of harmony and the end of war, do the missionization of the Trio, the subsequent emphasis on harmony and the capture of the Akuriyo constitute fundamental political changes in Trio society? The domestication of the Akuriyo should be understood alongside other examples of 'captive slavery' (Santos Granero 2009), mastery and familiarizing predation (Fausto 2001, 2008) in Amazonia. The following Trio story sheds some light upon how the Trio-Akuriyo relationship is situated in Trio thought.

Story of Aturai

The story of Aturai (from Koelewijn and Rivière 1987: 253–61) begins:

> Aturai lived long ago, in a time when there were many people. In the area of Samuwaka lived many Trio: Pïrëujana, Tïrïjo, Akïjo, and others. Some had come this way, to the Tapanahony: Waripi or Okomojana, who had mixed with the fierce Akuriyo. The Akuriyo and the Okomojana were trading-partners. In fact both the Akuriyo and the Okomojana were known as fierce people. The Pïrëujana however were trading-partners with Tïrïjo and Aramajana. They lived together, just as we now see Trio living here together with Waijana, and elsewhere [at Kwamala Samoetoe] Trio living together with Waiwai and Tunajana (Koelewijn and Rivière 1987: 253).

Aturai and his younger brother are kidnapped by the Akuriyo and Okomojana. Aturai learns that the Akuriyo plan to eat them both, so he escapes back to his own village. Once there, it emerges that he has superhuman abilities as a wrestler and warrior. He convinces the other Trio to prepare themselves for war, and they surround the Akuriyo and Okomojana village and kill everyone except one child. This child leads them to another village, where they try to kill everyone, but another child covered in eagle down, who first appears on top of the roof of a house, proves to move too fast for them to kill. This child, called Marïtïikë, turns out to have even greater supernatural abilities than Aturai, and he can hunt prodigious quantities of game using only a spear or a machete. Aturai, worried that Marïtïikë may seek revenge on the Trio, decides to give him a wife and thus make him 'junior' (pëito, 'jipëetome wapëjae' [Koelewijn 1984 vol. 1: 245]). Marïtïikë refuses to kill some relatives of the Akuriyo who had been killed by the Trio when asked to do so, because he has not yet been given a wife. The Trio kill many more Akuriyo. Maritïikë says that he is a Pianakoto. He is given incisions, and cleansed with a certain moss used for the purpose of cleansing prisoners of war. Finally Aturai is satisfied with the revenge he has taken.

The Okomojana and the Akuriyo now live peacefully with Trio people, primarily in Kwamalasamutu and Tëpu respectively; the Okomojana intermarry with and are treated as equals by Trio people, in contrast with the Akuriyo. Two factors may explain this difference: (1) the Okomojana, unlike the Akuriyo, already 'knew about' horticulture, and (2) the missionaries appear to have taken a less direct role in the integration of the Okomojana. The significance of these two factors will become clearer below.

In the story of Aturai, the 'fierce' Akuriyo and Okomojana literally eat their prisoners, whereas the Trio Aturai give his prisoner a wife in order to make him his 'subordinate' – illustrating a key strategy, which will be explained in due course. There are two outsiders in the story, in one case a Trio with a partially Akuriyo upbringing (Aturai), and in the other case a Pianakoto (Maritïikë), and each has prodigious abilities. The outsider, because of his supposedly greater knowledge of the forest and spirit world, is potentially dangerous, and the only way to benefit from his abilities without danger is to take control of him, by domesticating him through marriage.

The Akuriyo have been similarly domesticated in Tëpu, and their prodigious hunting abilities make them valuable servants for the Trio. Yet no Trio parents would want their daughter to marry an Akuriyo, because the Akuriyo lack the capacities and influence that are most valued. Although Akuriyo are recognized as great hunters and honey gatherers, they have no other skills that are recognized by the Trio. They are considered poor gardeners, they have few relatives, and they have no connections in the world of *pananakiri* and money. Akuriyo women's manioc processing skills are often derided with stories of how people were once poisoned because the prussic acid was not correctly removed. Trio people do not, however, merely see the Akuriyo as lesser human beings, with diminished social capacities and stunted networks of influence. Their difference is qualitative rather than quantitative, and stems from Trio categories of human personhood and marriageability.

Marriage and Manioc

Trio and Wayana shun marriage with Akuriyo, but marriage frequently occurs between Trio and Wayana in either combination of sexes. The exceptional treatment of the Akuriyo cannot be said to be due only to their former reputation for fierceness (the Okomojana have been able to intermarry with Trio to such an extent that they are now considered Trio themselves). Nor can it be fully explained by the contrived nature of coresidence with them, as a result of outside influence.[27] The more fundamental explanation is that the Akuriyo lacked the quintessentially humanizing food, bitter manioc. For Trio people, it does not matter that the Akuriyo may have had gardens and bitter manioc in the past,[28] or that they were allies of other *janas* long ago. Their lack of manioc is seen as the ultimate evidence of savagery, compared to which their inferior knowledge of Christianity is a mild stigma.

The 'domestication' or 'taming' (*ɯpamnehe* [W]) of other groups occurs throughout Guiana (Howard 2001). Once settlements are in contact, they maintain their relationship through a variety of prestations expressed in the institution of the alliance feast. As chapter 4 will show, these involve the prestation of manioc on the part of the hosts and that of game on that of the guests, metaphors of consanguinity and affinity, femininity and masculinity, respectively. The Surinamese Trio and Wayana, as Christian converts, had been convinced of the superiority of their newly modified way of life. When they went to contact other groups, it was not for the purpose of alliance in the conventional sense. Their purpose was evangelical, and as such it was to give culture, not to receive it; correspondingly, to give manioc, and not to receive it. The result was integration, or, in the case of the Akuriyo, incorporation and subjection: an unequal alliance.

Although they were not 'tamed' by the Trio or Wayana in the same sense as other Amerindian groups were, it is useful to compare the case of the Maroons (*mekoro*). Like the Akuriyo, Trio say that *mekoro* do not 'know about' manioc (although in fact they do grow it); also like the Akuriyo, they do not consider *mekoro* to be suitable marriage partners. The modalities of the relationship between categories of person are thus expressed in the reciprocal or nonreciprocal prestation of beer and women: 'real' people gave manioc to Akuriyo and Maroons, who are nevertheless classified as 'lacking' manioc; this marks them out as unsuitable wife-takers. The reason for the importance of lacking manioc is not simply that it exemplifies cultural difference. Instead, it shows that the Akuriyo's bodies are different, and is the strongest evidence of the fact, because for Trio people, manioc is the quintessential human food.

Now it is possible to understand the difference between the Trio's relationships with the Maroons and with the Akuriyo. The former were trading partners (*jipawana*), and as such neither wife-givers nor wife-takers (see chapter 3). Marriage alliances with them were never contemplated, and the relationship was largely articulated on an individual basis through trade. The Akuriyo, in contrast, came to live with the Trio because of an arbitrary decision made by outside agents.[29] They could not intermarry with them because of their bodily difference, but as coresidents their relationship needed to be expressed in appropriate terms. They therefore became servants: brideservants without brides.

Strategic Ethnicity

I have tried to show that Guianan ethnicity operates according to the same logic in a premission context of warfare and alliance succeeding one another, as it does when these practices have adapted to the projects of evangelical missionaries. Social organization thus appears to follow the same patterns of historical transformation as myth. The current tendency, however, is for leaders to assert their identity as a political strategy in its own right (Brightman 2008a). Amerindians, even those from the central highlands of Guiana, find themselves implicated in a wider world of international politics where their principal political capital is based on their 'indigeneity'. Many of the good Portuguese speakers among the Trio or Kaxuyana whom I met, such as Ronaldo, who was educated in Missão, or Ferrinho, who had worked a great deal with Brazilian gold prospectors, would often repeat phrases such as *sou Indio* ('I'm an Indian'), or *indio é assim* ('that's how Indian is'). These were not leaders, but ordinary men, whose contact with Brazilians had impressed upon them their identity. In Suriname and French Guyana, the Wayana and Trio's neighbours, the Maroons, because of their long history of trade with them, differentiate between distinct Amerindian groups. Brazilian gold prospectors, who have had a history of conflict with Amerindians, appear to regard them all as generic 'Indians'. Through the assertive manner with which they adopt this layer of identity, the 'Indians' themselves begin to use it for their own ends. As 'Indians', they know about the forest, and it belongs to them. The people who spoke to me about this, whether Wayana, Trio or urban Kali'na, all deliberately reiterated the stereotypical discourse that the 'Indian' belongs to the forest, he knows about its products, it provides his livelihood, and without it he dies. However, rather than reflecting a fundamental change of self-identification, these instances all involved individuals addressing me as an outsider and a white person. They were adoptions of a particular perspective as a social strategy.[30] The question of the extent of the accuracy of this image of the 'ecological' Amerindian deserves to be discussed separately, but the important point here is that it is used as part of a political strategy based on ethnicity.

In the village, ordinary alliance feasts and other rituals have taken on new forms, involving guitars, Christian hymns and Sranan *poku* sound systems (see chapter 4), but as with the production of 'traditional' craftworks, generic 'Indian' dances are put on to satisfy the stereotypes sought by film crews, researchers and tourists. In Tëpu, on one occasion a small group of Swiss tourists arrived unannounced, and the resourceful Kapitein Silvijn hurriedly mustered a dance troupe in order to earn money from the visitors; the dancers put on an impromptu parody of a Maroon dance that was more amusing to the local population than to the tourists themselves. The ironic nature of such a performance suggests that these uses of Amerindian ethnicity are not examples of cultural exploitation. They instead manifest the strategic use of a knowingly constructed ethnicity in order to obtain goods or cash.[31]

Leadership Inside and Out

The strongest constant element that can be observed in the pre-mission as well as in the contemporary patterns of supralocal relations on all levels is that relatedness is constantly being actively reconstructed and transformed. The scale of this has changed since missionization, and Trio people express great contentment at living in large villages, where they claim they are at peace with each other and can potentially marry a greater diversity of people. However, 'relatedness derives from both birth and conviviality' (Lepri 2005: 720), and the influence of a leader is strongest along the networks of consanguinity that loosely correspond to the *jana*.

Having said this, today's official Trio leaders are characterized by a twofold or double definition. On one hand, they emerge from society as men with exceptional capacities and strong networks of influence. On the other hand, they have been appointed – anointed, as it were – from outside, handpicked by missionaries and endorsed by the state. From the point of view of Trio people, it is the former that counts, but outsiders only recognize the official trappings of leadership: titles and offices, which were indeed, for a number of years from the 1960s onwards, made visible with official uniforms. Trio leaders thus seem to exemplify two contradictory theories of political power. As Marshall Sahlins writes, the first is associated with the widespread figure of the stranger-king, as well as Joseph Gumplowicz and Franz Oppenheimer's theories of the origin of the state in conquest: 'This conception of power as foreign to society has latterly given way to a variety of others – Marxist, biological, the social contract – alike in their understanding of political authority as an internal growth, springing from the essence of human social relations or dispositions' (1985: 76). Clastres's argument about the suppression of the emergence of the state is conceived in terms of this second field of thought, but ironically may have been improved had he argued in terms of the first. The only indigenous Amazonian leaders with real power to emerge outside contexts of warfare emerged just as sporadically, as messianic prophets, whose power derived from their association with the outside (Hugh-Jones 1994). Though far from being stranger-kings, they came to personify something foreign (except that, far from personifying the state, they tended to lead armed resistance against it). Similarly, as pastors and official leaders, the *kapiteins* and *Granman* may personify the power of the bible and the state, but it is primarily from an external perspective that they are quasi-stranger-kings. From a Trio perspective, however, these leaders are indeed an 'internal growth', a magnification of everyday masculinity, but this does not constitute a rejection of the outsider's perspective; instead, it is merely the expression of a different cosmological framework.

Notes

1. Suriname has the largest maroon community in the Western Hemisphere (Price 1976: ix). Often referred to as the Bush Negros (Bosnegers in Dutch; Businengre in Sranan), they include six tribes: the Djuka or Ndjuka and the Saramaka (each 15–20,000 people; the Matawai, the Aluku and the Paramaka, each around 2000; and the Kwinti, fewer than 500) (ibid.: 3–4). Greatly outnumbering the Amerindian population upstream, they dominate the middle reaches of the Saramacca, Suriname and Maroni rivers, and the lower parts of the Tapanahoni and Lawa, tributaries of the Maroni.
2. In exceptional cases, the leader may be a woman. There are two female *chefs coutumières* in French Guiana, among the relatively highly educated coastal Lokono and Kali'na.
3. Moreover, Article 13 of the Peace Accord of Lelydorp (1992) 'stipulates that the legal status, authority and the stipend paid to these authorities must be strengthened and increased and that the government will do so by enacting legal regulations after consultation with those concerned', although little change has occurred since the accord was signed (Kambel and MacKay 1999: 129) (the Peace Accord marked the end of the Surinamese civil war, the War of the Interior, which had begun in 1985. It was signed by representatives of the government and leaders of the Indigenous and Maroon insurgents [ibid.: 121]).
4. My own Wayana friends and interlocutors happened to be particularly close to André, who, together with Mimisiku, had adopted Gabriel as a boy when he fled from pelt hunters in his native Wayãpi territory in Brazil. I was aware of other Wayanas' negative opinions of him however, as a white interloper with no claims to Wayana identity at all. All of this further illustrates how ethnicity and identity are continually contested and dependent on context, particularly in Guiana.

5. As later chapters show, these are quintessentially masculine activities which it is odd to associate with a 'feminine principle'.

6. Schomburgk reflects on the disparity between endogenous and exogenous group names: 'The custom of each tribe of Indians having their own names for the adjacent tribes, as also for their chief rivers and mountains, renders it very difficult to identify the said tribes and rivers &c.' (1845: 83).

7. Although in this case intermarriage has been explicitly encouraged by a Wapishana leader as part of a land claim strategy (G. and L. Mentore, pers. comm. 2006).

8. Cf. Schomburgk 1845: 55–7; Coudreau 1887a: 351; Farabee 1924: 175.

9. Cf. Kuper 1982.

10. Here I use the term 'settlement' to distinguish the relatively impermanent villages of the past with the large conglomerate villages of today.

11. E.g. Harcourt's 1608 account of the Maroni (1928: 118).

12. E.g. Coudreau (1887b, c).

13. Carlin writes 'last week' as the most recent time referred to by *pena*, but I also heard it used in phrases like 'I ate a little while ago', or 'I have already eaten'.

14. Schomburgk (1845) refers to the 'Drio', and Coudreau (1887a) to the 'Trio' and the 'Chiriou'. Frikel was told that the name 'Tiriyó' derived from *Wátüre*, to kill using a club, and that this was the Tiriyó's principal arm (1960: 1). According to Rivière, 'the more easterly group of Trio call themselves ... Tirïyo', and this gave rise to the Maroon and Surinamese 'Trio', and the French and Brazilian 'Tiriyó'; only the western group of Trio called themselves Tarëno, and the Waiwai called them Yawï (Rivière 1969: 11). It appears that the situation has now changed, and all the 'Trio' call themselves Tarëno, except when speaking foreign languages. They are called *Tiliyo* by the Wayana.

15. It is difficult to categorize *tarëno* either as a proper name or simply as a noun referring to 'the people here'. I italicize it when the usage seems closer to the latter, and capitalize the first letter when the former seems to be the case. However, this ambiguity is worth noting, because it is also relevant to other 'ethnonyms', to various degrees.

16. Rivière (1969: 11) notes this possibility.

17. This information is coherent with Frikel's account (1960: 10–11): he was told that the Pïrëujana were composed of the Pïrëujana 'proper', and the 'Rãgú (piki)'.

18. This is probably true (cf. Dreyfus 1992). My older Kali'na interlocutors also told me that the Trio were fearsome warriors, as well as having powerful spirit songs.

19. From the seed of annatto or achiote, *Bixa orellana*.

20. Firefly people (Chapuis and Rivière 2003).

21. The names Piana and Pianokoto are used by Trio and Wayana, although the word for harpy eagle in both languages is *Piana*. I was unable to discover the meaning of the word *piano*. It is possible that it is a corruption of *piana*, pronounced deliberately differently to convey some peculiar attribute of the Pianokoto, such as strange form of speech.

22. The Wayana appear to have differentiated the Wayalikule ('long ears'?) from the Wama (*wama*, or *wama hale*, in Wayana, means arouman, *Ischnosiphon arouma*, a type of cane used for weaving, and of which people are said to have been made). Crevaux was told by his Boni hosts that the 'Oyacoulets' were tall and fair, and were named after their peaceful (but treacherous) greeting, 'Coulé-Coulé' (cf. *kure*, 'good' in Trio and Akuriyo) (1993: 70). Ahlbrinck met members of both groups in 1938 on the upper Oelemari but claimed that a woman he brought to Paramaribo was the last Wajiarikure (1956). André Cognat and Mimisiku both told me that they thought they had found the Wayalikule in the forest, until they identified themselves as Ak-

uriyo. The Wayalikule were also known to the Wayana at the time as the 'long ears' (Cognat and Massot 1977), a group reported to live on the headwaters of the Maroni since the earliest records. John Ley heard of 'Indyans with longe and large eares hangeing uppon their showlders' (Lorimer 1994: 207), and Harcourt heard that these long-eared natives were of enormous proportions (1928: 208). Fisher, Harcourt's cousin, heard that the long-eared Amerindians were extraordinarily kind and gentle (Harcourt 1928: 173), which suggests that this group, later reputed to be fierce, might not always have been so.

23. *Dasyprocta leporina.*
24. *Cebus apella.*
25. See Brightman and Grotti 2010 for further discussion of this topic.
26. Similarly, 'Whilst Tukanoans sometimes take Makú wives, Makú men do not marry Tukanoan women' (Silverwood-Cope 1972: 200).
27. Cf. Keifenheim 1997, on 'wild' Mashiku Amerindians 'pacified' by the Kashinawa: their status is ambiguously poised between those of 'brother-in-law' and 'slave'.
28. 'One Akuriyo woman said that her mother had told her about manioc bread' (Schoen and Crocker n.d.: 5).
29. In fact this took place almost by accident – it was not planned by the missionaries, who decided at the last moment to transport the Akuriyo to Tëpu because of serious deteriorations in their health following contact (Schoen 1971)
30. Cf. Vilaça 2006.
31. See Hugh-Jones 1992, who shows how Barasana employ whatever means necessary in order to obtain the things they want from white people.

Chapter 2

HOUSES AND IN-LAWS

> A fractal person is never a unity standing in relation
> to an aggregate, or an aggregate standing in relation
> to a unity, but always an entity with relationship inte-
> grally implied.
> —Roy Wagner, 'The Fractal Person'

As we have seen, leaders make groups by speaking about them and on behalf of them, and by representing, even 'being' the group. These activities are grounded in the space of the village, and more specifically, in the
house. Besides hunting, the principal activities expressing masculinity
involve making things, including woven artefacts, tools, weapons and,
above all, houses. This chapter will focus on how houses are made and
on how affinal and consanguineal relations converge in them. The term
'house societies' was coined by Lévi-Strauss (1983: 186; 1987: 151ff.) 'to
refer to societies that have hereditary ranking but without rigidly defined
classes, territories, or property rights (i.e. the bureaucratic state)' (Heckenberger 2005: 64). This strict definition, suitable for certain northwest
Amazonian and central Brazilian groups (Hugh-Jones 1995; Lea 1995)
does not apply to Guianan society, which lacks 'hereditary ranking'. However, it does preserve an estate of mixed principles, like canonical house
societies. There is much ambiguity in Lévi-Strauss's own writings on the
house, and much debate among other authors, as to the significance of
stratification as a defining attribute of house societies; such things as the

tension between alliance and descent (Lévi-Strauss 1987, in Waterson 1995: 50) or the centrality of 'monogamous marriage in both the symbolism and the organization of kinship' (Bloch 1995) may be more significant than the distinction between 'differentiated' and 'undifferentiated' societies (Howell 1995: 151). As in Langkawi (Carsten 1995), the house can be seen as a model for society, despite, or rather perhaps because of, its characteristic transience.

The concept of 'house societies' was conceived in order to understand 'societies made up of units which cannot be defined either as families or as clans or lineages' (Lévi-Strauss 1987: 151), in other words to address a problem also posed by Guianan ethnography. Rivière observed that 'as a building, group or category the visible Guiana house is a contingent entity dependent on its invisible counterpart' (1995: 204). This succinctly expresses in a concrete manner something fundamental to Guianan social organization. Political leadership and social organization are very closely linked to village foundation, the essence of which is housebuilding, and in the invisible archetype of the house we can see something of the cosmological reflection of concrete practice. If the clearing of land and the building of a house are assertions of leadership qualities, as I argue they are, then the house itself can surely tell us a great deal about the politics of family and village life. Indeed, just as a leader is creator and owner (*entu*) of the village, so a man is the builder and owner of his house, and this allows for the most powerful form of political expression because in Guiana, as I have mentioned, people vote with their feet: they do not hesitate to relocate when they have become discontent with their situation. The relationship between marriage and the house is also of great practical and symbolic importance, because of the practice of uxorilocality. Kinship, village foundation, housebuilding and property relations closely mirror each other and can be explained in mutually constitutive terms. These things are in fact 'transformations' of one another on differing scales.

Leadership, Inequality and the House

For Trio people, the transformation of space from forest (*itu*) into place, whether village (*pata*) or garden (*tëpitë*) is the defining act of appropriation that creates ownership and belonging. It is most of all through enacting such transformations that leadership emerges, and this can be seen very clearly on a domestic scale, that is to say, in housebuilding. As property, houses are inextricably associated with the individuals who have sponsored their construction. Ownership of a house is not expressed using temporary controlled possessive constructions (*X entume wae*), but using permanent possessive constructions (*tï pakoroke wae*). Houses are not exchanged, but instead when one is no longer wanted it is abandoned. However, the materiality of the house does express a certain level of continuity and of economic wealth. It is common to salvage whatever materials can be reused, such as hardwood houseposts, upon relocation. Because of the labour that is required to build any kind of house, and, nowadays, the cost of tools and certain desirable building materials purchased in the city, the houses that people live in or are associated with are clear indicators of their position and wealth. The most obvious and visible are the signs of material wealth – that is, objects that require cash to acquire them. These include corrugated zinc and sawn planks – the latter because of the petrol that is needed to operate the chainsaw in order to cut them. People often express the desire to improve their dwellings in various ways, and speak admiringly of such improvements, and disparagingly of old or poor-quality materials. The more durable the materials that are used, the more likely they are to be reused, and therefore such wealth visibly accumulates among those who have access to it, accompanied by prestige. A house may be said to express social organization in two ways: firstly, any house is the material expression of its builder's position as head of household. Secondly, the particular features and dimensions of a given house express economic wealth, the scale of labour that the builder could muster, and thus his prestige position relative to other housebuilders.

Village foundation is a political activity of profound importance. This has been widely acknowledged in Amazonian ethnography (Arvelo Jiménez 1973; Goldman 1963; Overing 1975). But neither Clastres (1974) nor Waud Kracke (1978), in the two most ambitious attempts to describe Amazonian leadership, recognize the significance of it; even Rivière, in arguing for the political foundations of settlement patterns in Guiana (1984), despite his argument's emphasis of spatial organization, focused on the negative part of the process, when coresidents split into rival groups until one relocates. This may be because village foundation involves the simple building of a house in a newly cleared location. Housebuilding is, however, on any scale a declaration of political autonomy. Building a house constitutes an assertion of independence on the part of a man who previously, in most cases, lived in the house of his wife's father (see below).

Leadership qualities are not only expressed in the act of relocation itself. Building usually involves a small amount of communal labour, although this is not an absolute requirement. When I went to collect strong saplings for rafters with Boasz, my grandfather, for example, my meagre efforts constituted more help than he would usually have had. The part of building that is most conducive to communal work is thatching. I tried to lend a hand at this, and for a beginner the intricate process of twisting fresh green bifurcated leaves of *wai* (T)[1] is slow work. Each new leaf adds only half an inch of progress along the batten and the process of making an entire roof is a long one. The more men perched among the rafters, the better. Labour is obtained not through the payment of cash, but by means of a complex mechanism of reciprocity. The workers treat the day of work like a relaxed party, and are provided with drink and sometimes food by the sponsor. Rather than constituting 'payment' for the work, these refreshments can be described as a token of reciprocity, of the fact that similar work will be carried out at some time in the future, or has been at some time in the past, by the sponsor for each worker when they in turn should require it. Nevertheless, the work is not explicitly regarded as being carried out in return for other work. The attitude of the workers is that a pleasant atmosphere of *sasame* (harmony, euphoria[2]) is created, by the sharing of *tënisen* (T) (beer), which is conducive to helping others (especially the provider of the drink – or rather, her husband). In order to muster workers, it is therefore important to have a good garden, producing plenty of manioc, and a wife who makes good beer. It is also important to have good relations with other men, and for one's own skills, especially those as a housebuilder, to be valued. A good hunter may also find it easier to summon a workforce because a person who earns his favour is likely to be sent a few choice pieces of meat, especially if he is also reasonably closely related.

It would be wrong to think of the process of organizing labour solely in terms of direct or indirect exchange, generalized reciprocity, submission to charismatic leadership or communal labour, but all of these play some role. It is useful to consider the relationships between housebuilders and their helpers; close kin often help, but usually only when they have a direct interest in the new building – son and nephews, for example. Otherwise, helpers tend to be affines who are in some kind of junior relationship towards the housebuilder; the most obvious of these is the daughter's husband. Indeed, Boasz and his son-in-law Gabriel, my friends and hosts, often worked together on the former's house, with the latter doing the hardest tasks. Akuriyo also normally help with building. As well as relationship status, inequalities in the village are revealed though housebuilding because of the importance of charisma and the resources required for generating a workforce. Men with less personal charisma, or less productive gardens, and younger men without subordinates (*pëito* [T]), tend to have more difficulty in mustering workers, and it is therefore common to find young men's houses in protracted states of partial construction. These differences in personal influence are also reflected in residence practices, as more influential men often have others living in their houses while less influential men often live in the house of another. They also partly explain the marked differences between the poorest Akuriyo house and the richest Trio house, as we shall see.

Households and Housebuilders

When a man marries, he lives in his father-in-law's house for a variable period of time. At some point, because of a dispute or the death of his father-in-law, or because the family has grown too large, and when he is strong and responsible enough, and sufficiently skilled in hunting, fishing and other masculine activities, he may relocate and build a house. This occurs according to exactly the same pattern as village foundation. Indeed, we should not find this surprising, as it was precisely in the developmental cycle of the family that Meyer Fortes and others found the intersection of the family and the political spheres in many types of society (Goody 1958). Building and the necessary organization of work parties are assertions of leadership on variable scales. On the most equitable level and smallest scale, two men of similar standing may work for each other on different occasions, each submitting to the other on the other's territory. In this sense, the domestic house is a microcosm of the village. Even local visitors to a domestic house are offered drink when it is available, and they bring conversation and animation – exchanging knowledge for drink. Sometimes they will bring meat. Thus the male visitor/dancer : female host/provider of drink dichotomy, as we shall see with regard to the *tukusipan* (below) and flute rituals (in chapter 4), exists on the domestic scale as well as on that of the collectivity as a whole.

This dimension of housebuilding manifests itself in different ways, which highlight the differences between individuals. There is another discrepancy between housebuilding and leadership: a village leader is openly regarded as temporary whereas a housebuilder is permanently its owner. This is expressed linguistically in the distinct forms of possessive construction used: temporary in the former instance (*pata entu*, village leader/owner), and permanent in the latter (*tï pakoroke wae*, I have a house / am 'with-house'). This difference is moreover at odds with real events: villages may outlast houses, and nowadays usually do. Village leadership has also become more durable and secure with missionization. The most likely explanation is a simple one: *pata* refers not only to place (village), but also to the people within it, and the relationship between a leader and his followers is constantly reaffirmed and potentially contested. This is consistent with Lévi-Strauss's (1943) reciprocal model of leadership. This explanation has implications for the role of leader itself, which poses a challenge to Clastres (1974): if there is a distinction between the roles of leadership and that of the household head, then the possibility arises that leadership can be treated as an institution, the public sphere may be said to be locally recognized and so, for what it is worth, Amerindian society may 'have' a state (defined as the public sphere as distinct from the private) after all.

However, it is worth remembering that in the past villages were often single domestic units, and this highlights that the leader and the house-builder are structurally equivalent; the distinction between the terms refers to the distinct activities of placemaking and representing the people who dwell in that place. There are many elements of consistency shared by the village and the house, and the purpose of this chapter is to focus upon the political significance of the latter, whether expressed in the dynamics of certain relationships between kin or affines, or in the foundation and maintenance of status.

In view of the permanent association between houses and their builders, and the fact that consequently a house is generally abandoned following its builder's death, we can see and explain many observable differences in contemporary building, which tell us much about Trio and Wayana society today. Differences between domestic dwellings reflect not only differences between individuals' ability to organize labour, but also their access to cash and other transferable resources. The manner of construction of foreign agents' building projects reflects their differing relationships with local people and highlights the economic influence they exert.

The House as Artefact

The house is a dynamic object, which manifests living relationships and the movement of people. Ordinary houses (*pakoro* [T/W]) can take on a variety of forms, but share a single basic design: Four vertical corner posts of hardwood (typically *kunawa*[3]), support horizontal lintels of lighter wood. At least one other, longer hardwood post, centrally placed, supports the middle part of the ridge purlin. The gable lintels carry vertical posts that support the ends of the ridge purlin at the gable; the side lintels and ridge purlin carry rafters, to support the courses of thatch. A ridge pole is laid over the rafters where they cross the ridge purlin, to carry the ridge thatch. The gable ends may be covered with thatch, the double battens either being connected to the last rafters in such a way as to form a flat gable, or else fanned out using further vertical posts supporting extra rafters to make a hood-shaped round gable or apse. In the latter case, the effect is to give the house a lozenge shape, a form known as *paiman*. The gable end away from the prevailing wind is sometimes left open. In the past, the eaves usually reached to the ground, but it is now more usual, in houses designed for sleeping in, to have walls made of planks, secured with nails, either closely fitting each other vertically or slightly overlapping horizontally. In other buildings used for cooking, eating, weaving, processing manioc and other activities, the eaves are lengthened using long palm leaves such as *kumu*,[4] or else the sides may be left open. Corrugated zinc is often used instead of thatch, both for main houses and outhouses, and, being only available to those who can afford it, has prestige value.[5] Flat roofs, inclined in order to let the rain run off, are often used for dog houses and cookhouses. They are made of old pieces of corrugated zinc, flattened oil barrels or old sections of thatching, or a patchwork of any combination of these. Some houses simply have beaten and brushed earth floors. This is the case for all houses that are not designed for sleeping in, with the following exceptions: the school, the clinic, the airstrip radio building, the Telesur radio house, the Jaraware library, the ACT buildings and dog houses. This last exception, which may appear incongruous, shows the great care that is taken of dogs. Although they often howl miserably while tied or chained into their houses, where they are often not fed in preparation for a hunt, the floor protects them from chiggers, enabling them to run faster. The buildings mentioned, as well as some of the main domestic houses, have floors made of planks carried on beams supported by the main posts, to which they are attached with dado

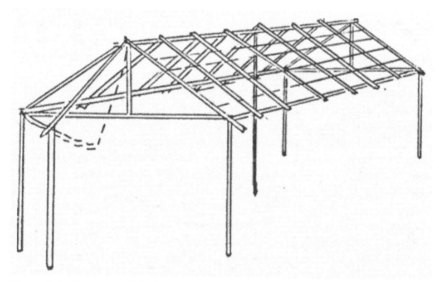

Figure 2.1. Structure of the basic domestic house.

joints – this type of raised house, now known simply as *pakoro*, is recorded by Frikel under the name *mekoro-pan*, because it had been adopted from Maroon house types (1973); the Maroons in turn may have adopted this form from the Kali'na, who Jean-Marcel Hurault records as using a similar design (1973).[6] In domestic houses, the floor is usually constructed high enough to allow the space beneath to be used for various activities, such as chatting, drinking and dancing. The planks used for walls are, in some houses, of a rough kind cut with a machete, but floors require well-cut planks made with a chainsaw. They are therefore expensive.

There is a clear correlation between the types of houses owned by people, their wealth and their position in the village. Economic difference is clearly visible, and materials from the city demonstrate a command of relations with the world of *pananakiri*. Douwe has a large, expensive house, with a plank floor and corrugated zinc roof, as do Silvijn, Bram, Levi and Boasz. All of them have two storeys, and Silvijn has enclosed the lower storey of his house and divided it into windowless rooms that are kept locked, and where he is rumoured to hoard a great store of manufactured objects. Akuriyo have modest houses with beaten earth floors, old thatched roofs and machete-cut plank walls. Sil's is particularly miserable, as his lack of a wife combined with his status as an Akuriyo makes almost inevitable – even more emphatically in his case than for any other Akuriyo, it is impossible for him to summon a work party. It is made almost exclusively of forest products, manifesting his association with that domain. It might be suggested that the Akuriyo choose to live in such humble houses because, as former hunter-gatherers 'proper' and forest-dwellers, they have a different relationship towards domestic space. However, their often-expressed desires to be like Trio people, and the practical impossibility for them to have 'better' houses for the reasons given above, make this seem unlikely.

Most people have houses whose features lie somewhere between these extremes, although there is a clear gap between the best Akuriyo house and the worst Trio or Wayana house. Mike's house stands out because as a Trio it is unusual for him to have machete-cut plank walls and no floor. However, he has a high roof of corrugated zinc without walls next to the dwelling-houses, beneath which the women (of which there are many in his household) regularly prepare beer. This seems to be the remnant of a long-postponed project to build a less modest house – but the zinc is put to good use. It is significant that the first of Mike's daughters to marry did so quite recently; with a son-in-law to help, Mike may well build further. Jip, who has a lot of money because of his entrepreneurship and his government connections, but who is unpopular because of his exploitative attitude to trade, has a small house, but it is decorated with every imaginable trapping: apart from a zinc roof and a plank floor, he has a glass window, and even a satellite dish. The house built by Silvijn as a 'hunting lodge' for the government official Meine, which I slept in during the first part of my stay in the village, has two verandahs, at the front and back, from which visiting government officials on one occasion idly watched over the villagers while sipping rum, and an outhouse (kept locked when the house is not being used), containing a European-style toilet, fitted with a reservoir to fill the cistern with rainwater. Adjacent to this there is a large midden; far from worrying that visitors may be disturbed by villagers dumping their rubbish next to their house, they consider it normal to leave rubbish and excrement in the same area, a liminal space regarded as neither wholly within the village nor the forest.

To see the way in which the patronage of outsiders functions in the village, it is useful to consider the various housebuilding projects that have been initiated. Aside from Medische Zending and the air authority, there are three main patrons in Tëpu: Meine, Cees Koelewijn and Amazon Conservation Team (ACT). Meine, although he represents the government ministry of social affairs, acts primarily on his own initiative, and in his own name, even if the funds he uses are provided by the state. Villagers therefore regard his projects as 'belonging' to him, rather than to the state. He has had the 'hunting lodge' mentioned above built for him, as well as an open-sided house with a 'bar', overlooking the river. The idea of having a bar in Tëpu was so extraordinary that I thought my interlocutor was joking when I heard the purpose of this new building, but upon closer inspection it was indeed clear that it was designed for this use and no other – there are even locally constructed wooden armchairs for Meine and his entourage to lounge in when they visit. Meine pays his workers well, in their own view; he also obtains building materials effectively, and he gives a regular payment to a brother and a niece of Silvijn (Sam and Monjiekë). These projects add greatly to Meine's personal prestige, upon which he relies for his influence in the village.

The Collective House

Leadership is even more closely associated with the collective house than with building projects sponsored by outsiders. The *tukusipan* (T/W) is a large, circular, domed house in the centre of the village (see illustrations 2.1 and 2.2). It has been a traditional feature of Wayana villages for as long as is known, but was adopted recently by the Trio. In the past, instead of a large collective house, the Trio village had an open space or plaza in the middle of the village, called the *anna*, for collective activities. Like

Illustration 2.1. The *tukusipan* in Tëpu.

the *anna*, the *tukusipan* is used for collective occasions, and rituals that invariably involve, and revolve around, the coming of visitors. Leaders occasionally summon the entire village there to make speeches. Outsiders without kin in the village are always taken to the *tukusipan* when they arrive, and when government representatives or other officials come they are entertained there. The building is also used for their official business, such as distributing pensions. In various ways, therefore, it can be regarded as the architectural expression of the importance given to relationships with other people from outside the village, as well as of the collectivity of local coresidents – it is by far the most impressive building in the village and, before there were schools and health centres, it was the only 'public' building.

Trio people call the big house either *paiman* or *okoropagë*, although there was some disagreement between interlocutors as to the correctness of these terms; the former means a lozenge-shaped construction with a pitched roof, like the domestic house design described above, and the latter is a large, round house, with a conical or domed roof. Although the Tëpu communal house is not a true dome, but has a short ridge – making it technically a *paiman* – local people tend to call it *tukusipan*, this term referring to the function rather than to the structure of the building. The *tukusipan* is situated in the centre of the village, and is a large domed structure with a central pole piercing the top of the dome through the centre of a *maluwana*.[7] Two concentric circles of hardwood posts support lintels from which spring slightly flexible rafters to the central post, allowing the thatch to take a domed, rather than a conical, form, the shape of the curve being fixed by the length of the battens. On larger structures an additional, inner ring of longer posts gives further support.

Both *paiman* and *tukusipan* are also the names of mountains or the large 'tepui'-type rock formations characteristic of the region. As Rivière suggested (1995, see above), the invisible house or rock archetype of the house found among many groups, notably the Ye'cuana (Guss 1989) does seem to exist among the Trio in some form, and the same is true of the Wayana. Visitors from other villages are traditionally lodged in the *tukusipan*. Its name means 'place of the humming-birds', expressing the association between visitors and humming-birds (Schoepf 1998: 115).

The collective labour and expertise required to build this structure is enormous compared to the building of an ordinary domestic house. All the able-bodied men in the village take part in its construction. The *tukusipan* structure, for the Trio, seems to have been adopted from the Waiwai *müimó* (roundhouse), although in Tëpu the structure is not a perfect dome, but a variation of the domestic house (*paiman, pakoro*) with increased overall proportions, a very high roof with a short ridge and a rounded lintel. The Wayana seem also to have used both types of structure – the imperfect or false dome is shown in Otto Schultz-Kampfhenkel (1940), whereas the true dome can be found today in Antecume Pata on the Litani. The Trio of Tëpu had a team of Waiwai to supervise and lead the building of their first *tukusipan* in 1974 (which, for the Trio – who at the time were

Illustration 2.2. The *tukusipan* in Antecume Pata.

the overwhelming majority in the village relative to the Wayana – was their first, and seems to have been a perfect cone structure, as was the case in Kwamalasamutu). This is significant because the Waiwai were acting as helpers to the missionary Claude Leavitt, and with their knowledge of building they brought knowledge of the Bible. The Waiwai are still revered by Trio people today, who say that they are highly knowledgeable and have enormous gardens; although they joke about the fact that they do not drink beer.

The sides of the *tukusipan* in Tëpu are walled with spaced planks, with about a plank's space between each one, letting in light while providing some shade on the sides exposed to the sun early and late in the day. There are two openings with hinged doors, one of which is at the nearest point to the river (north), and the other on the opposite side (south) (see figure 2.2). Near the latter is a small shelter, which serves as a cookhouse for collective meals. On the north side there is a table (see illustration 2.3), behind which sit figures of prestige, such as leaders and visiting officials, on collective occasions: the bureaucrat's desk has thus been firmly adopted as a symbol of authority. When visitors arrive, or men return from collective hunting or fishing expeditions, as part of the celebrations following the cutting and burning of gardens towards the end of the dry season, they dance anticlockwise around the *tukusipan* in single file before entering it through the north door, carrying what they have caught. The game or fish is displayed to all, and placed in the centre of the house, from where it is taken by the women, who dance, again anticlockwise, carrying it around the inside of the house for some time, and then out through the south door to prepare it for cooking.

The doors are not explicitly divided into a 'men's door' and 'women's door', but in practice there is a differentiation during these rituals, corresponding to the masculinity of guests and the femininity of hosts.[8] However, when visitors arrive by air from the city, the opposite door is used as an entrance door, and I once even saw it formalized with the creation of a gallery of palm fronds. Although there is a practical reason for this – the south door is nearer the airstrip – it also

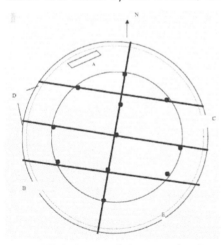

Key: A – Table for Captains and other persons of prestige.
  B – River side door
  C – Cookhouse side door.
  D – Cross beams.
  E – Bench along edge of entire wall.

Figure 2.2. Plan of the *tukusipan* in Tëpu.

Illustration 2.3. Leaders behind the table in the *tukusipan*, Tëpu.

constitutes an inversion of usual ritual practice, which underlines the fact that guests from the city do not have the same ritual associations. Most importantly, they lack the element of fertility discussed below in chapter 4.

The central pole has a symbolic significance, which is emphasized by the fact that, in many cases (though not in Tëpu) the central supporting pole is removed after construction and replaced with a shorter pole piercing the centre of the roof (and the *maluwana* painted disc when it is present) but not reaching to the ground, and therefore serving no structural purpose. It is often decorated with painting and adornment, and extends vertically high above the top of the dome; immediately above the point at which it pierces the dome there is often placed a ceramic object resembling a large upside-down pot, which is also pierced by the pole – this feature is present on the *tukusipan* in Antecume Pata and on a miniature *tukusipan* in one of the smaller subvillages on the north side of the river in Tëpu. Jens Yde speculates that the rectangular domestic houses of Guiana developed from the type of roundhouse with a central supporting pole – the presence of such a pole in rectangular houses indeed supports his hypothesis (see figure 2.1) (1965: 154–57). The central pole has been interpreted in other parts of Amazonia as an 'axis mundi'[9] or a 'phallic axis of fertilization', and the Waiwai material supports such a hypothesis: young men from outside the village dance with the new central pole before putting it in place (Fock 1963: 169; Rivière 1984: 85), and this practice is consistent with the Trio and Wayana rituals in which male dancers and musicians symbolically represent the outside. The pole piercing the pot above the roof can also be seen as a symbol of fertility – pottery is a quintessentially feminine product and 'pot' can be used as a metaphor for 'woman'.

The ritual importance of the communal house is materially expressed in the *maluwana*, a painted wooden disc made from a section of the *kumaka*,[10] and coloured with earth dyes or enamel paints (see illustrations 2.4 and 2.5). Although only previously known as a Wayana and Apalai artefact, it has been adopted in Tëpu, a primarily Trio village. It is designed to be attached to the centre of the domed roof of the communal house, *tukusipan*, with the house's central pole transfixing the disc through its centre. The design in an example I acquired in Antecume Pata represents water spirit-monsters (*mulokot*) and caterpillars (of two types, the especially powerful *kuluwayak*, and *ëlukë*), which are said to be the most powerful and dangerous types of spirit.[11] These are surrounded by a jagged ring representing silk-cotton tree spines, and another smaller ring of spines surrounds the inner hole through which the house pole is passed with obvious phallic symbolism. This is given further significance when the *vagina dentata* motif, associated in Guianan myth with a culture hero's relationship with the anaconda is taken into account (see below and Mentore 1993): the phallic house pole passing through the ring of *kumaka* spines surrounded by *kuluwayak* and *ëlukë* is, in this light, a dense

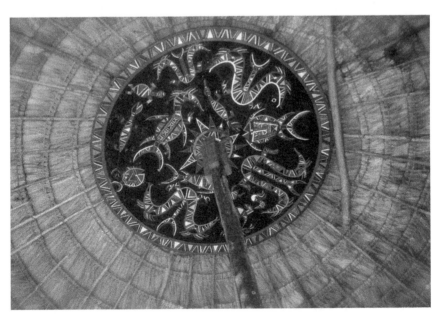

Illustration 2.4. The *maluwana* in the *tukusipan*, Antecume Pata.

set of images indeed. The image of the male principle at the centre and the female principle outside it may seem to contradict the ritual roles of women at the centre feeding visiting males, which accords with uxorilocal marriage practice. But the *tukusipan*, like the leader, represents the collectivity, and leaders, by their creation of a village, place themselves at its centre; while this represents affinity at the centre (cf. Viveiros de Castro 2001), it also represents a reversal of roles from another perspective: women thus come to represent affinity and the outside.[12]

Story of Mulokot (told by Gabriel)

A long time ago the Wayana saw it. He was a young man, he was neither young nor old. A man like me. Then what did he do? Nothing much, he went to get alaule (poison) to catch fish.… Then the Mulokot came. The man put alaule as before, 'yah yah yah'.… He said, 'what is it?' He looked carefully and listened but the water was very dirty where he had put the alaule, he heard 'kulo kulo' and 'muto-muto-mutom'. We've never seen the Mulokot because he isn't like a snake, he's a water spirit.

Then, he heard the old people telling stories. 'Where were you, yepe?' (said his friend) – 'I went fishing, to catch pakus.' 'What did you catch?' 'Nothing, just pakus, pacoussines, carp.' … They talked like this, the young Wayana and his friend. The old people were around the fire. The young people were behind them. Nearby. … Then they (the young men) say to each other, 'You know what I saw, my friend? … I don't know who it was. The water became very dirty. Mulokot dug, he ate earth.' 'What is he like? Is he like a fish?' 'No, he isn't like a fish. He is different, he has a special colour.' 'I see! … What was it like?' 'Like a fish, but not like a fish; he has something like body ornaments. He has something like a fin.' 'I see! No, it's Mulokot', he said (the elder). 'It was Mulokot. You mustn't touch it.'

Then someone said he wanted to go and see. 'Where did you see it? What did you see', he said. 'I don't know.' 'The elders say it's Mulokot!' 'I want to see it.' … They went over there. 'Is it here?' He put alaule as before, 'tïh'. … When he turned round after killing the fish, Mulokot appeared. 'It's him! Do you see him? He is quite big. A fish, a bit like a fish but not like a fish.' 'There he is!' 'Is he there? Can I kill him?' 'No. You mustn't kill him.' 'Can I kill him?' 'You can if you want, but I don't want you to.' Then, he struck him.… But he isn't like a fish; he goes 'tokolon-tokolon kolo-ko-lo-kolo-kolo-kolo muto-muto-mutom', he digs the earth straight away.… The first Wayana was further away than his friend. 'Have you killed him already?' 'Yes, I've already killed him.' He brought an arrow and came nearby to see. But he (Mulokot) wasn't dead; he had left; it was hard to see. The two Wayana left, 'tenh'.

'Are you back?' said the mother of the second Wayana 'Yes, we're back.' 'Do you want to eat?' (he didn't have a wife). Then he said, 'Bring (food),

I will eat.' He was a bit sad, because Mulokot was hurting him. Then, she gave him manioc juice with chilli-peppers: 'tei, tei', and some cassava bread on the fan. Because in the past there were no bowls. Then, he saw the Mulokot in the manioc juice, in a pot, 'tih' (there was just a bit of liquid there, but Mulokot was in it, 'wei-wei-wei' [playing]). He didn't dip his bread in the juice. He just ate the bread, 'kom-kom-kom'. He saw him (Mulokot). He said to his mother, 'take it away'. 'OK.' His mother took it away, and she gave him banana juice in the calabash. 'Here is your drink.' 'OK', 'kïlïk' (he took it), he saw Mulokot in the drink, he saw him in the cassiri, in the banana juice, in the sugar cane juice, always in the liquid. Then he went to bathe, but he (Mulokot) is still there in the river.

The Wayana began to grow thinner. Then he said he wanted to go in the forest, he wanted to drink the juice of a liana there, but Mulokot was there. He said 'Solo-lo-lo' [he's in there]. Then he went into the forest, to the top of a little creek, he thought Mulokot was not there. Then, he went 'tih' to where the water came out of the mountain. But the Mulokot was still there. 'Enma (I'm very thirsty)', he said, 'I'm very hungry'; he was a bit thin. He ate only sugar cane, but not cassava in cassiri. He preferred drink, he wanted cassiri. But there was always Mulokot, as before. ... Then ... the Wayana died. He didn't want to see the Mulokot any more; he disappeared – 'tenh'; he had gone into the forest. 'I'm going hunting', he said to his mother; he said 'I won't come back, I'm going to die in the forest.' He went to the forest in the morning. ... Under the mountain: 'tulu-lu-lu', he heard the water, he went to drink it, then he went to drink the water under the mountain, 'tën' – he thought, it seemed to him Mulokot wasn't there. 'I'm going to drink it because I'm very thirsty', he said. Then he went very fast, 'tuh-tu-tu-tu', he ran, afterwards he drank the water, but after he drank it the water became like a storm, then, the water became very big like the sea, 'toh, koh-oh-oh-oh'. The man was never seen again because Mulokot had eaten him. The elders say that you mustn't touch Mulokot, you mustn't kill him, and you mustn't kill a water spirit. ...

The next morning his friend [first Wayana] went to see him 'tenh' [he went to look for him in the forest]. But the little creek had become as big as the sea, there were no more trees in the forest, the water was like the sea, very big. It was very frightening, one couldn't look at it. 'Eh, my friend has died because of Mulokot.' He returned to the village. Then he went to the mother of his friend and said, 'My friend is dead.' Then his mother cried. Then all the elders went to see in the forest, even the Wayana's parents, but they couldn't find him. The water had become like the sea, there were no more trees, the water was very high.

Esoteric knowledge is a marker of authority, and the elders' power is thus shown to depend not upon their social position but upon their knowledge of cosmology. The water spirit *mulokot* is said to have created the Wayana, and caterpillars are revered and feared as perfect symbols of the outward transformations and deceptive appearances characteristic of the spirit world. Mulokot is associated with the primordial flood in a myth that emphasizes that the water spirit is greatly to be feared. The *mulokot* and anaconda are often mentioned almost interchangeably in daily discourse, the former being the 'master' or 'spirit' archetype of the latter and regional variations of myths of the origin of cultural attributes give either anaconda or *kuluwayak* the role of archetypal Other from whom these attributes come. The anaconda also shares the significant attribute of transformability with the caterpillar, and this transformability takes the form of a shedding of skin. Skin, clothes or outward appearance are frequently associated in Amazonia with change of perspective (Rivière 1994; Viveiros de Castro 1998), which is exactly what occurs when people become human in acquiring human attributes: they begin to see like human beings. Another association is widely made in Amazonia between the shedding of skin (particularly that of snakes) and immortality (Gow 2001), and as I will show, immortality, in the sense of social continuity, is a key purpose of the use of the *tukusipan*; this continuity takes place through another transformation: that of others into kin.

There are other elements to the *maluwana*'s attributed powers. Gabriel and other Wayana told me that it serves the village as protection against spirit attacks. Rituals such as the *marake* ceremony are conducted beneath it, in the *tukusipan*. A 'real' *maluwana* (i.e. made for this purpose) must be made in isolation, particularly from women, by a shaman; work is only carried out on it in secrecy, while chanting specific *ëlemi* (spirit songs), at times when the village was at low levels of risk from spirit attacks, and would have to stop, for example, when a woman gave birth to a child, only to resume when the child was strong enough. 'Real' *maluwana* are now rare. They can be as large as 1 metre and 80 inches diameter – the size of the object in illustration 2.5, which was made by Kuliyaman, the last man highly respected as a maker of *maluwana* in French Guyana and

Illustration 2.5. The last 'real' *maluwana*.

Suriname, who died in 2001. Only in the Wayana communities living beyond the Tumucumaque mountains in Brazil are there said to remain men knowledgeable enough to make 'real' *maluwana*.[13]

The isolation of the maker of the *maluwana*, described to me by several different interlocutors on different occasions, contrasts with that given to Rivière by Colson (1995: 196n.). According to her, all the senior men are involved in painting the *maluwana*, suggesting that the object is an expression of the collectivity. Rivière speculates that it is made of hard wood, and that it is transported to a new village when an old one is abandoned, 'thus symbolizing continuity as well as collectivity'. Although *kumaka* is in fact a soft wood, and I have seen no evidence of a *maluwana* being brought to a new village, I suspect that Rivière is correct about its symbolism. According to Schultz-Kampfhenkel (1940: 168–9), the Apalai *maluwana* was painted with human hair – hair, like feathers, bone and beads, is associated with durability and protection from spirits. Certainly, the knowledge of the cosmos that is represented by the *maluwana* is one of the few, and most important, elements of continuity in a society little interested in genealogy. The question of whether the *maluwana* is made in secret by a shaman or collectively by senior men, as Colson suggests, does not affect the conclusion that it is associated with the collectivity; I suspect that in the past a small group of senior men with sufficient esoteric knowledge may have made the object collectively, but in isolation from the rest of their relatives for the safety of more vulnerable individuals. However, the shaman's position as affine to the rest of the collectivity (Vilaça 2006), or as oscillating between the perspectives of affine and kin (Gow 2001), does qualify him uniquely as a maker of this object that, like himself, mediates between inside and outside.

The position of the *maluwana* under the centre of the roof in the *tukusipan*, and the explicit relationship between the transitory wood and thatch communal house and its rock archetype, together with comparative Amazonian evidence (e.g. Guss 1989; Hugh-Jones 1995), reinforce the interpretation of the *tukusipan* as a microcosm of the universe. The spiritual agency or power given to the images on the 'real' *maluwana* ensure that the *mulokot* and the *ëlukë* are present as the ceremonies take place beneath, but safely contained in their circle of *kumaka* spines.[14] As the people reinforce their humanity through dance, blowing and flute playing, and through ritual stinging of candidates for the *marake* with the abdomens of wasps protruding from the *kunana* mat, they taunt the spirits with a celebration of the cultural attributes that, according to myth, their ancestors took from them in exchange for nothing at all.[15]

The *tukusipan* is the focus of all collective festivities, as I have mentioned, and is the place to which visitors/dancers come bringing knowledge and power, as I will discuss in more detail in chapter 4. It can be regarded as symbolizing the collectivity in a state of openness to the outside. By analogy with the domestic house, since it is made collectively, it is owned collectively. At the physical and social centre of the village, it is also its symbolic entrance space. In Tëpu, all new arrivals in the village except close relatives are conducted first to the *tukusipan* for an audience with one or both Kapitein. The *tukusipan* itself, the *maluwana* and the flutes played on ceremonial occasions all serve to control visitors to the village. As visitors/dancers are structurally or ideally potential husbands to the local women / providers of drink, the *tukusipan* also constitutes the theatre for the enactment of the first stage in the creation of the most important 'made' relationship of belonging: that between father-in-law and son-in-law.

The importance of this for leadership is clear: it is the leader who organizes the construction of the *tukusipan*, and it therefore represents him and by extension his authority in the village. Its function as the theatre of contact between the villagers and the outside world of both humans and spirits mirrors the role of the leader, as mediator between the village and the outside. The *tukusipan* may even be regarded as the state in miniature – the material manifestation of the public or collective sphere. Within it, 'overt' political processes are performed, such as receptions for government representatives, as well as the festivities that restate social and cosmic order.

The matter of the distinction between public and private spaces, and their correspondence with overt and covert politics, is worthy of a short digression. It was central to feminist anthropology in the 1970s and 80s, and had significant influence on Amazonian anthropology at the time. As Henrietta Moore points out (2013), Jane Collier and Michelle Rosaldo's classic article on the subject (1981) showed that in brideservice societies, marriage is the primary means by which both men and women establish relationships with other individuals (beyond the household, one must add), make political claims and initiate personal strategies. Marriage is a highly political relationship for these reasons. Writing about the *tekatawa*, the physical public arena in which chiefly dialogues take place among the eastern Parakanã, Fausto describes how it is 'diametrically opposed to the space of habitations' (i.e. domestic living spaces), and that the point of this is to 'create an auditory barrier between the men's and the women's collectivities' because women are not allowed to hear the transmission of ritual songs (2001: 225). Another characteristic of the *tekatawa* more pertinent to the present case is that it constitutes a 'public sphere of debate founded on a discursive modality which is opposed to the intimidating speech of warriors' (ibid.) – it is a space for leadership as mediation, as opposed to warrior chiefliness. As Laura Graham (1993) has argued, however, the public sphere in Amazonia does not have the same basis in public debate between presumably autonomous individuals as it does in the Western tradition as described in particular by Habermas (1989). In contrast, 'the Xavante ... see discourse as the public product of multiple selves, a veritable collage of voices' (Graham 1993: 736). Among the Trio and Wayana, the process through which this collage is produced is less formalized, since they lack age-sets and men's councils. They have nothing as marked as the relationships of dominance that are reinforced through Xavante chiefly dialogue. Yet it is clear that one cannot assume that Trio and Wayana leaders are merely 'individually ratiocinating speakers who articulate their views autonomously' (ibid.). I consider it unlikely that leaders in any society can be accurately described this way, but Trio and Wayana people do not share these kinds of liberal assumptions about actors as wholly autonomous individuals.

Scale and the Household

The scalar relationship between village and household can be seen physically in the presence of a miniature collective space, a plaza (*anna* [T]) formed by the circular grouping of the buildings formed by at least one domestic house, its cookhouse and various other outhouses (see figure 2.3).

The domestic house (*pakoro*) in many ways expresses the same social relationships as the collective house but on a smaller scale: a house is part of the biography of its builder,[16] the former with the biography of the individual man, and the latter with that of the village, and marriage is of central importance to both. The relationship between these types of space can be represented as follows:

Tukusipan/anna : village ::
mini-*anna* : domestic house

Each domestic house contains (with a few exceptions) a builder/

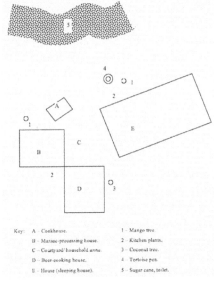

Key:
A – Cookhouse.
B – Manioc-processing house.
C – Courtyard/household *anna*.
D – Beer-cooking house.
E – House (sleeping house).
1 – Mango tree.
2 – Kitchen plants.
3 – Coconut tree.
4 – Tortoise pen.
5 – Sugar cane, toilet.

Figure 2.3. Plan of Boasz's house in Tëpu.

founder, his wife, their children (at least their daughters), perhaps one or more sons-in-law and their children. The house of my host in Tëpu, Boasz, is a perfect example,[17] extending to four generations: it contains him, his wife, Eva, their widower son, Sem, and daughter, Amelie, her husband, Gabriel, their daughters, Melissa, Emma, Mila and Lola, their son, Felix, Melissa's husband, Robert, and their daughters, Kiki and Lena. If we consider only the married couples in the household, we have Boasz and Eva, Amelie and Gabriel, and Melissa and Robert (see figure 2.4).

The relationship between father-in-law and son-in-law is neither warm nor cold, but it is restrained. The latter shows a certain amount of deference, but this is not 'extreme' as it can be in central Brazil (Turner 1984: 341). They occasionally engage in activities together, usually to do with housebuilding or maintenance and garden preparation. Although they often eat together, and talk freely to one another, they always remain slightly reserved in one another's company. The relationship is palpably, if subtly, authoritarian. When Gabriel is away in his other village, Antecume Pata, his son-in-law in Tëpu, Robert, is noticeably more relaxed and less industrious. Gabriel himself showed quite different sides to his character when in Antecume Pata, where he is more autonomous and proportionately more relaxed and self-confident, compared to his shy, reserved aspect when in Tëpu (cf. the Kayapó son-in-law's 'relative constraint upon self expression' [ibid.]). For instance, in Tëpu in the evening Boasz would often play the role of the knowledgeable head of household, telling stories of the old days, or retelling tales from the Bible. Gabriel would never do this in Tëpu – although he did tell some myths that he emphasized were 'just for fun'. However, when I followed him to Antecume Pata, he suddenly started to read the Bible often, and retold Christian stories. Knowledge of the Bible is considered particularly powerful and is an

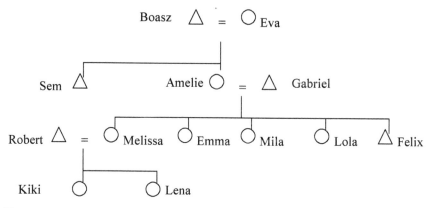

Figure 2.4. Boasz's household.

important attribute of a leader. But to share such knowledge is also part of a leader's responsibility, just as a household head feels a responsibility to share such knowledge with his family.

Whether on the scale of the village in the *tukusipan*, or on the scale of the domestic group in the *pakoro*, this relationship between father-in-law and son-in-law, the soceral relationship, is at the core of central Guianan society, but its basis in turn lies in the influence of a man over his daughter, where almost all elements of inequality are present: gender, age and generation. Yet the relationship is nonetheless complementary, for who will take care of a man without daughters in his old age? The daily intimacy of household activities, through mutual grooming, feeding and nurture, and simply being together, are what constitute the essence of the good life for Trio and Wayana. It would be misleading to explain these relationships solely in terms of power or control, once they have been created.

Consanguinity, Affinity and the 'Atom of Politics'

In Guiana, as among the Kagwahiv in Kracke's account, the father-in-law's dominion, or 'soceral authority', provides an idiom for all authority, and it is here that we can speak of 'control', albeit based on the loving, intimate relationship between man and daughter, sister or wife. Duties to the father-in-law are often the same as those a follower owes to a headman, but the headman is also conceptualized as a father to the collectivity (Kracke 1978: 34). The term *peito*, existing among many Carib speaking peoples, has been given a range of meanings from the potentially equal 'brother-in-law', through 'son-in-law', to the totally inferior 'slave'. There is also a verbalization of the concept *apotoma*, from *apoto*, which Sergio Meira glosses as 'helper', 'servant', 'used in situations in which the "helper" is, in some sense, at an inferior level with respect to the "helpee" [*sic*]' (Meira 1999). Rivière (1977: 40–41) identifies it more generally with affinity, and explores the link between affinity and relationships of superiority-inferiority. Among some groups, such as the Trio, the relationship (denoted by *pito* [T]) is relatively egalitarian, tending towards 'brother-in-law', but among other groups, such as the Wayana,[18] *peito* (W) takes on the potential connotations of servant or client. I would stress that this is a relative and not an absolute difference, which has partly to do with the stronger tendency of the Trio towards group endogamy, but as we shall see there has been some crossover between languages and associated practices, and this historical development highlights more general features of regional power relations.[19]

The father-in-law is ideally and terminologically equivalent to the mother's brother, bilateral cross-cousin marriage being the general ideal in Guiana. It provides the key not only to understanding kinship in the region, but also to understanding political relations, because it is the point at which consanguinity and affinity meet, and at which one man may have authority over another who is not his son. This relationship, in its political dimensions, appears to embody something fundamental in a manner similar to the variable structure surrounding the avunculate, composed of brother, sister, father, son, which Lévi-Strauss named 'the atom of kinship' (1958: 62). In Guiana, we do not find the same bewitching clarity of complementary sets of oppositions in this structure as Lévi-Strauss himself found elsewhere: here, if authority tends to be more strongly vested in the WF/MB,[20] it is also the case that all of the other relations in the set are relatively 'free and familiar', and indeed even the soceral relationship is hardly 'marked by hostility [or] antagonism', though it may be characterized by some 'reserve' (ibid.: 60). This observation merely confirms that the avunculate is the sole locus of authority here, and highlights that it is also the closest relationship of asymmetric affinity (cf. Fausto 2008). Insofar as it is the kernel of those relations, however minimal, of difference, power and control that exist in Guianan societies, I therefore suggest that we can regard the avunculate, at least for the Guiana region, as the 'atom of politics'.

The power of the soceral relationship has already been stressed by some Amazonianists. Terence Turner argued that it was the structural axis of central Brazilian social dynamics (1979, 1984; Viveiros de Castro 1996). Notwithstanding the Trio example, Rivière suggests that 'in all Carib societies the relationship between affines – and specifically between parents-in-law and their children-in-law – is always asymmetrical in nature, and this being the case, affinal relationships offer the best idiom for expressing political relationships that involve domination and subordination' (1977: 41). The ideal village is composed of a leader and his sons-in-law, who are the subordinate in-marrying husbands of his daughters. Thus, in Guianan society, there exists a hierarchical principle whereby '"wife-givers" are superior to "wife-takers"'.[21] I would add that even the relationship between brothers-in-law who have exchanged sisters (an often-stated ideal scenario) would be asymmetrical, as each party would regard himself as a wife-giver, and the associated feeling of superiority would not necessarily be cancelled out by his having received a wife. One should add to this that the exchange of sisters, even in the rare cases in which it actually occurs, is scarcely ever simultaneous; more generally, as Turner puts it, the developmental cycle of the household over time is characterized by the 'asymmetrical staggering of the process through which male and female offspring of a family become detached from it and attached to their families of procreation' (1984: 341). Thus in a relationship between objectively equal parties, each considers himself in credit with regard to the other, and from their respective points of view each is superior to the other.[22]

Symmetry and Asymmetry

This last point calls for a return to the question of the relationship between the Trio terms *pito* and *pëito*. Both words are used by Trio speakers, as well as grammatical extensions of '*pëito*'(T) such as '*epëetoma*' ('working for someone'), or '*X ipëetoton*' ('those who work for X'). Carlin glosses '*ranti ipëito*', for example, as 'government his-servant' (employee), and notes that the term denotes a 'reciprocal … [relationship] with a hierarchical basis. … Generally a *pëito* became a brother-in-law to the ruling family. That is, he was given a wife, and thus he and his children could enter the kinship structure' (2004). It is in practice a clearly distinct word from '*pito*', which is more usually applied between brothers-in-law, whereas '*pëito*' refers primarily to employees and Akuriyo. As mentioned above, Rivière (1977) has suggested that the terms have common origins, although *pëito* clearly means something approximating to 'servant', and *pito* is associated with a highly reciprocal form of exchange relationship.

In fact, to be more accurate, Rivière connects the Trio term *pito* to the pan-Cariban variations of the term *poito/peito*, and does not mention the Trio term *pëito* even in the comprehensive discussion and tables in his 1969 monograph. His view has been challenged by the linguist Sergio Meira, who identifies the existence of the Trio term *pëito* (spelt *pëeto* by Meira), which he argues is 'a more likely cognate' than *pito* for the other Cariban words denoting affinal asymmetry (1999: 590). It seems to me that if Rivière did not note the usage of *pëito*, it is very likely that it was adopted later by the Trio from the Wayana, as a way of articulating the new relational modalities that emerged in the large mission station villages that they came to share with Wayana people (whom they now often marry) before Meira's arrival.

Meira offers no alternative etymology for the term *pito*; however Luiz Costa has argued that there are also theoretical grounds for believing the terms to be entirely separate: 'Whereas the ultimate destiny of *poito* is to be assimilated, *pito* cannot be assimilated' (2000: 21). *Pito* is a term for distant affines, whereas *poito/pëito*, whether as war captives, slaves or sons-in-law, are eventually to become kin. My feeling is that the problem with this distinction is that it relies upon definitions of consanguinity and affinity that are more rigid than those actually used by Trio people themselves. What in fact characterizes their usage, and their relationship towards consanguinity and affinity, is a certain creative ambiguity. The difference between the Trio terms *pito* and *pëito*, even if the latter is a recent adoption from Wayana as I suggest, does indeed correspond to cat-egorical distinctions that correspond to social practices, but it is more in terms of symmetry and asymmetry (Fausto 2008, 2012), than of consan-guinity and affinity, that the distinction is to be found.

I have considered this problem elsewhere in relation to the Trio's treat-ment of the Akuriyo (Brightman and Grotti 2016), so here I will limit my discussion to the role of alterity in marriage and social reproduction. The assimilation of alterity is a theme that arises in numerous ways in Trio daily life. Cannibalism is a common theme in Trio and Wayana myths of alterity, including in everyday conversation.[23] Eating the heart and cer-tain other parts of the enemy, and drinking his blood, is said to have given extra vigour to the warrior (cf. Chapuis and Rivière 2003: 431ff.). Ronaldo told me that his own grandfather, a Kaxuyana shaman, ate his enemies during his people's wars with neighbouring groups. Kuliyaman's (Wayana) story of the war between the Upului and the Tïlïyo[24] even con-tains a cannibalistic comedy of errors, as characters accidentally eat the wrong people and frantically try to cast spells to avoid the consequences (ibid.: 509ff.). In the Trio story of Aturai (see chapter 1), the eponymous culture-hero and his brother are captured as children by the Okomojana or the Akurijo, according to different versions of the story (Rivière 1969a: 263; Koelewijn and Rivière 1987: 253ff.). The 'Okomojana' version has it that Aturai learned from the Okomojana the practice of having affines, and when he escaped to his own people he taught them to marry women other than their own mothers, sisters and daughters. In the 'Akurijo' ver-sion, the Trio practice of slave-capture mirrors the Akurijo practice of cannibalism – each appears as equivalent to the other. The associations between affinity and warfare, and between cannibalism and the capture of prisoners, are consistent with the idea that warfare is a form of exchange – it is negative reciprocity, but reciprocity nonetheless (Lévi-Strauss 1943). The sharing of bodily substance was also the ritual expression of peace agreements: Trio and Wayana used to mark the end of periods of warfare with a ceremony that involved the leaders of the opposing groups drink-ing each other's blood.

Such an exchange between structurally equivalent (if not necessarily equal) partners could be a precursor to trade, and here we can return to the term *pito*, to consider its relationship with two others: *jahko* and *-ip-awana*. The former is a term of address for a man who is not genealogi-cally related, but it is often translated by Trio people as 'brother', though it is a reciprocal term, lacking the asymmetrical inflections of ordinary Trio terms for brother, which indicate 'elder' (*piipi*) or 'younger' (*jakëmi*) status. The second term, usually found in the possessive form *jipawana*, can be translated as 'my friend' or 'my trading partner'.[25] It denotes a relationship that involves potential danger, and is associated with a myth, which takes the form of a cautionary tale, in which a man, called Alatïwo in the Wayana version told to me by Gabriel, is persuaded by his *-ipawana* to climb a tree to take an eaglet from its nest. Alatïwo's 'friend' removes the ladder, revealing that his idea was a ruse to rid himself of Alatïwo, whose wife he covets. The eaglet's father arrives, and promises to help Alatïwo to avenge himself, if he marries his daughter. Alatïwo agrees, and his new father-in-law makes him an eagle 'costume'. Alatïwo then learns to hunt like his father-in-law with the 'arrows' of an eagle. Alatïwo and his father-in-law remove their eagle costumes to enter Alatïwo's former village, presenting themselves as mere strangers who want to trade objects. Alatïwo is carrying a very beautiful magical bow, made by his father-in-law; his former friend wants the bow, and Alatïwo gives it to him; then, when he tries to use it, the bow breaks and kills him. In the end Alatïwo returns with his new father-in-law to live with his eagle wife.

The story's emphasis on the trading partner relationship between the protagonists (in Wayana, *yepe*), and the importance of trade objects in the story (the magic bow) make it clear that this a story about the limits of trust that one should have in one's trading partner. But it would be rash to suppose that the story is merely concerned with the dangers of making friends with distant others: a Trio version of the same myth collected by Koelewijn involves two brothers who quarrel, instead of trading partners, but is otherwise practically identical (Koelewijn and Rivière 1987: 114–17). An *-ipawana* is usually addressed either as *jahko* or as *pito*, and the former's translation as 'brother' by Trio people is consistent with the Trio version of the cautionary myth.

If the terms *jahko*, *-ipawana* and *pito* can sometimes be interchangeable, this can be understood in terms of Eduardo Viveiros de Castro's notion of potential affinity: he argues that affinity is pervasive in Amazonian societies, and that this '"figurative" affinity is the *source* of both "literal" affinity and the consanguinity the latter breeds ... because particular relations must be made up of and against generic ones; they are results not starting points' (2000: 25). The possibility of 'literal' affinity is recognized when the outsider is addressed as *pito* (cf. Viveiros de Castro 1993: 168), whereas addressing him as *jahko* is a form of consanguinization in its own right, iterating a 'consanguineal' relationship that bypasses marriage.[26] Rivière found that the *-ipawana* was 'ideally' addressed as *pito* (1969a: 79), and it is worth considering why this might be: addressing an *-ipawana* as *pito* implies that the interlocutors' exchange relations could potentially be formalized through marriage. In contrast to *jahko* (which suggests a generic consanguinity between parties and therefore implicitly excludes the possibility of exchanging marriage partners), *pito* evokes the idea of sister exchange – for instance, Karl, a man only a little older than me, suggested to me on one occasion that we could call each other *pito*, saying, 'I'll give you my sister, if you give me your sister.' The verb used was -*karam*-, 'give', as used both for objects and for people. Goods are never exchanged directly for women (cf. Descola 2001), but if the same partners exchange both women and goods, then this seems to be regarded as preferable. *Pito* thus expresses a stronger feeling of trust than *jahko*, hence the stated preference for -*ipawana* to be addressed as *pito*.

Despite this, I found that Maroons tend to be idealized as perfect -*ipawana* although they are not regarded as potential marriage partners at all: could this be because one can expect them to remain at a distance? Although Maroon trading partners can be addressed as *pito*, the possibility of them actually becoming literal wife-givers or -takers is absent: they can remain in the realm of alterity or potential affinity as sources of the powerful and desirable objects that can only come from beyond the pale.

Yet potential affinity, Viveiros de Castro has argued, encompasses consanguinity even at the level of the village, the house, the couple and the dividual person (2000). It therefore must apply both to *pito* and to *pëito*: both are affinal terms; the difference may be that the former emphasizes relative symmetry, and the latter, asymmetry, but perhaps the more important difference is that a *pito* is a potential *pëito* – the Trio relationship terminology and marriage practice are such that the distinction between brother-in-law and son-in-law (on which Costa's argument relies) can often vanish. Theoretically, the Trio ideal of marriage with ZD allows the creation of (literal) affinity within the consanguineal house, making the domestic house a self-sufficient unit. It reduces the ideal of coresident endogamy to its logical minimum scale. Ego's WF is his ZH, meaning that the usual authority of a wife-giver (WF) is cancelled out by the fact of his being also a wife-taker (ZH). This helps us to see why *pito* can refer both to a brother-in-law (ZH) and to a son-in-law (DH, ZS) – the two can be, and ideally are, the same person.[27]

An illustration of the way in which Trio and Wayana imagine potential affinity at the heart of uxorilocal conjugal relations can be found in the following myth, told to me by Gabriel:

A young girl saw a caterpillar on a *kupë* tree in the forest near the village. It was a very fat *kupë* caterpillar. 'Oh, what a fat caterpillar', said the girl. Several caterpillars on a *kupë* do not leave quickly to find another tree, not before eating all the leaves. 'Oh, what a caterpillar!' Perhaps it could become my husband, she said. She wanted the caterpillar to become her husband. 'You could just become my husband', she said. She spoke all alone, but the caterpillar had heard what the young girl said. Then, it was already the evening. So, the caterpillar comes: '*Tïh!*', there!, it was like a young man.

'So, what did you say to me?'

'Oh! Who are you?' she said.

'It's me!' said the caterpillar, 'what did you say to me?'

'Nothing', said the young girl, 'I didn't say anything, what did I say?'

'Well now, let's see, you said to me: "you could become my husband".'

'Ah, she said, it's the *kupë* caterpillar.'

Tïh! There, it's a boy. It's a young man, he was painted, he had colours. *Kupë* has the left leg painted *pahye* colour; on the right leg, it's *kulumuli* design, the leaves of *kulumuli* were of different colours; there, like that, he was beautiful.... [The caterpillar/man became the girl's husband].... But his body paint always stayed on him, it did not come off in the rain, it stayed there. Because he, the caterpillar, he was the *kupë* kind, which has beautiful colours.

But none of the other people had *kupë* colours, only he had them. One morning he said to his wife, 'Can we go and pick the fruit of *kupë* (*pisuku*)?'

'Right, let's go.'

They went on foot through the forest to the *kupë*. She thought he was going to climb like the Wayana, who climb to pick things. It was a very big tree, it wasn't possible to climb on the big branches. The *kupë* was all alone, it wasn't next to other trees.

'How are you going to climb?' said the girl.

There, '*tïh!*', there were lots of *kupë* fruit, but very high.

'I'm going to climb', said the caterpillar/man.

He, the caterpillar, he knew how to pick the fruit, because he was a *kupë* caterpillar.

'Listen to me!' he said, 'you are too near me, go a bit further away, so that you cannot see me', he said.

'Why?' she said.

'No reason, just to see me from far away.'

He thought that she wouldn't want to see him, that she would be afraid. He didn't want her to say, 'Oh! what a big caterpillar!' So, he said to her 'go a bit further. Then, I'll go away; if I come back, I'll call: "*ëë*". Then you can come'.

'Go on, climb', she said, but it was difficult to climb.

'I told you I'm going away, so go a bit further away from me,' he said, 'it's less dangerous if we leave each other.'

'OK', she said, and she obeyed.

Then, she went away, but not very far. But she saw what he did when he climbed on the *kupë*, the *kupë* tree is white, like that one over there, it's all white. He was a very fat caterpillar, he was very beautiful, like the *ëpkui* caterpillar. But the *kupë* caterpillar is not the same as the *ëpkui*.[28] It has different colours, like the *lasta* fish.[29] The *kupë* caterpillar is a bit shiny. The *ëpkui* caterpillar is not like that, it's all black, and a bit yellow; it's different from the *kupë* caterpillar, it's also a bit blue.

The young girl said: 'Ah yes, it's true', she had understood what was happening, she went a little further away and hid behind a tree. Then, he was no longer a man, but had become like the caterpillar next to the tree trunk. So, '*tumpak!*, he went up, '*munïk, munïk, munïk*', he climbed, he climbed up to the top like a caterpillar, he didn't fall.

'Oh! What a big caterpillar' – as he had expected, she said, 'what a big caterpillar!'

So, she went home.

He had often used to go away, but this time he didn't return. He went back to his own place.

That's all, his wife went back to the village, she went back home, because she had seen her husband becoming a caterpillar, that's all.

[the girl tells her mother]

'Oh dear', said her mother, 'he will not come back, you have seen that he is a caterpillar.'

That's the ancient ones' story of the *kupë* caterpillar. It was my grandfather who told it to me. Before, a few caterpillars of the *kunani* [fish poison] kind used to transform themselves too, one could not speak to them, or else they would immediately transform themselves into men.

There are two features of this story I would like to emphasize here: firstly, the ease with which a nonhuman (caterpillar) can turn into a human as a result of one speaking to it, and the ease with which it can transform back into a nonhuman again when one sees its nonhuman origins. This can be taken as illustrating the persistence of (potential) affinity in an in-marrying husband. The second feature that is relevant is the repeated emphasis on the beauty of the body markings (or body ornaments) of the caterpillar-man. The importance of this becomes clearer when we compare a Trio version of the same myth. In the Trio version, a married woman called Wirijepïn has an affair with a caterpillar-spirit. When he is accusing her, he tells his mother-in-law that he has seen his wife with someone else whom he could not see clearly: 'He looked much better, he looked very handsome. He wore feathers around his arms and a feather-crown on his head' (Koelewijn and Rivière 1987: 223). When Wirijepïn disappears, having eloped with the caterpillar-spirit, her mother seeks the help of a shaman, who allows her to speak to the spirit. The woman addresses the spirit as her son-in-law:

> 'I want to see you', she says, 'I want to know what my son-in-law looks like.' The shaman goes into a trance and rubs medicine on the woman's body, then Wirijepïn and the caterpillar-spirit appear, sitting next to each other. 'He looked like a caterpillar. The caterpillar was beautifully painted. "But ... you are ... he is ... a caterpillar!" she said to her daughter. "Yes, that is him. But he is not a caterpillar, so don't kill him." ... "He looks awful", her frightened mother said. "I don't want to see him, your husband looks horrible. Come, let's go!" Wirijepïn obeyed her mother and went back to her village.'

The beauty of the caterpillar-spirit is important here. So long as Wirijepïn sees him as a man, she is captivated by his beauty, but her mother breaks the spell by saying that he is ugly – and a caterpillar, not a man. This association of beauty with an in-marrying man may help to explain an enigma mentioned in a footnote by Meira, which is that the term pëito is also associated with beauty: as he writes, 'curiously enough ... pëeto-me, formed with the attributivizer postposition –me ... idiosyncratically means "beautiful, handsome"' (1999: 590n. 5). Just as other objects of beauty such as body ornaments and designs for bodypaint, basketry and beadwork are invariably said to come from the outside, so it is with in-marrying men.

I have tried to show that the difference between the two key Trio affinal terms pito and pëito is one of degree and not one of kind. In case of any remaining doubt, it should be noted that an actual son-in-law can be addressed as jimuku, 'my son', if consanguinity is to be stressed, and the choice of terms – pito, pëito, jimuku (and others; see Rivière 1969 for detailed discussion) – depends on the actual situation at a given time, the affective nature of the relationship, and the other genealogical or affinal ties existing between speakers. Finally, if pëito expresses a more asymmetrical relationship than pito, this is also a difference of degree due to the fact that a pito lies closer to the edge of the sphere of influence of the person who addresses him as such.[30]

Leadership and the House as Idea

My argument so far can be summed up as follows: leadership is founded upon a basic hierarchical principle governing all social relations in Guiana. The key to understanding this principle is the soceral relationship, and the data presented on the house demonstrates how it is expressed upon different scales, from the most intimate domestic sphere to the theatre of external relations. Part of the role of the leader is to expand both of these fields of influence. When residents of Tëpu are asked why they think it is a good thing that the missionaries and other outsiders brought resources, such as a church, school, clinic and innumerable goods, and communication tools such as air travel and radio, the first response is invariably that it has enabled them to live together in peace, in a large group. A large village, or cluster of villages, allows the creation of larger webs of affinity, of potential kinship, through reciprocal activities such as the frequent drinking parties hosted by different *pakoro*, as well as the occasional collective ones held in the *tukusipan* (see chapter 4). The number of potential spouses is thus maximized, and the reproduction of the group ensured. These questions of marriage, leadership and residence are inherent on differing scales in the *pakoro* domestic house, and in the village or collective *tukusipan*: the household head contains the relationships of which the household is composed, and the village leader similarly contains the relationships between all the households of the village. The leader, in turn, is defined in opposition to the outside.

The outside, or the forest (*itu*), as opposed to the village (*pata*), although it is conceptually the place of the radical other or enemy, is nevertheless part of the lived environment of 'real' Wayana or Trio. Tim Ingold (2000) has convincingly criticized the assumptions underlying the conventional differentiations between nature and culture that characterize many explanations of the evolution of human architecture. He shows that dwelling is logically prior to building, and that the latter is merely an expression of man's 'being in the world'. But in stark contrast to Ingold's model, the Trio house is built following an idea perceived to be universal, and this invisible idea is regarded as prior. On the overtly political or public level, the *idea* of relocating will precede the action. Trio and Wayana people regard the social environment, including the human, political environment but also those of game and other animals, and of spirits, as inscribed on the landscape in the form of houses. They domesticate the world by recreating it in their own image. The historical changes that have given new scale and form to village and housebuilding materials and created new types of social relationships can be seen to fit into the same dwelling structures that express social continuity. Like myth, therefore, material culture also adapts and absorbs history, preserving the same sets of relationships with different constituent elements.

Political action and change are intrinsic to living in the world for the Trio and Wayana, just as they are for any other humans, and in this chapter I have shown that building is an expression of politics and kinship. By the same logic as that which places dwelling prior to building, therefore, I suggest the sociopolitical house is prior to the physical house, although both constitute architectural reflections of society. Following Lévi-Strauss, we can say that the Guianan house is 'a fetish in the Marxian sense … the representation of a relationship between allied (wife-giving and wife-taking) houses' (1987, in Gillespie 2000: 8), but we need to be more precise. It represents the ideal of local endogamy confronted with the reality of conjugal autonomy, as men marry into their wife's father's house and later establish their independence by building their own. It is thus a fetish of the continuing dynamic alternation between consanguinity and affinity, and a crystallization of the hybrid network of relationships of which it is composed.

The use of the house in studies of society is, as Susan Gillespie has observed, 'especially concerned with how local life – the actions and structural integrations of groups within particular political and economic contexts – is intertwined with genealogy, that is, kinship through time' (2000: 2). However, in Guiana it is debatable to what extent, and in what way, houses represent continuity or 'objectify perpetuity' (ibid.). On the one hand, they are concrete manifestations of an ideal 'invisible house' or stone house (see above), the *maluwana* being a further objectification of the continuity of the collectivity. On the other hand, the house represents and contains the soceral relationship and the conjugal unit, both of which are formed by discontinuities: a newly married man leaves his father's house, usually forever, and eventually he may build his own house, causing his wife also to leave her parents' house. The house can thus be seen as representing the antithesis, or the denial, of genealogy as a foundation for continuity.

Notes

1. *Arecacea, Geonoma* species.
2. To some readers, it may seem surprising to find happiness and euphoria associated with one term, but I believe the translation is the most suitable, for reasons that will become clear in chapter 4.
3. Unknown species.
4. *Oenocarpus bacaba.*
5. As it makes the house hot during the day and cold at night, its only practical qualities are its durability and ease of installation; the former quality also has symbolic importance.
6. Indeed I have visited a Kali'na house of this type myself. However, Peter Rivière tells me that there were houses with raised floors at Alalaparu in 1963–64 and that the

first one was built at Paloemeu while he was there; the builder explicitly told him he was copying the missionary house (pers. comm. 2008).

7. See discussion (below) of the *maluwana*; for this word, I use the Wayana spelling throughout.

8. Yde notes a 'tendency' among the Waiwai to use the door nearest the river as a 'guest door' (1965: 152). Cf. the highly organized and cosmologically charged Barasana house described by S. Hugh-Jones, in which space is explicitly gendered (1979, 1995). As Rivière has noted, 'not all communal roundhouses have more than one door, but where they do the main door at the front is usually associated with men and male guests, and the other door or doors with women' (1995: 193).

9. A 'means of communication', a 'connecting link between the earth and other cosmic levels' (McEwan 2001: 184).

10. Silk-cotton tree, *Ceiba pentandra*.

11. The design also includes smaller images of tortoises and fish, which, some disapproving older Wayana told me, are a recent innovation of young artisans to decorate trade objects. However, I have observed similar decorations on old *maluwana* clearly made only for ceremonial purposes, including one in Antecume Pata made by Kuliyaman, suggesting that the real cause for disapproval may be the profane context of the production of *maluwana* for trade (in both cases these secondary images are 'just for decoration'). As well as the usual *mulokot*, *kuluwayak* and *ëlukë*, a *maluwana* pictured in Darbois 1956 depicts many different animals such as frogs, monkeys, deer, herons and the giant anteater. An Apalai *maluwana* pictured in Schultz-Kampfhenkel 1940, almost identical in style to the Wayana equivalent, has the *mulokot*, *kuluwayak* and *ëlukë*, and white herons. In all *maluwana* I have seen, however, there is an inner and an outer ring of wedges representing *kumaka* spines, enclosing the spirits' and other creatures' images.

12. Cf. Grotti 2007, who shows how women can become ritual predators

13. *Maluwana* have become quite commonly available in tourist souvenir shops on the coast, and are usually made by Wayana who have migrated to the city, or by residents of the Trio village of Tëpu who have adopted the craft to trade *maluwana* as a commodity. I collected another *maluwana* in Tëpu, made at my request by Luuk, a young man of mixed Trio and Wayana parentage who had married a Trio woman. Interestingly, Luuk signed and dated the object, suggesting a quite different role for it as an art object and conveyor of his individual agency.

14. The 'serrated border motif' elsewhere in Amazonia has been interpreted as serving 'to mark the threshold between the everyday world and a different order of reality' (McEwan 2001: 193).

15. Cf. Beaudet 1997: 143–56, who proposes this function for the almost identical Wayãpi *tule* flute ceremony. The Iatmul ceremonial house post presents an intriguing comparison: while being carved it must be hidden from the uninitiated, and it carries an important association with the *bandi* initiation-ceremony candidates: the carving process is analogous to the *bandi*'s scarification, and it is painted with the same coloured mud as when a *bandi* returns from the river after the scarification from the 'third crocodile' (Moutu 2003: 91).

16. In northwest Amazonia, especially among Witotoan groups, there is a more formalized version of this: ranked housebuilding rituals with corresponding house types enable men to ascend the social hierarchy through their career (S. Hugh-Jones pers. comm.).

17. This house was in fact built by Gabriel, Boasz's son-in-law, but it is spoken of as Boasz's house; Gabriel merely built it for him as part of his brideservice.

18. Where, according to Rivière (1977), the son-in-law's behaviour is expected to be still more submissive, although in my experience, perhaps because of a long period of intermarriage and coresidence with the Wayana, the Trio son-in-law is just as submissive.
19. One of the Wayana terms used to refer to war prisoners was *peito*, which Chapuis translates as 'obligé' (person under an obligation). Dreyfus refers to Navarette's description of the same practice among Arawaks (Lokono) in the sixteenth century, emphasizing the marrying-in of male and female prisoners (1992: 92n.). Hurault (1968: 74) gives a more general definition of the term, stating that all other men in a village are called *peito* (which he translates as 'vassaux' [vassals]) in relation to the leader.
20. i.e. wife's father/ mother's brother, who belong to the same category and are ideally the same person.
21. While this is also true of some other language groups, Rivière argues, others show different patterns, particularly patrilineal social formations practising virilocal residence, such as those of northwest Amazonia: for them affinity cannot express asymmetry, and marital exchanges between the corporate groups tend to be balanced and express alliance. Among the patrilineal Yanomami, affinity is an expression of political friendship (albeit fragile) (1977: 41).
22. Writing about Gê dual organization, Lévi-Strauss makes the mirror image of this observation: 'Even in these relationships of subordination, though, the principle of reciprocity is at work: the moiety that wins primacy on one plane concedes it to the opposite moiety on another' (1944b: 268, in Lévi-Strauss 1991: 314).
23. Cannibalism, as a mode of 'familiarizing predation', is of course an important trope for the reproduction of society in Amazonia (Fausto 1999, 2007).
24. Tirio/Trio 'proper'.
25. Cf. Santos-Granero 2007.
26. This appellation, which suggests consanguinity, concurs with the Piaroa practice of using kin terms for nonaffines (nonrelatives) in other territories, to circumvent the dangers that arise in affinal relationships when the demands of reciprocity are not met (Overing 1983–84: 343).
27. Lévi-Strauss calls this 'avuncular privilege', and notes that 'the double right of the uncle over the niece and of Ego over his cousin … can be in conflict in the case of bilateral cross-cousin marriage' (1969: 433–34) – this is presumably one reason why marriage with a sister's daughter remains on the level of an ideal, rather than a norm. Another is that FZD is M, and MBD is ZD, making the system almost equivalent to one of patrilateral cross-cousin marriage – which, Rivière argues (1969a: 278) following Lévi-Strauss, can only work on a small scale. Indeed, it seems that the practice of marriage with a sister's daughter, more common in the small, ideally isolated settlements of the past, has virtually disappeared in today's larger collectivities, in which there is a greater number of potential spouses.

Nevertheless, the ideal of marriage with ZD represents the *idea* that the balanced reciprocity achieved through sister exchange, may be achieved by other means and perpetuated. Moreover, it cancels out the relationships of superiority – inferiority between in-laws, making the WF's authority null, because WF is ZH, or *pito*, i.e. an equal. Marriage with ZD is therefore an egalitarian, harmonious ideal, because MB is ZH. The gift of a sister is likely to reduce or negate the need for brideservice. However, this ideal can be regarded as the obverse of reality: because in most cases in practice one's wife's father will not have previously received one's sister in marriage, bride-service is justified – so hierarchy, inequality and the authority of MB prevail.

28. Here the transformation seems to be into a different species of caterpillar from the original one – the reason for this is not clear.
29. Trio and Wayana people have taken to calling a species of fish (which I have not managed to identify) 'rasta fish' because of its green, red and gold colouring.
30. Another way of looking at this is to consider the *pito* relationship as a symbolically symmetrical relationship representing actual asymmetrical relations – compare Turner on moieties: 'The transformational relation between the symbolic representation and the oppositional relation it symbolizes ... consists in the replication of the dominant member of the latter as the structural model of *both* of the opposing terms of the former' (1984: 338).

Chapter 3

TRADE, MONEY AND INFLUENCE

Men's capacity thus includes their ability to enter into
relations with different others. The effect of these relations is to particularise individual persons by virtue
of their specific ties. If big men or great men encompass this diversity within, then perhaps they manifest
as a characteristic internal to theselves what each
man may also conceive as a possibility inherent in the
creation of any external relationship.
—Marilyn Strathern, 'One Man and Many Men'

When I first arrived in Tëpu, I was shown to the 'guest house' by a
group of men, some of whom carried my belongings, and when I entered
the surprisingly imposing building, I found a stern-looking, thickset man
in a dark shirt seated waiting at a desk. This was Silvijn, the village Kapitein. He addressed me courteously and confidently, using a mixture of
languages including Sranan Tongo, English, Dutch and Trio, and asked
me who I was, whether I was in good health, whether I was a Baptist, what
I wanted to do in the village, and what I would give to him in return.
He told me that he knew Paramaribo and many other cities, and he had
been to America. He talked at length, with much repetition, while others waited patiently. His long speech seemed typical of the Amazonian
chiefly dialogue I had read about, but one thing that I had not expected
was its often bizarre eclecticism. It brought together the evils of tobacco
and alcohol with the relative benefits of different Christian churches, the

love of languages and the problems of goldmining in the area, subjects that are all connected in this region, but their juxtaposition in the speech seemed to me as random as the passage from one language to another. I later found that Silvijn fluttered from one thing to another as energetically in his daily life as in his speeches, and that his activities were just as studiously cosmopolitan. He travelled constantly, greeted every person who passed, and interrogated them with a directness uncharacteristic of ordinary Trio, when he was not busy hunting, fishing and clearing gardens.

Here was an Amerindian leader who more than fulfilled his role as it had been described by Montaigne, Lévi-Strauss and Clastres. While he no longer had to lead his men into battle, he still had to expose himself by being the first to interact with strangers; but rather than this being to 'gamble his prestige', it seemed to me that his very prestige depended on this communicative aspect of his role. Moreover, I soon learned that the emphasis he placed on communication was not motivated simply by prestige, but rather by an idea of good living and a sense of responsibility to mediate the necessities of good living to local people. This did not, however, prevent him from ensuring that the choicest fruits of his excursions and privileged relations with outsiders were kept for himself, his close kin and especially his wily and demanding wife and father in law.

Economic Influence

The division of labour between men and women is the only one in traditional Guianan society, with the exception of the role of the shaman. The security of intermarriage with coresidents, and the political (as well as economic) benefits for a man of having his sons-in-law live with him, support indigenous ideals of endogamy, which are often expressed in terms of 'living together', and maximizing the number of consanguineal relationships. This ideal is balanced in practice by an enthusiasm for communication between localities. The two are reconciled by transforming outsiders into fully sociable human beings. Relationships between individuals are not primarily motivated by economics, despite the importance of trade, as we shall see. The nuclear family may be the atom of economic self-sufficiency, but it represents a logical minimum unit of subsistence, and certainly not an ideal social world. Feeding close kin is given priority, but the good life is symbolized by the multifarious social effervescence of ritual feasts, which expand sociability and in which leadership plays a fundamental role.

In an attempt to describe the economic foundations of Guianan society, Rivière argued that the only important form of property or wealth was women, since people, or labour, were the only 'scarce resource' (1983–84). But as Audrey Butt Colson (1973) and Simone Dreyfus (1992) have shown, Guianan Amerindian groups have been involved in trading networks since before the European conquest, and Rivière himself (1969: 51–55) has shown that the Trio were among them. Trade goods, especially manufactured metal tools, and the gold and jade of pre-Columbian times, have always been, by definition, coveted items. Even the voluntarily isolated Akuriyo/Wajarikure were far from indifferent to 'trade' items; on the contrary, they stole metal goods from Wayana and Boni camps (Cognat and Massot 1977), and there can be little doubt that the prospect of material wealth was a strong motive for their acceptance of sedentarization. The account that Mimisiku gave me of his first encounter with the Akuriyo shows that they were not indiscriminate in their desire for goods, however: 'They only wanted knives, machetes, hooks and matches, that's all. They didn't like sugar or rice, though we brought them a lot of things.' There has been a tendency to discuss trade and external relations and convivial, local sociability separately, and this needs to be addressed, for the true importance of each lies in the relationships between the two. Clastres suggested that the foundations of Amazonian society are not economic, but political, and consist of the control of the leader by the rest of society. Because of this, the leader is indebted to society for the privilege of his role, and must repay his debt by fulfilling the constant demands of the people (Clastres 2010: 203ff.). If this is the case, then what the leader brings to the village, be it food, people, trade objects or fine words, contributes to the people's sense of well-being – to the sense of contentment and conviviality that having and obtaining wealth brings. A study focusing on material objects in Trio social networks in the small village of Amotopo has shown that the *kapitein* is far from being the most important acquirer and distributor of goods, and that women play an unexpectedly important role; however it is the *kapitein*'s eldest son who is most 'active in exchanges with outsiders' (Mol and Mans 2013: 313). Since his father has succeeded in maintaining his son as coresident, it is unsurprising that the latter plays this key role, especially given younger men's greater mobility and openness to the outside, and in doing so he appears to be taking on some elements of his father's leadership.

Exchange and Trade

Each time I left the village, several days before I was due to travel, people would come to ask me for things. 'I want some fishhooks – the little ones for catching minnows, gold ones'; 'I want some big fishhooks for catching *aijmara*'[1]; 'some binoculars'; 'some clothes: shorts, tee-shirts'; I want some glass beads: some black shiny ones, some white ones', so it went on, and I soon had a long list of objects of desire. At first it seemed to me that these demands were addressed to me because I was a *pananakiri,* and so must be rich. To some extent this is true, because as someone perceived to be an urban dweller, I was believed to have easy access to money and manufactured objects. However, it soon became apparent that they were not trying to take advantage of me as an outsider – indeed, the more I got to know people, and the more I was addressed by them as kin, the more things they would ask me for. I also came to realize that the same thing happened to anybody who travelled to the city. Although people were perfectly conscious that objects had to be acquired through purchase and trade, the distribution of those objects among coresidents was a matter of sharing, and not of calculated exchange.

The consequence of this is that those who have better access to money and things have more to share with their kin when they are at home. By cultivating social networks individuals can increase their influence; meanwhile, and no less importantly, they thus expand their sphere of familiarity and conviviality, which promotes their well-being and that of their kin. The Trio and Wayana see a direct link between trade, leadership and ritual specialization: leaders' access to trade and to means of transport and communication complements and consolidates their role as leaders, and the same can be said of both shamans and church elders. Only a few individuals are able to travel for trade, partly because of the risk associated with people and places distant from one's kin and place of residence, but also, in today's world, because of the sheer cost of travel to the city. Trio people, when they go to the city, do not usually shop around for the best price when they want something, but instead they rely on individual relationships that they have cultivated with their trading partners, *jipawana.*

Trading with Maroons

This relationship is characterized by delayed reciprocity. Fernando Santos-Granero (2007) has discussed relationships of this kind in terms of friendship, which he argues Amerindians seek as an 'alternative' to relationships of kinship and affinity. He highlights the attraction of trust and security that they represent, and sees their importance as 'enlarging an individual's sphere of safe relations' (ibid.: 15), and that they 'may have played a key role in the establishment of ancient Amerindian macropolitics' (ibid.). The *-ipawana* relationship is of great importance today, but it was most clearly expressed in the trade relationships with Maroons. Trade with the Maroons diminished considerably during the course of the twentieth century, with the arrival of Brazilian traders looking for rubber, brazil nuts, animal skins and gold, and later of government agencies, south of the Tumucumaque, and of missionaries on the northern side. However the Wayana of the Lawa and Litani have never stopped trading with the Maroons, although the latter have lost their monopoly on industrial goods. Maroons were more important than other Amerindian trading partners for two significant reasons: firstly, because they were of greater economic importance, since they had a monopoly on metal and other manufactured goods before the arrival of missionaries, and secondly, because they constitute a 'pure' form of trade relations since marriage between Amerindian and Maroon was considered impossible, relations with them being artificially facilitated through fictional, processual kinship rather than by ordinary affinal mediation (see chapter 2). Indeed, the Maroons are said to have been made into humans by Trio people. A myth told to me by Boasz[2] describes how a Maroon spirit was 'saved' by a Trio who pierced a hole in his bottom to give him an anus, thus making him into a tube, and so able to process food like a human.[3] Commensality is a marked feature of Trio-Maroon relations, and indeed a *jipawana* is treated as far as possible as a kinsman.

Another myth[4] emphasizes the ambiguous nature of Maroons, and raises the complex question of substitution. Here, a Trio woman called Matukuwara initiates trade relations with some Maroons while the Trio men hide in the forest. She and a Maroon drink some of each other's blood to share substance and become allies. The Maroons are very demanding, and want Trio children in exchange for trade goods. The Trio give them children at first, but finally refuse, saying, 'Children are not like things, they are not trade goods. Let's just trade goods, because they are not irreplaceable.' Because the alliance with the Maroons is initiated by a woman in this case, sister exchange and intermarriage cannot take place. This device thus expresses the fact that exchange of people for people does not occur between Trio and Maroon; meanwhile, the refusal to exchange people for things marks a division between trade and intermarriage, and between human and nonhuman (Descola 2001).[5] However, a caveat should be added to this formula, that it depends on a perspectivally variable definition of humanity. Matukuwara refuses to exchange her own children because they are her kin and therefore from her point of view they are human. This allows us to understand how an exchange of slaves could take place in the past in various parts of the Guiana region (Whitehead 1988: 57) and elsewhere in Amazonia (Santos Granero 2009): at the moment of exchange neither party regarded them as kin, and they could therefore be acquired as property, since they were not fully human. They were subsequently classified as sons-in-law, allowing them to be integrated into the kinship system.

Despite the perils of travel, when relations were established between trading partners they seem to have lacked the ambiguity characterizing relations between affines. My adopted grandfather Boasz spoke with affection about his *mekoro* (Maroon) trading partner, and compared his relationship with him to his relationship with me: like me, the *mekoro* would come to stay in his house, where he was fed and looked after, but this never led to any suggestion of marriage alliance. As discussed in chapter 2, the *mekoro* trading partner seems to epitomize Viveiros de Castro's category of 'thirdness' (following Charles Peirce), transcending the dualism of consanguinity and affinity or kin and strangers, but remaining in the realm of 'potential affinity' (2002: 153).

The consanguinization of the *jipawana* makes sense in the light of Amazonian strategies for appropriating outsiders, such as pets or enemies, which have been aptly described as modes of 'familiarizing predation' (Fausto 2001). As we have seen, *jipawanas* are addressed as *jahko*, which means something like 'comrade', and is sometimes translated as 'brother'. Several of my *jipawanas* addressed me as *jahko*, and those who fed me called me *jimuku*, 'son'. This is as we might expect, but others called me *pito*, an affinal term. Similarly, Mokha, Kapitein Silvijn's father-in-law, who looked after Peter Rivière during the latter's visit to Tëpu in 1978, also described him affectionately to me as his *pito*. In general, the distinction between *pito* and *jahko* expresses the degree of trust and reciprocity between persons. Both relationships inevitably imply indebtedness for goods or services, which are founded upon a certain level of trust. I have explained in the previous chapter the reason why, contrary to what one might expect, it is the affinal term *pito* that expresses a greater degree of trust between -*ipawana* than the consanguineal term *jahko*.

Money

Changes in trading practices have increased in pace over the last five decades. Such was the trading power of the missionaries, that the abundance of goods at their stations attract people to settle there. Control of manufactured objects is now a pervasive feature of leadership throughout Amazonia (cf. Freire 2002), and the introduction of air travel has increased its intensity enormously but it is clear that the relationship between trade and leadership is not a recent development. Trade goods and the knowledge obtained from trading partners reinforce the prestige of the few individuals who can obtain them. Today it is no longer only personal charisma and skill that is required, but also greater access to urban contacts and to sources of cash. Such specialism is somewhat mitigated by the fact that it is now possible for relatives to remain in contact with each other over long distances by radio and letter. People who go to live in the city are able to trade forest products and traditional artefacts, and to use the cash raised to purchase manufactured goods, which they send back to their relatives. Although a certain level of education and the correct social contacts are necessary to live in the city, this activity is open to more people than was that of the specialized regional trader; also, significantly, it constitutes a new form of activity in that these individuals act on behalf of their close kin at a long distance, often over a long-term period – something that only new forms of communication (radio and air travel) permit. One important element, which can be regarded as a form of communication in its own right, and which makes visits to the city both possible and more attractive, is money.

Guianan people have been aware of the existence and use of money since the earliest days of colonization, even if the cash economy took a far longer time to penetrate to the interior than that of trade objects. Robert Harcourt was given ornaments by 'Carib' (probably Kali'na) Amerindians, one of which is a 'moon' (crescent) shape, which he estimated were made from gold and copper in a ratio of one to two; 'All which things they assured mee were made in the high Countrey of *Guiana*, which they said did abound with Images of Gold, by them called Carrecoory' (1928: 108). There is a hint of the myth of El Dorado in this account, but '*karakuri*' is the word that Trio people use today for money, the source of which remains to them mysterious and quintessentially white. Thus, both European and Amerindian situate the object of value in the territory of the Other. Money and objects of trade are seen as potent, even when they may appear to be mere tokens with no inherent practical use.

Money has now established itself in Tëpu and Antecume Pata as a token of exchange, even between coresidents. However, Trio people generally use it only to purchase industrially produced goods originally introduced from the coast: petrol, tinned or dried foods, metal goods, etc. They almost never use it within the village to purchase meat, and never to purchase garden products. They do not, to my knowledge, use it to pay coresidents for labour (for example, for help in cutting new swiddens), although it is used by outsiders to pay for Trio labour. Money regularly changes hands for the sale and purchase of manufactured goods, by and from *chinesi* (shopkeepers), but indirect exchange and delayed reciprocity are the norm: the fewer and more distant the ties of kinship between individuals, the more likely it is that money will be used to allow immediate reciprocity. Conversely, closer kin practise more delayed reciprocity and, in the intimate social relations of a household, sharing is the prevailing mode. The differentiation of exchange relationships according to social distance can be clearly seen in large villages in which there are frequent interactions between people who are genealogically only distantly related if at all.

In Tëpu, there are some regular paid posts, but there are fewer opportunities for occasional work. Both are referred to as *orokome*, which derives from the Sranan term for work, *wroko*. Paid jobs tend to be distributed along family lines, and certain families have therefore monopolized access to cash. In almost all cases, these are the families of village leaders and ritual specialists (shamans or church elders). There are some established Trio entrepreneurs who buy goods from the coast to sell in the village, and obtain quantities of game to sell on the coast. In Tëpu, such entrepreneurs have in all cases begun with some kind of paid post such as schoolteaching, which has provided them with initial capital and some knowledge of city life. All of this amounts to a clear pattern of emerging economic inequality, whereby those who have closest ties to the families of village leaders and ritual specialists, especially church elders, have increasing access to cash and industrially produced goods, at a rate much faster than their less well-connected coresidents.

In the past, the possibility of social fission and relocation restrained economic inequality and the acquisition of wealth in the long term, because a village leader, who had greatest access to resources, was obliged to give them away to maintain the loyalty of his coresidents. Although this Clastrean generosity can still be seen in some of today's leaders, the relative permanence of village location has changed the balance between social fission and the circulation of goods, ensuring that money and material wealth can be accumulated. Money plays an important role in this change of balance because it can be used in transactions between fairly distant affines (who now live in the same village), thanks to its ease of transaction and its association with instant reciprocity. However, it is difficult to say to what extent the changes that the use of money has brought about, while they may be radical in material terms, constitute fundamental qualitative alterations of Trio or Wayana society. Change is a gradual process: the same patterns and structures, and the same motivations and relationships, persist.[6] However, material wealth is increasingly translated into opportunities for education and employment for children, leading to the further monopolization of cash sources by certain families, and raising the prospect of the emergence of a class system among one of the world's most 'egalitarian' societies.

Here there is no sharp distinction between short-term exchanges for the fulfilment of immediate needs (in which money is used) and long-term exchanges involved in reproducing the social and cosmic order (Parry and Bloch 1989). Different forms of exchange are instead intricately bound up with each other, and trade is just one sphere in which sociopolitical relations are enacted and manifested. Indeed money today performs a facilitating role in social relations mediated through exchange, much as Martin Holbraad has argued: 'the multiplicity of money renders it supremely suited as a medium of exchange, where "medium"' is understood as a synonym of "environment" as well as "object"' (2005: 232). It seems to me that a more apt characterization of 'medium' than 'object' or 'environment' would be as a 'communication facilitator', and this would certainly describe the role of money. In this respect it is subordinate to the greatest and most concrete facilitator of communication, which is physical mobility. Money is essential for mobility using today's favoured modes of transport: motorized canoes and above all aeroplanes.

The Politics of Air Travel

Ronaldo, a Kaxuyana married to the daughter of my host Boasz's son Jesper, who lives in Missão, came to Tëpu on foot to visit his wife's grandparents, bringing his wife and daughter. He said that he intended to see the coast, particularly Cayenne. He gave no reason for wanting to do this except 'just to see'. His plan was to return to Missão and catch some songbirds on the savannah – some twa twa and some pikolet.[7] Then he intended to travel to Maripasoula and sell his birds there or on the coast, and to travel along the coast as far as Macapá, from where he would fly to Missão. In this way, long distance travel to visit relatives, particularly when it involves crossing between river systems, is done increasingly by air instead of by canoe and on foot. People in Antecume Pata who told me that they intended to go to the Jari to see relatives said that they would not go on foot. Instead, like Ronaldo, they would go to St. Laurent or, preferably, by air to Cayenne, travel along the coast by road or air to Macapá, and from there take a FUNAI flight.

Flight is in some ways seen as a more powerful version of river travel. The word for an aeroplane is *kanawaimë*, 'great canoe'. Like canoes, aeroplanes permit access to worlds that are distant both geographically and socially. The attractions of flying are manifold. They are primarily practical and economic: being able to transport goods or people by air, because of the great distances that can be covered in short spaces of time, enables places to be visited and goods to be obtained that have greater value than those that can be produced in or otherwise obtained from the forest or river. The cost of obtaining them is such that they remain scarce, and gives importance to a few individuals with access to flights; having said this, it is worth asking to what extent the goods are sought after for their own sake, and to what extent their value is determined by the rarity and power of the social relations they represent.

Airborne Evangelism

The aeroplane has played a vast role in the recent history of the remote central areas of Guiana. The Brazilian Trio were sedentarized in one of the first 'trinômios', or frontier stations combining protection of strategic national frontiers with the 'civilization' of the Amerindian inhabitants (Frikel 1971: 109; Hemming 2003: 390–91). Meanwhile in Suriname, the government cut airstrips for mission stations in strategic locations near international borders and at the intersection of the large Palumeu and Tapanahoni rivers.

According to some accounts, the Door To Life missionaries played a fundamental role in the creation of airstrips in Trio and Wayana territory. A missionary historian writes:

> God had simultaneously, [sic] placed the burden of the Wayanas and Trios on the hearts of Bob Price and Eugene Friessen, co-founders of the *Door To Life Ministries* (DTL) of Philadelphia. In June 1959, the two winged their way in a single-engine Piper Super Cub from Philadelphia to Suriname. Winning favor with the Suriname officials, they penetrated the uncharted territory in a government-approved survey. The door had been opened. ...
>
> In 1959, there was no Mission Aviation Fellowship in Suriname, but the Suriname government was eager to open its undeveloped interior. When the government saw what foolhardy American missionaries could do with a tiny Piper Cub, they went to Florida and bought four of them. When DTL crashed their Piper on a beach near a Wayana village, the government asked DTL pilot, Eugene Friessen, to fly for them. Many jungle airstrips would be necessary to develop the country, so the project was dubbed, *Operation Grasshopper*. Since these airstrips would be essential to the advance of the gospel, a little prompting from a couple of missionary enthusiasts had made the government of Suriname a partner in the Great Commission. (Conley 2000: 388–99)

The creation of these missionary stations marked the beginning of a period of rapid change. Airstrips allowed the stocking of medical posts and shops. Taking advantage of the Trio and Wayana's existing dependence on metal goods obtained from the Maroons along trade networks following the rivers, missionaries took over the Maroons' market by offering better goods for a fraction of the price or as a reward for loyalty. The missionaries nurtured the association of the newly available goods and healthcare with the church, and encouraged the Trio and Wayana to believe that medicine was effective only by the grace of God and therefore that churchgoing and prayer were necessary for the maintenance of good health (Cognat and Massot 1977; Rivière 1981). Today, the aeroplane has become a part of everyday life, and it is common in dry season for more than one flight a week to come to Tëpu bringing health workers and medicine, fuel, government delegations, NGO workers, researchers and many kinds of manufactured objects, as well as providing a way for people to travel to and from coastal urban centres.

Unlike in Brazil, where FUNAI provides free flights to the city, flying is expensive for Amerindians in Suriname and in French Guiana. In the remote southern Surinamese villages of Tëpu and Kwamalasamutu, certain individuals benefit strikingly from their privileged access to flights. Those who have strong links to the government or to missionary organizations frequently enjoy flights at low rates or free of charge. Church elders, who, as we have seen, are often official leaders, are sometimes able to influence missionaries into giving them free flights, and the latter sometimes fly them to the city or to other villages for meetings or training. Some also benefit from a lenient credit system with MAF, the missionary air service, whose staff assume that churchmen are more likely to honour their debts.[8] This reinforces the necessity for personal connections for access to the networks of trade and travel, persons and objects that air travel represents.

The City, Prestige and Mobility

The city, which the Trio refer to using a Maroon loan word, *poto*, still retains some of the mysterious allure that it had a generation or two ago when few Trio people had ever visited it. Much has changed however, as the self-deprecating humour with which Boasz told the story of his first visit to Paramaribo illustrates. He described how, as a young man, he was walking along the street there and began to feel hungry. A Hindustani man called him over, saying 'come, come to my house'. The man gestured to him to sit down, and offered him food and drink. Boasz ate and drank, and felt glad to have made a new friend. After a while he got up to leave, and then the Hindustani man asked him for money – 'karakuri, karakuri!' Boasz didn't have any money, and the Hindustani man grew very angry, shouting and waving his arms about. In the end the police came and Boasz was brought to the police station where he spent the night in the cells. Several decades later Boasz could laugh about this episode but at the time it must have been a traumatic experience.

Many Trio and Wayana choose to fly to the city using the connections described above, and when they return to the village, the motivation for enduring the hardship of city life becomes clear: they wear their experience like a badge of prestige. For example, Sem, a member of my host family, lived in Paramaribo for a long period, where he was being trained as an electrician by the government. When he returned to Tëpu, he immediately assumed the prestigious role of *mahto entu*, or 'generator owner'. He did little else, spending entire days lying in his hammock, being served food by his elderly parents, and only going fishing or hunting once every few weeks – most of his meat and fish was brought by an Akuriyo. When he did go, it was for prestigious major expeditions to bring back large quantities, in which he could easily afford to participate, being the owner of a large motor, and having access to cash, and therefore to fuel, through his paid work and his various connections. He could often be heard explaining to other people how life worked in the city, the prices of things and where to obtain them, particularly to his parents, whose attention and interest suggested respect – his knowledge was apparently ample compensation for relinquishing the more traditional responsibilities of a Trio man.

Although Sem has many of the social attributes favouring leadership, he lacks the personal qualities of a leader. However, his case illustrates the fact that air travel and the consequent increase in cosmopolitanism has paradoxically reduced people's mobility rather than increased it in an important sense: because of it, people travel much less in the forest. One must also take into account the fact that his wife died some 15 years before of cervical cancer – as did the wife of Pepijn. Both deaths were regarded as spiritual retribution for the two men's excessive hunting for the bushmeat trade. As a result Sem had less pressure to hunt – no longer having a father-in-law – and may also have been reluctant to do so for fear of further angering the spirits.

The trade expeditions mentioned above show that at least some individuals were able to travel long distances in the forest, but the division of labour between the Akuriyo and the Trio and Wayana shows that the fine-grained knowledge of the forest and its infinite paths trodden by different kinds of creatures (game animals and others) is diminishing among the latter, who freely admit the Akuriyo's superiority in this domain (and in no other). In fact, this change began with the advent of dugout canoes,[9] and the shift from interfluvial to riverine habitat: with this the acquisitive and imaginative gaze of the Trio and Wayana gradually began to point downstream to the source of manufactured goods instead of into the forest and below the surface of the water.

Air transport has come to encompass other forms of mobility in Tëpu. Travel on foot and by boat between villages has been superseded whenever possible by air travel. Fuel and motors are always brought by air. Notes are even sent by air between literate residents and coastal-dwelling relatives. So it can be said that air travel has become the mode of transport *par excellence* in Guiana, its consequences reach into every aspect of village life, and anyone aspiring to a role of leadership must ensure access to it. This may seem to offer a powerful economic basis for the emergence of a strong form of political power. However, a closer look at emerging forms of entrepreneurship show that this is by no means necessarily the case.

Air Entrepreneurship

It is arguably vital for leaders to have access to trade, but trade does not necessarily make a leader. Networks of objects and persons are now more implicated in air transport than in any other form of mobility, and these networks are highly valued for social and material reasons. Highly prized items such as corrugated zinc sheets, fuel, motors and industrially produced cotton must all come from the city. Various indigenous products are traded for the tourist market,[10] but more lucrative trade items are bushmeat and 'exotic' animal species. Certain food items are sent to urban-dwelling relatives, particularly manioc bread and dried game or fish. This is important as a means of preserving over a great distance the bonds of nurture characterizing relationships between kin (see Grotti 2007). But when the logic of economic gain takes over from the logic of conviviality, trade can diminish a person's influence.

Jip has been the most successful among the residents of Tëpu in obtaining the favour of Meine, the representative of *Socialezaken*[11] with responsibility for the villages of the 'hinterland'. Shortly before one of Meine's flights is due to arrive, Jip sends not only Akuriyo but also other Trio to shoot the favourite game and catch the favourite fish of coastal consumers: usually *kurimao* (paca)[12] and *aijmara* (aimara),[13] respectively. For these he pays a tiny fraction of the price they fetch on the coast. He stores them in his large, top-loading refrigerator, the only one in the village. On one occasion he sent 30 aimara, each weighing about 10 kilos, to the coast. He paid the fishermen 4 SRD per kilo, and in Paramaribo aimara sells for at least 20 SRD[14] per kilo (in Maripasoula it is worth €5 per kilo, and in coastal French Guiana the price is higher still). Because the flight is paid for by the government, he has very few costs. He benefits in a similar way from the transportation of goods from the coast to the village. They come on government flights, free of charge, but he sells them for prices the same as, or even higher than, his competitors. He can charge higher prices than them because he has a more consistent and plentiful supply – the other *chinesi* Jack and Jayden need to pay for the transportation of the goods they sell. For example, he sells flip-flops worth 2 SRD in Paramaribo for 6 SRD; Jayden sells the same items for 4 SRD[15] but rarely has them in stock. As a result of this attitude to trade, Jip is unpopular among many people in Tëpu, who see him as stingy; his stinginess with goods and money manifest a social parsimony – a lack of conviviality. This suggests an exception to the correlation between leadership and access to economic relations: if such access is not accompanied by generosity and the other 'classic' personal qualities of leadership, then it does not make a leader.

However, the case of another entrepreneur, who specializes in the trade in exotic animals, shows how economic initiative can combine with leadership qualities. Thijs's contact in Paramaribo orders particular species for clients, which are transported by air.[16] Most commonly, Thijs sends emerald tree boa,[17] dyeing poison frog[18] and cock of the rock,[19] for which he receives 84 SRD, 6 SRD and 350 SRD, respectively.[20] He told me that he would be prepared to catch any animal he was asked for, including (in theory) jaguars and king vultures.[21] The high value of the most rare and difficult-to-obtain species is unsurprising in economic terms. However, it illustrates that the relationship between distance and prestige is not confined to the village, and its importance even for a client in another continent has repercussions for the villagers.

As with the bushmeat trade, there is a division of labour involved in obtaining live animals. Akuriyo have a particular talent for trapping as well as hunting, and they have few alternative sources of cash. Thijs told me that he pays them, for example, 5 SRD for a humming-bird and 75 SRD[22] for a toucan.[23] The discrepancies in local and international prices, not to mention the total mutual incomprehension evident in the relationship between local people and nonembedded conservation organizations, highlight an incipient economic hierarchy extending far beyond the village, with the Akuriyo at the bottom and buyers knowingly flouting international regulations on endangered species at the top. Within Tëpu, however, Thijs's activities bring him wealth and prestige befitting his position as *Basja*.

Thijs's adaptability to a demand shows something of the perspectival transformability that is one of the capacities characteristic of leaders; although catching pets is by no means a practice alien to Trio people, Thijs often catches species that would never be considered pets by Trio people themselves (e.g. reptiles). Thijs's case offers a revealing comparison to that of Jip. In both cases a new form of trade is taken up in response to the demand of *pananakiri*, and in both cases the familiar division of labour appears with the exploitation of Akuriyo and their hunting skills. However, in contrast to Jip, Thijs he is popular; he frequently visits a wide range of people all over the village with his calm, friendly demeanour; he is generous; he plays the guitar in the church and leads the singing of hymns (see chapter 4); altogether, he has the qualities of a leader that seem merely to be confirmed by his appointment as *Basja*. All of this begins to show that the foundations of leadership are more than material, and are as much a matter of personal capacity as of influence.

Public Speaking

Speech has political consequences. Gossip can break as well as strengthen social networks, and the exclusions of persons from and through gossip are as important as the interactions it constitutes: it can act as a form of sanction for unacceptable behaviour, and in its most negative form among the Trio and Wayana, it becomes an accusation of sorcery. This rarely occurs within the sphere of the village, perhaps by definition, because an accusation of sorcery in a village could lead to its division, or, conversely, an accusation may follow a political division and lead to physical separation[24]; sorcery accusations can thus be co-opted into the machinations of rival factions (Rivière 1970). Leaders now use the rhetoric of Christianity to discourage people from using sorcery. As a result, skill in speech, always an important attribute of leadership, has become still more important. The capacities of a leader include the rhetorical skill used in public speaking, which is related to myth-telling, but distinct from it. Speeches are made for various purposes, but tend to emphasize and encourage collective harmony (*sasame*)[25] and to make reference to the conviviality characteristic of everyday life. They thus tend to follow the strategy of extending the latter to the wider collective audience, expanding the subjective sphere and encouraging all the listeners to share the same ontological perspective. In light of this, as I mentioned in this book's introduction, it is difficult to agree with the classic models proposed by Clastres and Lévi-Strauss whereby the leader's words would be exchanged for, or counterbalanced by, some other prestation on the part of the 'community', for the leader's main objective is to generate solidarity with the rest of the community that he himself represents.[26]

The charisma required for making public speeches is the same quality as that demonstrated in the ability to tell stories well. In addition, in contemporary Tëpu it is clear that only individuals who have certain official roles ever make public speeches. The most important among these are the roles of church elder and of Kapitein, but those of *Basja* and B.O. (*bestuursopzichter*) (both minor, government-appointed administrative posts) are also relevant. They are important in that as state or church posts in an officially recognized village they give their holders the pretext for public speaking and the fostering of community beyond the smaller units of 'traditional' villages. In most cases, public speaking involves a long harangue, with a great deal of repetition and rambling, and sometimes with the aid of a megaphone. These speeches, entirely out of harmony with the tenor of daily interactions, and their content, peppered with references to the foreign and exotic, highlights their esoteric nature, resulting from the speaker's access to a specialized form of knowledge; once again, the official roles contribute to this sense. This esoteric or religious nature of public speaking is the reason for the phenomenon that Clastres suspected when he wrote that 'in the discourse of prophets lies perhaps the germ of the discourse of power' (1974: 186).

I will limit the discussion of public speaking here to the everyday roles of the two village captains in Tëpu, reserving special forms of speech for chapter 4. The Hoofdkapitein, Douwe, does not speak publicly as much as Silvijn, and when he does so it is more often in church, i.e. in the religious, rather than in the secular domain. He has a more subdued style compared to the charismatic mode of Silvijn's interventions, but both leaders speak in similar ways whether in church or in the collective house or anywhere else in the village. The principal difference between church speaking and others is that the former includes reading from the Bible, and extensive commentary on readings, as sermons, which tend to reiterate elements of the stories concerned, while making little attempt at relating these to elements of the audience's daily lives. The formal qualities of the church elder's or leader's speech in the church are similar if not identical to those of leaders' speech elsewhere.

The relationship between Douwe's role and that of Silvijn may be compared to those of 'horizontal' and 'vertical' shamans (Hugh-Jones 1994) in other parts of Amazonia: the former are younger, more charismatic and tend to transform themselves and be involved in shamanic warfare and spirit attacks, whereas the latter are older, less dynamic, but very knowledgeable: they are the repositories of myth and other forms of cultural knowledge.[27] The younger captain, Silvijn, emphasizes through his speeches his social, horizontal connections with the human world as well as mundane forms of esoteric knowledge such as foreign languages; this and his tendency to travel a great deal demonstrate an ability to 'transform' himself. The older captain is less mobile, and uses his authority in a less dynamic way, taking a conservative approach to decision making; by speaking in church he emphasizes his vertical connections with the spirit world and his esoteric knowledge of the world of myth into which Christianity has become incorporated. The contrast between the two leaders highlights that the life cycle of the leader, like that of ordinary men (see above), is significantly manifested in terms of communication networks: the younger leader specializes in visible and material networks, whereas the older has a monopoly on knowledge and invisible, spiritual networks.[28] This echoes the observations made above about myth-telling and about visiting: the latter is primarily a young man's activity, whereas myth-telling is an older man's skill. In terms of communication, younger men can thus be said to communicate with the visible and material world and older men with the invisible and spiritual world. Put in more abstract terms, younger men communicate through space and older men through time as they converse with the invisible world of mythic time. The latter tends to be privileged and considered more powerful, which begins to suggest how age hierarchy is understood and how it translates into the realm of leadership.

Literacy

Many elderly people are unable to read, but the generations that went to school in the 1960s and 70s have rudimentary literacy skills, and a handful can read and write well. Most of these have obtained posts as teachers, pastors or radio operators. Those who were too young to go to school until the 1980s missed many years of education because of the disturbances caused by the civil war, but most people can read and write at least a few words (the Akuriyo are a notable exception to this: most can make out no more than a few letters of the alphabet). Although a small library was inaugurated in Tëpu by Cees Koelewijn during my fieldwork, the principal reading material remains the Bible,[29] and a copy is usually carried to church even by those who cannot read. The church elders are chosen partly for their ability as readers, an important element of their role being to read aloud from the Bible. Since most church elders have leadership roles (either official or unofficial) and vice versa, as well as a church elder being in itself a form of leadership, the ability to read well has great importance. In this regard, it is worth noting the correlation between the readings chosen and the leaders' speeches described above: in both cases, the emphasis is placed upon living well and on domestic and social harmony and conviviality – in short, on peace. The text of the Bible takes the place of the traditional rhetoric of leadership, fulfilling the same role.

Ordinary Trio and Wayana have become far more than passive consumers of the written word. They use writing in a huge variety of ways: During celebrations, people write festive messages such as '*sasame*' ('happy', 'harmonious'), or '*1 Januari*' (for New Year) on pieces of paper that they attach to themselves using pieces of string. Most Trio adults have words tattooed on their bodies, usually the names of themselves and their closest kin, abbreviated to a few letters so as not to endanger themselves by communicating the entire name – even if only their Christian names or nicknames, and not their secret shamanic names, are used; one man has his Brazilian nickname, Ferrinho, tattooed on his forehead. Writing is partly a mode of adornment, part of the beauty and goodness that are equated in the word *kurano* (T). Names written on the body also communicate an individual's position in the social network, being a part of which is essential to making her/him human – it is thus an inscription and reiteration of humanity, and a way of asserting one's own perspective, similar to the reiteration of 'I' in 'strong' talk and in some shamanic dialogue.

For the Trio and Wayana, writing has thus become more than a symbol of 'whiteness' or Christianity, and they have transformed it into a tool to facilitate indigenous processes. José Antonio Kelly has suggested that literacy enables people to manage the 'transformational axis' of relations with white people (2003: 110), and if this is true then it is in this sense of transforming the uses of writing. However, this means that by adopting *pananakiri* methods such as writing, Trio and Wayana people do not necessarily place themselves in the social position of white people quite as Kelly suggests that Yanomami do. Although in the hands of a *pananakiri* the pen is still symbolic of Panankiri practice, in the hands of a Trio or Wayana person today it can become an indigenous instrument of sociality. For this reason, there is no 'axis' or continuum between *pananakiri* and Wild people. Both are 'others' and the Trio and Wayana transform the power of both for their own ends.

Metaphysical Communication

Relationships with the spirit world are characterized by transformation of external attributes and shifting perspectives. Control of these processes of perspectival transformation is an important aspect of leadership and explains why many authors have found Amazonian leadership and shamanism to be closely related, but it also shows that there is more to the relationship than control over the 'mystical' means of reproduction (Santos-Granero 1986, 1991, 1993). For instance, Trio and Wayana shamans do not simply 'control' game animals, but must enter into complex processes of communication with them, and although shamans have special abilities to participate in these processes, they should be seen in more than economic terms. The ability to communicate negatively, or to overcome an adversary in a relationship of negative reciprocity, is highly valued and respected among the Trio and Wayana, and this ability and power is admired in a shaman as much as his knowledge (indeed the two are not separable), because it enables him to protect the village from spirit attacks. Spells or spirit songs (*ëlemi* [W]) can be cast by people who are not shamans. Some are used to precipitate sexual encounters, and others to attract game. The Trio's reputation for powerful *ëremi* (T) still extends great distances: an old Kali'na man in Awala told me that even there the Trio are still known as irresistible seducers and powerful hunters because of their reputedly powerful knowledge of love and hunting spells. The power to influence another human or nonhuman person by metaphysical means exists through song (*ëremi*), through blowing smoke or air (usually part of the role of the *shaman*, although I once saw an ordinary Akuriyo blowing on a rag before surreptitiously shaking it against the neck of a drunken Trio who had maligned him), or through water (singing into a gourd of water before giving it to the patient to drink), but in all cases it involves blowing, if we include the controlled passage of air from the mouth in song and speech as forms of blowing.[30]

The more powerful the shaman, the further away he can exert his influence. There is a qualitative difference between ordinary people, who can cast 'contagious' spells, and shamans, who can travel metaphysically and send invisible arrows great distances. This corresponds to a quantitative difference between shamans according to how far they can exert their influence. Thus, once again, people are differentiated by the amount of power and influence they can exert, in this case by virtue of communication with the spirit world, and this further contributes to the capacity of a leader.

Bible Economy

An equivalent kind of metaphysical displacement can be seen in church elders and missionaries. Although their discourses and their rituals differ from those of shamans, their social role is a direct continuation of that of the traditional ritual specialists. We have already seen that their access to air transport and links to churches and other religious organizations such as MAF permits them to access far off places more easily. Their travels and their knowledge of the scriptures, their ability to 'see' the stories of Jesus, are, in terms of the pre-Christian foundations of their cosmology, modes of communication with the spirit world – a world with which ordinary people can at best communicate to a limited extent.

Evangelical contact expeditions form a pattern across the region. The Trio were originally evangelized with the help of the neighbouring Waiwai,[31] and Trio missionaries have been active among the Apalai and Wayana of the Paru de Leste (Barbosa 2002: 136) and the Waiãpi of French Guiana (D. Davy pers. comm. 2006). I learned from various interlocutors in 2011 that there is also an ongoing Surinamese Trio evangelical campaign to Brazil to convert the Zo'é, an isolated group protected and monitored by the Brazilian Indian Agency (Grotti forthcoming). The fostering of negative attitudes towards 'traditional' beliefs was begun by the Protestant missionaries of the Unevangelised Fields Missions in Suriname and Guyana, and strongly contrasts with the gentler approach to evangelization taken by the Franciscan missionaries of Missão Paru de Oeste, but the training and deployment of Amerindian missionaries and their constant travelling from village to village ensures that there is much exchange of belief and practice across the international borders.[32] Wayana and Apalai from Brazil participate in annual 'Bible conferences' organized by native evangelists, with discreet support from outsiders. A Wapishana pastor who accompanied me to the Waiwai village of Erepoimo in Guyana in 2003 told me excitedly about the 'Bible conference' that took place in Mapuera in Brazil every year. For him, he told me, it is very much a Christian event; for the village captain of Erepoimo, however, the purpose of the pilgrimage to Mapuera is primarily to visit relatives; in either case the importance of communication is paramount, whether with the most senior 'messengers of the word' or with kin who are otherwise only contacted by radio.

My Wayana and Trio interlocutors in Tëpu were keen to inform me of the presence of missionaries from the United States and Holland at the conference, to emphasize its importance. On the other hand their excitement was not sufficient to motivate them to build the extra accommodation necessary to host the occasion, which is one reason why it did not take place in their village. Such conferences have more value for the visitors than for the hosts: although there is much to be gained from having an excuse to welcome visitors, guests who are uninvited, unknown or too great in number would not necessarily be desirable. The Bible economy of Guiana is perhaps the most far-reaching network of social relations – and of invisible spirit power – in the region. Kapitein Silvijn was taken by American missionaries to the United States for training, as he used to enjoy telling me, which illustrates how direct relations with faraway lands and peoples are deliberately used to nurture the prestige of key individuals. Moving in the other direction were gifts that illustrate the Bible economy in its most concrete sense: when I returned to the village after a break in 2003, I found the newly constructed Jaraware house, built at the initiative of Cees Koelewijn for the preservation of Trio culture, was filled with cardboard boxes containing black plastic-bound copies of the complete New Testament, which had finally been translated into Trio by the first missionary to work among them in Suriname, Claude Leavitt (Leavitt 2004). The church elders distributed the copies throughout the village, and from then on churchgoers were to be seen carrying them in special cloth bags, also supplied by the missionary organization.

Leadership and Influence Beyond Consanguinity

As Joanna Overing first noted (1981), the fusion of similar and dissimilar elements is the essential condition for creativity, or for social renewal, in lowland South America. The ability to access and control people, knowledge and objects from far away is of prime political importance, and the utmost concern for the aspiring leader. This control of communication involves the mediation of affinity, and allows the management of social reproduction. The ability to communicate, whether by physical displacement, through sound (verbally and musically), or metaphysically (by shamanic transformation and the transmigration of souls) is therefore fundamental to leadership as a quality rather than as a binary relationship between a leader and his coresident followers. This is what brings about the eclecticism that struck me when I first arrived in Tëpu: the leader must cultivate eclecticism to be able to communicate widely and to show that he can do so. It brings him prestige, but prestige is not an end in itself; instead, it serves to maintain the position of an able communicator who appears primarily motivated to foster the well-being of the community and to maintain its existence, by constantly expanding the field of conviviality and subjectivity, while mediating between it and the outside world. This eclecticism, or cosmopolitanism, which is necessary for the renewal of the collectivity, is embodied in the leader. In this way, through networks of communication, the collectivity is a hybrid and the leader the hybrid *par excellence*, who centres difference in himself and transforms it into the good life of the community.

Notes

1. Aimara, *Hoplias aimara*.
2. Another version of this myth appears in Koelewijn and Rivière 1987: 265–66.

3. See chapter 4 for further discussion of tubes.
4. Koelewijn and Rivière 1987: 267–70.
5. Hugh-Jones has argued that in some Amazonian cases persons are in fact exchanged for things (2003).
6. Cf. Gordon 2006.
7. Larger-billed seed-finch, *Oryzoborus crassirostris*, and Lesser seed finch, *Oryzoborus angolensis*, are popular pets and fashion accessories, among Creole men on the coast. Many young men in Tëpu also keep them and take them everywhere in the village – even placing the cage on a rock by the river when they go there to wash (it is said that letting these birds see new surroundings and hear new sounds enhances their singing ability). A pet shopkeeper and birdsong trainer in Paramaribo told me that males that sing very well can fetch prices in excess of €5000.
8. MAF is the Mission Aviation Fellowship, a worldwide organization entirely staffed by evangelical Christians. It provides the infrastructure necessary to install and maintain missions in remote locations, creating in each one a channel of communication through which many kinds of relationship can flourish.
9. According to previous authors, the Trio and Wayana first obtained dugout canoes from the Maroons, only making their own from 1952, and previously only used bark canoes, which are more suitable for the small creeks (Frikel 1973: 41; Lapointe 1972: 11). However, Peter Rivière has expressed doubts that at least some Trio were not making canoes earlier than this (pers. comm. 2008).
10. These are also sent to the village of Palumeu downstream for sale to 'ecotourists'.
11. The Ministry of Social Affairs.
12. *Agouti paca.*
13. *Hoplias aimara.*
14. About £0.80 and £4, respectively.
15. About £0.40, £1.20 and £0.80, respectively
16. The survival rate for these creatures is already poor for the journey by air and would be prohibitively small by river.
17. *Corallus caninus.*
18. *Dendrobates tinctorius.*
19. *Rupicola rupicola.* These nearly all die before reaching the coast and are extremely rare. Thijs took me on one occasion to see their 'lek', the males' famous competitive dance, but in the spot where, he insisted, there were usually large numbers at that time, there was nothing at all.
20. About £17, £1 and £70, respectively, in 2004. Specimens of dyeing poison frog bred in captivity marketed as 'Surinam Cobalt' are sold online by Patrick Nabors at http://www.saurian.net for US$55, but a wild specimen would be worth a great deal more.
21. *Panthera onca* and *Sarcoramphus papa*, the creatures traditionally most feared and associated with shamanic power. Any concern over possible spiritual repercussions may be dissipated by the knowledge that the animals would end up far away, in the United States or Holland.
22. About £1 and £15, respectively.
23. *Ramphastos* species.
24. Violence is rare as a sanction, although I heard from several sources that missionaries in their heyday encouraged it by taking it upon themselves to beat unfaithful Trio wives. This is also mentioned by Frikel (1973).
25. For further discussion of this, see chapter 4.
26. Cf. Durkheim on the public orator: 'he is a group incarnate and personified' (2001: 158).

27. This also recalls de Jouvenal's distinction between *dux* and *rex*, taken up in an Amazonian context by Kracke (1978).
28. Silvijn also speaks in church, but his speeches are more dynamic and focused upon promoting *sasame* (see chapter 4); for instance, he frequently leads hymns.
29. Claude Leavitt's translation of the New Testament, recently reprinted (Leavitt 2004).
30. The importance of blowing is discussed in chapter 4.
31. Dowdy 1963; Frikel 1971; Howard 2001.
32. Frikel attests to this when he refers to the "'Messengers of the Word" Indians, of Trio and Waiwai origin, principally coming from the American mission of Araraparu' (1971: 6).

MUSIC AND RITUAL CAPACITIES

Music ... gives the innermost kernel preceding all
form, or the heart of things.
—Arthur Schopenhauer, *The World
as Will and Representation*

I now return to the political dimensions of different forms of communication and movement, in order to explore how leadership achieves and maintains solidarity on a level beyond the domestic. Lévi-Strauss's observation that 'the chief must be a good singer and dancer, a merrymaker always ready to cheer up the band and to brighten the dullness of daily life' (1944a: 25) has not subsequently been taken up by many authors, least of all by those focusing on politics and leadership. The various angles from which I have so far examined Guianan leadership and society have consistently led to a focus upon 'relations' rather than 'things'; things draw their significance from the relations in which they are implicated. Nowhere is the enactment and creation of relations more concentrated and refined than in the 'bursts of breath' (Hill and Chaumeil 2011), or the 'heterophonic blasts' (ibid.: 27) of wind instruments. In this chapter I shall discuss musical rituals and aspects of the material culture associated with them, as well as certain forms of 'musical' verbal communication (cf. Menezes 1978).

The leader has a special capacity to charge social relations, and notably to control affinity. Among his means for doing so are speech and music.

The boundaries between lexicality and musicality may often be blurred or subverted by various types of sound (Hill 2011).[1] When the distinctions between musical and nonmusical sound are increasingly unclear, it may be asked whether we should be speaking of music and dance rather than of larger categories of sound and movement. But if we can establish the existence of a continuum between more and less formal, and thus more and less musical, then it is legitimate to speak of music if we bear in mind that we are referring to a quality rather than to a thing. The musical quality of certain types of communication is the key to their political significance (Menget 1993: 65), and I suggest that this is because music allows leaders to exercise their capacities within a culturally resonant aesthetic realm (cf. Blacking 1974: 98).

Musical instruments, which in Guiana are predominantly aerophones of various types, are used in ritual contexts in which social formations and dynamics are particularly visible. They are highly gendered, and the ability to play well is expected of a leader. As tubes, they both symbolize and provoke transformation, and they are used in rituals that transform and order the knowledge and power of the outside for the benefit of the collectivity (Brightman 2011).[2] The Wayana and other Guianan groups regard several forms of artefact as persons (Van Velthem 2001), especially in ritual contexts, and the flute as tube clearly represents the body. Their

Illustration 4.1. Various types of flute.

tubularity is also the negation of their genderedness, as Stephen Hugh-Jones has pointed out with regard to myths of gender in northwest Amazonia: the body as tube can be seen as a 'reflection on the bodies of men and women, on the congruence between the form of their genitals, and on their respective reproductive capacities' (2001: 252).

Their role in promoting and embodying continuity lies not just in the material object of the instrument, but also in the music itself: instrument and sound endlessly represent and reproduce archetypal or prototypical forms.[3] The ritual occasions on which this takes place bring together otherwise independent family units to form a collectivity, and thus structure collective life. This chapter will show that by examining music we can more clearly see leadership at work, giving order to society. During musical rituals, similar and dissimilar (present and mythic time; consanguines and affines; hosts and visitors; affines and ancestors) are fused through the transcendence of their difference. The renewal of society that takes place through ceremonial feasts is, in material terms, a reciprocal transaction: men/fertility come from outside, and are given beer by women from inside. Because there is no differentiation between the world of the dead and the spirit world, and the transformable, ambiguous environment of the outside is the realm of nonhumans and distant affines alike, it is logical to conclude that the dead are brought back to life through these ceremonial feasts. But the idealized interpretation of what is occurring collapses the difference between the visitors and hosts, so that the presence of reciprocity is denied. The result of this is that reciprocity does exist as a mode of predation, but it is disguised as sharing, just as relationships with outsiders exist in daily life despite an ideal of endogamy.

Structured Sound

In this chapter I will present the different kinds of music to be heard in the villages of Tëpu and Antecume Pata. This includes the traditional forms of aerophone music and song as well as the recorded Maroon, Creole, Brazilian and evangelical Christian music more frequently heard today. It also includes certain forms of speech, showing there is no clear distinction to be made between song and speech, either in formal or functional terms. I will approach music as structured sound, which gives the additional advantage of minimizing ethnocentric bias in the definition of the 'musical', and in doing so I follow Anthony Seeger (1987). As he argued, it is possible to distinguish technically between categories of speech/song by structure of text, phonetics, tempo, pitch and timbre. Whenever temporal and tonal structures are more highly formalized than in everyday speech, the effect is to produce a more musical form of communication: structured time produces rhythm, and structured tone produces melody. The same criteria can apply to dance steps and to instrumental music: dance is structured movement.[4]

I also wish to emphasize that music is indeed a mode of communication – perhaps even the supremely social mode of communication precisely because of its privileging of form over content. The greater the scale of social formation providing the context for a piece of musical communication, the more structured that form of communication appears to be, and in this fact lies the explanation for the importance of music for leadership and political organization. It is true that the formalization of language into ritualized speech, 'intonings' or song, and of movement into dance, reduces the amount of rational 'communication', arguably allowing ritual to act as an instrument of power (Bloch 1989). But if we do not reduce communication to the verbal expression of propositions or concepts (which represents a value of Western society), and understand it instead as making knowledge (broadly defined) 'common' by diverse means, and encapsulating such things as human substance and vital energy, then we can arrive at a richer and less conspiratorial understanding of its political dimensions.

Tortoiseshell Pipes: Individual and Collective

Although the word *ruwe* (T; *luwe* [W]) can signify any kind of bamboo instrument, as well as the bamboo plant itself,[5] the Trio of Tëpu also use it to refer to the musical instrument composed of a small set of five bamboo panpipes (*ruwe*) and a tortoiseshell friction drum (*sawaru*).[6] The front edge of the sternum or ventral plate of the tortoiseshell is smeared with *mani* resin[7] so that it causes the shell to vibrate when rubbed with the edge of the palm of the hand. The shell and pipes, usually attached loosely to each other with a length of cotton string, are held by clasping the shell to the ribs with the left elbow, holding the pipes in the left hand to leave the right hand free to rub the shell. Once the resin is warm, this rhythmic rubbing produces a sound that can be described as something between a hoot and a dull, rasping wooden squeak. The sound of the panpipes is similar to that of Andean panpipes, except that only small pipes are used (the longest rarely exceeding twenty centimetres), and although several players may play together, there are no orchestras playing *ruwe* with different tonal ranges. Newly cut bamboo is preferably used (particularly for dances), which further accentuates the contrast between the pipes' clear timbre and the duller hooting of the tortoiseshell.

Illustration 4.2. Pepijn, Ruben and Guus play *ruwe* and dance.

The *ruwe* has been said to be primarily an individual instrument (Beaudet 1997), but in my experience, although it does not require more than one player, it is used almost exclusively during collective celebrations. I have seen up to three *ruwe* players playing together using the hocket technique,[8] while dancing, on several occasions (see illustration 4.2). Various different melodies, always at roughly the same tempo,[9] are played; these are named after animals, such as *sawaru* (tortoise) and *kurairu* (chicken). The rhythm of the *ruwe* friction drum is that of the collective dances that take place at Christmas and New Year – these are the names now given to the celebrations that take place almost continuously from mid-December to mid-January, giving Christian and international license to festivities that have long taken place at this time of year towards the end of the dry season: a time of abundant fish and game, epitomized by fish-poisoning expeditions,[10] and a time of respite between the arduous tasks of clearing new gardens and of planting cuttings and seeds in them (which takes place when the rains arrive). A single, seated *ruwe* player often signals the beginning of a session of collective dances in the *tukusipan*, an invitation to people to arrive to drink and dance.

Lodewijk Schmidt describes a Trio dance festival beginning with bark trumpets being played in the forest near the village (in Rivière 1969: 246–47), and the association between the flutes and the forest remains today: celebrations begin in earnest when certain products are brought to the village by a group of men. On separate occasions these products were: game animals from the forest, fish from a poisoning expedition or an assortment of items of basketry. It is easy to see that the first two of these products follow the pattern that will by now have become familiar: things or beings from outside the local group (household, village) are brought into it by domestication or incorporation – in the case of meat and fish, this is achieved by cooking the flesh and combining it with the quint-essential domestic, human food, manioc bread. However, the basketry products require more explanation. These were brought to the centre of the village by a procession of relatively young men who, before they could reach the *tukusipan*, were waylaid by older men, grinning and playing the fool, and tugging at the woven objects (see illustration 4.3). There then followed, as with the fish and game on other occasions, a carnivalesque parade in the heavy backwards and forwards dance step (see below), in which baskets were jammed onto heads and other parts of the body and vast amounts of beer were drunk. It was explained to me that this was a brideservice ceremony: young men had made these pieces of basketry for their wives' fathers, and by tugging at the objects the older men were per-forming their role as demanding fathers-in-law.[11]

While it may seem incongruous that a parade of basketry to celebrate marriage follows the same pattern as parades of game that celebrate the social incorporation (by cooking and eating) of wild animals, in fact it makes sense when local forms of alliance are taken into account. Hus-bands are regarded as coming from outside – which is logical when uxo-

Illustration 4.3. Men tug at baskets brought to the dance by 'sons-in-law'.

rilocality is the norm, as we have seen – and they must be domesticated, for example by giving them beer. Their contribution of basketry is significant, not only because weaving is one of the skills that defines the male role, but because it stands for both the domesticated male (man as husband), and the powerful or skilful male (man as leader). Weaving is the main male domestic activity, and thus complementary to men's other principal occupations, hunting or fishing, which take place outside the village, but more than this it permits women to carry out their activities: the fire fan (siparu), the manioc squeezer (matapi) and the sieve (manare) are all essential for manioc processing and cooking.

Weaving is also commonly associated with quasi-magical or shamanic power, and woven designs are regarded as being potentially dangerous, as the spirits represented are said to risk becoming real if the representation is too perfect (P. Rivière 1994; Van Velthem 2001). High value is commonly placed on technical and artistic skill in Amazonia, and manifested particularly through basketry (Guss 1989: 70), and skill in 'craft' in general is an important attribute of leaders in a wide range of societies (Helms 1993). Among the Trio and Wayana, making a ruwe, as much as playing it, demonstrates skill and knowledge, and it is necessary to go as far as the Brazilian watershed to find suitable tortoises.

What applies to skill in producing artefacts also applies to skill in playing music (Helms 1993): ritual knowledge is highly valued, and the players of the ruwe are among the most respected men in the village. Although they are the players, their relationship towards the dancers is like that of conductors to an orchestra: the organized chaos that celebrates the coming together of affines to merge as a collectivity of shared substance finds coherence in the steady metre of the stroke of the hand on a tortoiseshell. Musicianship can thus be seen as a perfect metaphor for leadership, as ritual order emphasizes and exaggerates social order, and the musician is to the former as the leader is to the latter. But the relationship between musicianship and leadership is more than metaphorical and, as we shall see, leaders themselves often fulfil their role through music, in ceremonies and through formal dialogue.

Rattles and Shamanism: Percussion and Harmony

The kind of specialist knowledge that leaders demonstrate in rituals such as those described above brings us into the realm of shamanism, of specialist knowledge of the spirit world, and the characteristic musical instrument of the South American shaman is of course the rattle. The Trio shaman's rattle contains stones, kuri, that are the physical manifestations of his spirit helpers, *ikopija*. I knew that most Trio shamans had been convinced by missionaries to throw their rattles into the river – except for a handful that were taken to the safely distant custody of the Pitt Rivers Museum in Oxford by Peter Rivière. I therefore did not expect to find either shamans or rattles during my fieldwork in 2003–5. However, at the most important of the dance ceremonies in Tëpu described above, the procession of returning hunters and dancers was led by a man shaking a rattle (*maraka*).[12] Dressed in a large headdress of scarlet macaw feathers mounted on a cloth band featuring the stars and stripes, with a thick sash of orange beads across one shoulder and solidly built but old enough to be a great grandfather, his movements were energetic but solemn (see illustration 4.4). He was Paul, the father of Karl; Karl was married to Leia, the daughter of the 'headcaptain' of Tëpu, Douwe. Paul is also a pastor and leader in his own village, Palumeu. The first time I saw him leading the largest annual celebrations in Tëpu I was surprised, but I gradually realized that his role fits into the general pattern whereby knowledge, people and other resources are brought into social space from outside; this was part of a ritual expression of this pattern. As leader and pastor of another village, he was an ideal person to fulfil the role: pastors have most of the same qualities as shamans (specialist knowledge, contact with the spirit world, knowledge of archaic or foreign languages), and most of the important pastors I knew were the sons of shamans. Moreover, by having his own son marry the daughter of Tëpu's most senior figure, he had given human resources to the village as well as these less tangible ones. Even

Illustration 4.4. Paul leads the dance.

if his rattle is no longer said to contain spirits, it plays the same symbolic role as the shaman's rattle of old. It is partly a sceptre of power, partly a container of knowledge; but perhaps most of all, it structures time by shaking a beat for dancers to follow. This structuring of time brings people out of the ordinary, prosaic temporality of daily life and into the rhythm of the celebration of collective sociality, which brings affines together (often quite literally, as these festivities are frequently the scene of flirtation and seduction between potential and future spouses).

Following the rhythm set by the *ruwe* of local men or, on special occasions, the *maraka* of the dance leader, is the thump of the heavy step of dancers. In the past this was usually accentuated with a sound board (*tëpa* [T], *ehpa* [W]) shallowly buried above a pit; although these are rarely used today, the deep bass of the powerful sound systems (discussed below) provides an equivalent effect. Rattling seeds (*kawai*)[13] attached to the women's festive bead aprons (*keweju*, usually decorated with geometric designs representing jaguars or caterpillars), or to dancers' legs below the knee, further punctuate the rhythm. The dancers frequently make a loud-voiced plosive 'brr' sound through their lips in time with the music. The dance step is always heavy, steady, a quick but lurching march: a heavier, longer step with the forward foot followed by a shorter step with the rear foot. This heavy step is in stark contrast to the light, silent passage of the hunter in the forest, and its heaviness accentuates the humanity of the dancer. The short-long beat alternation gives an effect similar to a swing rhythm (cf. Beaudet 1997: 212). Meanwhile the sound of the *kawai*, like nut kernels or seashells, produces the jingling of many light, small, hard objects jostling together as they move in a harmonious whole: a fitting metaphor for the social effect of the dance. The sound they produce is described as *sasa*, and this is said to be the root of the word *sasame* ('like' *sasa*) (Carlin, in Rivière 2000). *Sasame* refers to the state of harmonious euphoria, of being many people together physically and socially. It is the feeling sought by the participants in collective celebrations of all kinds among the Trio and Wayana. This *sasa* rhythm is led by the shaman-leader-outsider, who shakes his rattle and leads the dance. As I have shown, musical instruments and leadership are closely associated in a variety of ways: making and playing them show the skill valued in leaders, and the occasions upon which they are used are those upon which leadership qualities come into their own.

Capacity, Blowing and Song

Like the rattle, another type of action closely associated with Guianan shamanism is blowing: the shaman typically blows tobacco smoke on the patient, paying particular attention to the affected area of the body. This has obvious parallels in aerophone instruments. As well as with healing and the renewal of life, blowing is also associated with the transmission of shamanic curses. It is closely related to certain types of song, and it is considered to be powerful in similar ways to song, particularly spirit songs; for this reason, it has been described as a form of 'silent sound' (Sullivan 1988: 434); indeed, in shamanic séances, secret chants are often rendered so quietly as to blend into silence, leaving only the sound of breath. Blowing may thus be regarded as a type of highly esoteric song. Spirit songs (ëremi), can be used for various purposes: healing, causing illness, seduction and hunting. Their use is today largely restricted to healing, and there is one powerful practitioner in each of the villages of Tëpu and Antecume Pata. In Tëpu, there is Bram, who was a member of the Akuriyo expeditions and, like his brother, Levi, who is the main church leader in the village, he is a church elder and son of a powerful shaman. He uses various lianas, and other plant remedies, of which he has such knowledge that his healing powers are famous across hundreds of miles – he has occasionally been flown to other villages to treat urgent cases. He typically boils the liana in water, and chants in an archaic or stylized language into the water before administering the liquid to the patient.[14] In Antecume Pata, there is Kutaka, an Apalai who, before he migrated to the village in the 1970s, was feared far and wide as a powerful and dangerous shaman. He does not use lianas, but instead chants into a gourdful of ordinary water before giving it to the patient to drink.[15]

I have shown that not all song involves the collectivity, and neither is all singing carried out by men. When women sing, except in the church context (see below), it is in the domestic sphere, and songs tend not to invoke spirits or to be attributed special powers. But women do sing mourning songs, which are part of the process of safely 'deconstructing' the person after death. On one occasion I heard such a song, which Eva broke into alone immediately upon hearing the news that her 'sister' in another village had died. She sang what was to my ears a beautiful but desperate-sounding, descending melody in Wayana interspersed with heavy, sharp breaths out and in, giving a halting, sobbing rhythm. Her mourning was an entirely individual affair, and her close kin and cohouseholders behaved as though nothing were amiss, even laughing and joking about other matters.

In general, powerful song seems to be a male privilege. Although older women have better knowledge of songs, this does not earn them any particular prestige. In contrast, the powers of men such as Bram and Kutaka make them highly respected figures. The content of the songs is incomprehensible to ordinary people, which adds to their mystery. It is also important to note the different uses of these chants, which represent the domains that are seen as important fields of chiefly and manly activity, as well as being metaphors of each other: healing and causing illness; seduction and hunting. As among the Achuar, the hunter can attract his prey using seductive techniques such as odours and sounds (Taylor 2000; cf. Détienne and Vernant 1974). Shamans are frequently represented as causing and curing illness by interacting with the spirit world as a hunter interacts with his prey. Leadership, masculinity and shamanic knowledge can thus be said to be as closely intertwined today as they were in the past, despite missionary influence; in fact, although outside influence changes its modes of expression and its outward appearance, it appears to have little real influence on the underlying mechanisms of leadership and politics. The leader's primary role being to communicate and to mediate; by bringing new musical forms and new material culture into play and monopolizing new forms of esoteric knowledge he is performing the same function as he did before the first missionaries arrived.

The Music of the Other

Leadership is exercised through music just as much in its newly introduced forms as it is in the *marake* and other collective ceremonies such as drinking parties for visitors, and in shamanic and other esoteric chanting. Contact with urban people, Creoles and Maroons has brought new musical forms that also bring people together by providing a collective focus and a common rhythm. This produces further occasions for men to demonstrate their skill and knowledge, either separately from other forms or at the same time, in heterophony.

Church Music

Cheerful hymns and festive songs performed with accompaniment on the guitar, accordion and electric piano are perhaps the most lasting liturgical legacy of the evangelical Christian missionaries whose influence reached its height in Tëpu in the 1970s (Antecume Pata was kept resolutely free of missionaries by André Cognat, although local people can often be heard listening to cassettes donated by the missionaries in Anapaïkë). Like most Christian evangelical church music, these are always in a major key. The more radically inclined among the missionaries deplore indigenous melodies, which often sound plaintive by comparison.[16] For example, a missionary involved in the Akuriyo expeditions makes the following comment in one of his reports: 'The influence of Bram[17] living amongst them has had a great impact upon them. Late into the night I hear the Akurijos singing the Gospel songs. Quite a difference from a former expedition when I heard them chant in the minor key from 7 PM until 2 AM' (Yohner 1970a: 6). It is clear from the context that the chanting 'in the minor key' refers to the often melancholy character of traditional song, and that the shift from this to the joyful tones of Christian songs of praise symbolizes an important breakthrough on the part of the Akuriyo in the eyes of the missionary.

Today in Tëpu there is usually music in the church every Sunday and sometimes during the week; in addition, evenings of celebration in the *tukusipan* are sometimes begun with a prayer and a hymn. The men (it is always men) who play the instruments are either among the most influential and important men in the village, or are charismatic and ambitious, and sure to grow in influence in the future: Thijs plays the guitar, Jack (president of Jaraware stichting [the local cultural association] and brother of Silvijn) plays the accordion and Robert (son of Julia and son-in-law of Gabriel) plays the keyboard. Playing these instruments gives these men another opportunity to cultivate a skill, a form of knowledge that encapsulates something of the capacities of urban people and Christianity. The singers sing in a nasal, twanging style that is in stark contrast to the very open-throated clear tone of traditional songs.[18] However, the even articulation of the strong beats of the 2/4 metre prescribed by the missionaries in hymns is subtly giving way to a syncopated rhythm, contemporary renditions being influenced by the omnipresent reggae and *forro*[19] of the Caribbean and Brazil.

Sranan Poku Sound Systems

Late in the evenings during periods of celebration, and at various times during the day almost whenever or wherever beer is being drunk, sound systems of various sizes (from small stereos to large, powerful speakers attached to car radios) can be heard playing dancehall, reggae or *forro* hits, styles locally known by the Sranan word for music, *poku*. These may be relatively local Maroon hits from Maripasoula, or those of international stars such as Sean Paul. The owners of the sound systems remain close to their machine, to control it and display their position as 'owner' of the music. Teenagers, young men and women, and sometimes younger children, dance in Tëpu in the relatively subdued style of Surinamese reggae stars in music videos, but in Antecume Pata the influence of erotically charged dancehall dancing styles (such as *bouké*)[20] has arrived from Maripasoula. Once again, music and dance provide a way of gaining prestige and demonstrating status by showing knowledge of pieces of music and dances from the urban centres, and displaying ownership and control of the sound system.[21] As Levi told me, in the past Trio people had flute music, and now they have *poku*, but they serve the same purpose; indeed, on one occasion Mimisiku commented to me on the 'power' of *poku* music.

In the cases of both church music and *poku*, ownership and skill in using instruments mark out individual men as having privileged access to knowledge. Whereas the knowledge of flute music described above comes from the spirit world and from the forest, the knowledge of these types of music comes from exchanges with urban, non-Amerindian others. These types of music may be said to have greater political significance today than indigenous, aerophone-based music, although the reasons for this are more clearly seen in the light of an understanding of the latter. It is common to hear *poku* music in heterophony with aerophone music – a fact that supports the suggestion that they perform similar social roles.[22] Despite this, there has been no perceivable formal influence of any extraneous music upon indigenous music[23] – this is a phenomenon that Jean-Michel Beaudet has called 'impermeability' (*étanchéité*), and that he argues is widespread throughout Amazonia (1997: 166). This supports a broader observation that indigenous symbolic ecology conceives of a simultaneous structural equivalence and ontological distinction between types of extraneous knowledge and resources: while they may be used for the same purposes, they are nevertheless kept separate. The importance of privileged access to different kinds of others or to the outside for leadership and historicity will be discussed in greater detail below, but first I shall consider the importance of speech as an index of sociality, because of the way in which it draws together indigenous and exotic forms of music along with more overt manifestations of leadership roles.

Speech as Music

Ethnomusicologists have debated whether certain forms of melodic and/ or rhythmic speech should be considered as music, particularly when they are not thought of as such by the cultures that produce them (Nettl 2005: 22). As Seeger (1987) has demonstrated, there is much to be gained by classifying speech forms according to their formal characteristics on a continuum with music. I have already considered types of chanting and blowing and shown that there are certain equivalences between these and flute music. But when even some of the most everyday forms, such as a woman urgently telling her child to be careful near the fire, sometimes fall into repeated cadences with an effect approaching that of song, we inevitably wonder where the boundary should lie. Yet even this example can be said to fall into a general pattern whereby hierarchy and the definition of social formation are made apparent through more structured forms of speech. The woman's gentle admonishments echo on the most intimate of scales the leader's harangues to the villagers that are, according to classic definitions (Clastres 1974; Lévi-Strauss 1944a), fundamental and definitive of his or her role.

As Jacques Lizot observes for the Yanomami, chiefly harangues and even important conversations among nonchiefs frequently employ the same 'virtuosity' (2000), a rhetorical skill the exercise of which I suggest serves more to draw attention to itself than to the content of the speech. These speeches display tonal and temporal qualities that have a life and a logic of their own, independent of content. On many occasions in Tëpu, Silvijn spoke to the village, particularly when communal feasts (see above) or official government visits brought almost everyone together in the *tukusipan*. He would sometimes use a megaphone (see illustration 4.5), but he was skilled in projecting his voice and for longer speeches he would manage without it. These speeches were long harangues, telling everybody to behave themselves – for example, not to let children drink too much beer and play near the river, not to fight; to be careful with their shotguns and ammunition,[24] and to be generous in sharing food (notably with visitors, e.g. myself); and, above all, to be *sasame*. The speeches would sometimes last as long as an hour, spoken in monotone, with each phrase ending in '*irë apo*' ('that's about it') in a lower tone. The audi-

ence would sit on benches all around the edge of the *tukusipan* while Silvijn stood behind the table at the midpoint of the longer section of wall between the two doors (see figure 2.3). The overwhelming impression was of the performance of a role, as much on his part as on that of the villagers. People remained silent or whispered to each other, but few showed real interest in the content of the speech, fidgeting and looking around themselves all the time – adults and children alike. Silvijn himself showed surprisingly little interest in what he was saying, but spoke constantly, barely pausing long enough to draw breath. Other leaders or officials in the village would often speak in public in similar tones, but

Illustration 4.5. Silvijn addresses the village.

for much shorter periods. Douwe, the headcaptain, gave similar speeches from the same position in the *tukusipan*, but his were far shorter and less frequent. The *basjas*, particularly Storm, would sometimes walk around the village using the megaphone to harangue people repeatedly against drunkenness.[25]

While the megaphone can obviously be seen as analogous to the aerophones described above, the formal, authoritative style of speaking is itself of greater importance. The ability to speak at length, to adopt the correct tone and timbre expected of a leader, is, like songs and dances, also an esoteric and prestigious form of knowledge. By comparing them with flute music and considering its musical features, we can solve the puzzle of why Amerindian leaders' speeches often seem so empty of content.[26] Their more obviously political nature helps us to see the political importance of dance ceremonies. Meanwhile the focus of dance ceremonies – that is, the mediation of the relationship between inside and outside, consanguinity and affinity, for the sake of social continuity and renewal – should lead us to conclude that chiefly dialogue is indeed a form of exchange, as Clastres and Lévi-Strauss suspected; but not so much between leader and community, as between inside and outside the polity, *through* the leader.

Ceremonial Dialogue

Chiefly dialogues have been portrayed in the past as prestations; both Clastres (1974) and Lévi-Strauss (1944a) have described leaders as giving words and/or things in exchange for women and allegiance, and Lizot notes of the high value placed on rhetorical skill in Amazonia, 'dialogues are primarily exchanges in the course of which the objects communicated are words' (2000: 166). Patrick Menget (1993: 68) distinguishes ceremonial dialogue (used between villages and upon intensely dramatic occasions) from political discourse (in which the chief addresses the village), and it is the latter to which Clastres, Lévi-Strauss and Lizot refer. Menget rightly presents ceremonial dialogue as part of a chief's role in defining the boundaries of the polity (cf. Rivière 1971; Chernela 2001), and points out that political discourse should be seen as part of a leader's range of personal skills (Menget 1993: 68). I suggest in addition that insofar as political discourse is a prestation, it has the effect of dissolving the social difference between leader and community, thus creating a shared subjectivity that obviates the need for reciprocity.

I include ceremonial dialogue in a chapter on music because the most chiefly kind of speech, the various forms of ceremonial dialogue[27] used in the past for parleying between unrelated men from different villages, is also the most highly stylized: it uses archaic and highly metaphorical language, is highly rhythmical and makes extensive use of tonal and lexical repetition.[28] As Greg Urban (1986) and Christine Beier, Lev Michael and Joel Scherzer (2002) have shown, similar forms of ceremonial dialogue are found throughout Amazonia. Beier, Michael and Scherzer point out that discourse forms and practices cut across genetic linguistic families and 'intersect, overlap and co-occur with one another in particular genres or in particular discourse settings' (ibid.: 125), showing a history of cultural diffusion by communication and contact across language groups. They note that special languages are commonly used in ceremonial dialogue and other esoteric speech forms, usually involved in 'political discourse, curing practices, and life-cycle rituals such as puberty rites and funerary rites'. Ceremonial dialogue has been associated with interethnic relations of potential hostility, and with the exchange of goods, sharing of communal traditions and balance of powers (Urban 1986). Aurore Monod Becquelin and Philippe Erikson (2000) see its role as that of regulator in the domains of space (arrivals of visitors, war), time (evoking the time of origins or death) and relations with the Other – the 'notional' domain. Erikson (2000: 131, 133) notes that Amazonian mask rituals often have the visitors incarnating the dead of their hosts, and greetings in general in Amazonia tend to express doubt over the ontological status of the interlocutor, and constitute part of a process of reinsertion into the sphere of the social. This role of regulator in several domains recalls other forms and objects of communication that I have been discussing, such as the house and flutes.

Although ceremonial dialogue no longer exists as a set of distinct practices among the Trio, I argue that it is closely related to contemporary forms of dialogue and music,[29] and it is useful to present these here to clarify the importance of certain features of these current usages. Three forms of ceremonial dialogue have been identified by Rivière (1969a, 1971) and further analysed by Carlin (2004), and their principal features are summarized in the table below.

The two forms of *turakane* speech, *nokato* and *sipësipëman*, are broadly similar and differ only in degree of strength and formality, but their existence as distinct forms emphasizes that there is a hierarchy of categories of ceremonial dialogue corresponding to the speakers' social and geographical distance. Otherwise, the main differences are between *turakane* and *tesëmïken*. These can be seen as complementary forms, because *turakane* is conducted between non-coresidents, one of whom has travelled, and *tesëmïken* is conducted between coresidents prior to or following a journey. There are three stages to the *turakane* dialogues: the visitor presents himself, then negotiates with the host after stating his intentions

Table 4.1. Ceremonial dialogue (based on Rivière 1971 and Carlin 2004: 20–29).

Type of dialogue:	Turakane		Tesëmïken
	Nokato	Sipësipëman	
Occasion or purpose	Receive visitors or announce arrival in village Trade Obtaining a wife		Communicate intentions or news, esp. before or after journey. Persuade. Restore relationships.
Relationship of speakers:	Different agglomerations and groups	Different agglomerations but same group	Coresidents, kin (imoitï)
Number:	2		2 or more
Gender:	Male (rarely female)	Male (occasionally female)	Male or female
Age:	Older	Middle to older	Any adult
Posture:	Seated on stool	Seated or standing	Seated or standing
Position:	Anna (centre of village, male space)		Any (inc. domestic area)
Word ending phrase:	Kara, tëme, taame or karahke	As for nokato but less frequent	
Response to speaker:	Mm (grunt)	Mm or Irërë	Irërë ('that's it' (emph.)), nna
Language:	Archaic	Somewhat archaic	Ordinary
Strength:	High	Medium	Low
Length (time):	Up to 24 hours	Several hours?	Short
Other features:	Competitive		Non-competitive

and finally, all being well, he is welcomed into the village. The last two stages are almost sung and, as Carlin notes, 'all the forms of dialogue are highly rhythmical, with the stronger types being chanted or almost sung rather than spoken' (2004: 23). The language is 'archaic and stylized, and semantically opaque' (ibid.) – form takes precedence over content. The words repeated after each phrase have no meaning to the Trio, and serve instead for rhyme, rhythm and assonance, as do the repeated responses. The most formal, rhythmical and melodic form is nokato, and the least is tesëmïken. The fact that, as Fock notes (1963: 220), speakers often do not listen to one another, and if they are of different 'linguistic stock' they each speak their own language, highlights that this privileging of form over content is due to the fact that these speech forms are communication acts *par excellence*: they are rituals for the establishment of communication, and express communication itself; any further signification is secondary. Even if the Trio do not appear to have used ceremonial dialogue with non-Trio in recent memory, regional patterns of ethnogenesis (discussed in chapter 1), and widespread nature and probable diffusion from a common origin of ceremonial dialogue itself (Beier, Michael and Scherzer 2002), show that there must almost certainly have been some such usage in the more distant past.

During the negotiation stage of the *turakane* dialogue, the host disparages what the visitor has to offer and doubts his good intentions and trustworthiness, saying that other visitors have cast spells and caused illness. Good health and strength or hardness are mutually associated, and expressed in one word: *karime*; also, particularly in the phrase *karime ijomi* ('he has strong speech'), this word denotes persuasiveness (Carlin 2004: 21). All of these are qualities expected and required of a leader, and the association between leadership and ceremonial dialogue is further reinforced by the fact that 'hardness' is also a quality of the original stone archetypes represented by the *kororo* stools upon which the speakers of *turakane* sit.

The rhetorical skill and even the form of ceremonial dialogue are also found in other speech forms, which differ from it in degree rather than in kind. Trio leaders today receive visitors (including non-Trio) in a way that diverges from the ceremonial dialogue format only in that the most distinctive rhyming phrase endings and other musical qualities have become much less pronounced. The content of the dialogue with a visitor is the same. A visitor to a Trio village must always present him- or herself to the village leader to be asked whether (s)he has any diseases, and what (s)he wants. This was precisely my experience on first arriving in Tëpu: I was summoned to a house, where I sat opposite Silvijn, who, as well as asking the customary questions in Sranan, gave me a long speech in a mixture of languages, as I described at the beginning of chapter 3.

When leaders perform the role of church elder, they give another set of formal qualities to their speech, seeking to replicate the pedagogical and priestly tone of the American or Dutch missionary. At the same time this is mixed with other features: their speech continues to contain many of the formal qualities of the chiefly harangue, both in its intonation, and in its punctuation with *irë apo*. However the elders also frequently read passages from the Bible, and when they do so their speech is often more stilted. All of this performance takes place in a particular setting that emphasizes the authority of the priest-elder, who stands facing the congregation in the building that represents for the Trio not so much the authority of the Church as the power of *Kan* and *Jesu*: the singular authority uniting and defining a monotheistic religion.

All of the forms of ceremonial dialogue are used as mediation in situations where conflict is likely to arise, and this is also true of both chiefly harangues and the contemporary reception ceremony of visitors that I have just discussed. This shows an important feature of Trio political action: conflict is always avoided where possible, and it is part of the leader's role to mediate in situations of potential discord. Moreover, it is worth noting that the seeds of local conflict always appear to be sown through gossip, which is the least formal and most everyday of all forms of speech. This presents us with a telling paradox: that it is at the most intimate level of communication that the forces for the disintegration of society most commonly operate. The chief's dual role as social centre and as mediator with the outside, and his mastery of formal and quasimusical speech modes can be seen as a foil to this paradox, constantly acting to mitigate its effects.

Another political corollary to ceremonial dialogue is that of social and political identity. Rivière states that *turakane* was only used among Trio, and that it can thus be seen as defining political and moral boundaries (1971: 306). While this may have been true for these particular forms, however, a more complex picture emerges when we consider ceremonial dialogue in general. Among the Waiwai, the use of the *oho* chant in preparation for action such as a dance festival or collective work manifests social hierarchy: a *yayalitomo* leader gives a message using the *oho* chant to his 'deputy', who passes it on to an 'employee', who then brings it by the same means to the *yayalitomo* of another village (Fock 1963: 208). It has also been suggested that ceremonial dialogue is generally associated with hierarchical, as opposed to egalitarian, organization (Erikson 2000 in Beier 2002). Although Rivière contrasts the Waiwai usage described by Fock with that of the Trio, among whom such a manifest 'administrative hierarchy' (1971: 307) is absent, it is the case, as I have shown, that Trio leaders do use formal speech to communicate with the village. Leaders punctuate their speeches with *irë apo*, as they harangue their *pëito* (followers) to motivate action, in a way that bears comparison with the 'administrative hierarchy' of the Waiwai. This comparison blurs the distinction implicitly made by Rivière and Carlin between ceremonial dialogue (with non-coresidents) and chiefly speech (to coresident subordinates), and shows that they belong to the same order: both suppress difference, but at different levels. Fock's Waiwai example describes the passage of a message down a social hierarchy as it leaves a village (from leader to messenger); the message is then received by the leader of another village. Once again we are reminded of the leader's role as representative of social space or place: as well as being mediator with the outside (and therefore receiver of visitors), he is at the centre of society, and when his word is passed to more junior individuals (in age, prestige and kinship distance), it radiates from the physical and social centre to the periphery.

Music and Leadership

An important feature of the 'strong' speech of the leader is that it helps to forge unity, to create a shared perspective among covillagers. The converse of this is the fact that it is the more everyday and intimate form of speech, gossip, that leads to discord and causes social disintegration. The scheme below can help us to understand why this is, and in doing so points to the essence of the leader's role. It is clear from table 4.2 that if we progress along any of the continua represented, from right to left, we do not move simply from individual to collective, but instead we move first from individual to collective and then back to individual again; or alternatively, from fragmented to cohesive to fragmented. Seen in three dimensions, it would in some respects be possible to connect the extreme left of the table with the extreme right. This is consistent with the idea, found in Guianan indigenous ontology, that each person contains the universe, or, as a Waiwai man put it, 'men rule the universe; women contain men' (quoted by Williams 2003: 425).

Lévi-Strauss condensed numerous Amerindian myths involving tubes into a formula whereby '1. the hero's body enters a tube which contains him. 2. A tube which was contained within the hero's body comes out

Table 4.2. Musical continua.

```
<.... Less formal/hard .................. More formal/hard .................. Less formal/hard ....>
<.... Kalau ........ marake ........ visitors or new year feast ........ beer party ........ daily meal ....>
<.... Deer bone flute ... claw flute .... waitakala clarinet ... ruwe pipes .... deer bone flute ....>
<.... Church hymns/guitar, accordion, piano ................................ Poku/sound system ....>
<.... No kato .......... sipësipëman .......... Chiefly harangue .......... tesëmïken .......... gossip ....>
<.... Piai chanting & blowing ................................................. mourning song ....>
<.... ëremi chanting ......................................................... ëremi chanting ....>
<.... Light steps ........................... Heavy (dance) steps ........................... Light steps ....>
<.... Monophony ................ Polyphony ................ heterophony ................ monophony ....>
<.... Outside/beyond society ................. Collective/social ................. Individual/Inside ....>
<.... Fragmented .................................... cohesive .................................... Fragmented ....>
<.... Masculine .................... Marriage/Sexual complementarity .................... Feminine ....>
<.... Death ................................. Fertility ................................. Life ....>
<.... Shamanic knowledge, skill ........... Leadership ........... domestic knowledge, skill ....>
```

of it. 3. The hero's body is a tube either into which something enters, or out of which something comes. From extrinsic at the outset, the tube becomes intrinsic; and the body of the hero passes from the state of contained to that of container' (1985: 216). This offers a good illustration of what happens during flute rituals and their various analogues that I have discussed: visitors' ceremonies, involving different types of flute, the *ruwe*, and even Creole and evangelical Christian music. If we consider once again that the flute, as the archetypal musical instrument, has as its principal quality the ability to mediate between inside and outside, consanguinity and affinity, then we can see that in relations with the outside – whether it be the spirit world, the government, the church or people from other villages – they have a vital role to play. In Lévi-Strauss's terms, the leader, like the hero, using the flute-tube, transforms the encompassing-outside-affine into encompassed-inside-kin.

Heterophony

All of this could be seen in terms of creativity, and the leader's role at the forefront of the musical process could be understood as that of creator. However, existing anthropological definitions of creativity do not quite fit. For example, Smadar Lavie, Kirin Narayan and Renato Rosaldo introduce their collection of articles on the subject as follows: 'Creative processes emerge from specific people, set in their social, cultural and historical circumstances. When distinct visions and traditions come together, expressive cultural forms often become politically charged because different actors have unequal chances to make their voices heard' (1993: 6). James Leach writes of the 'distributed creativity' of Reite people who see themselves as each the product of relationships with other people (2004: 169). The role played by particular individuals, the juxtaposition or combination of different 'visions and traditions', the importance of networks of relationships and the political dimension of creativity are clearly recognizable.

But in Guiana it is not cultural creativity that produces music; on the contrary, it is the creative power of music (music that is learned from the nonhuman environment) that reproduces culture and people. The leader who organizes a dance ceremony is not its sole creator, but his[30] relationship to the whole is equivalent to that of the other participants to the various parts. To return once more to the metaphor of an orchestra, he is like a conductor, the participants are like the musicians and the dance's archetype in myth is like the composer. But the result is not musically harmonious; instead, forms of music with different origins are played simultaneously, producing heterophony. This is by no means 'sonor chaos', but represents an aesthetic of heterogeneity (Salivas 2002), reflecting the convergence of disparate elements in a reproduction of primordial origins: visitors reincarnate ancestors, and alterity becomes the origin of society.[31]

Music and Difference

All of the musical forms used by the Trio and Wayana manifest an asymmetrical relationship between the bringers and the receivers of music, whether it is brought by male visitors from other villages, by culture heroes from the nonhuman inhabitants of the forest, by cosmopolitan youths from the city or by church leaders from the world of Christian evangelists. This relationship is not coercive; instead, it may be regarded as an articulation of society's organizing principles, or an expression of cultural or moral values. Guianan societies are frequently referred to as 'egalitarian', on the basis that their leaders' lack of coercive power implies the absence of social hierarchy. But ritual practice demonstrates that asymmetry of social categories is reinforced or reiterated on ceremonial occasions to renew its invisible presence as the underlying ordering value of everyday life: gender roles, the relationship between inside and outside and particularly relationships with various kinds of 'other', upon whom society depends for marriage, subsistence and cultural life.

Flutes and, by extension, other musical forms, help to mediate these relationships with the outside. Insofar as they are regarded as living objects, or bodies, we can identify in the ceremonial flute the quality of 'thirdness' (Viveiros de Castro 2002; see chapter 3). As tubes that are both containers and contained, encompassing and encompassed, they are agents that do not fit into either of the opposing categories of consanguinity and affinity or kindred and strangers, and that instead act as mediators between these categories. They are in this sense communicators *par excellence*, and as such leaders are their human counterparts.

Notes

1. In support of this approach, neurological data shows overlap in the neural networks and modules processing language and music (Mithen 2006).
2. Cf. Chaumeil 2001, who shows the creative/transformative power associated with Yagua blowguns, and Erikson 2001: 101, who proposes calling blowguns 'total social objects'.

3. Cf. Panare male initiation rituals that promote social continuity by reproducing the activities of 'ancient people'; Henley compares the feeling that this produces to the Trio *sasame* (see later in this chapter) (Henley 2001: 216).

4. Cf. Gell 1986; Kaeppler 1986, 2000.

5. *Guadua* species, probably *Guadua angustifolia*.

6. Red-footed or yellow-footed tortoise, *Chelonoidis carbonaria*, *Chelonoidis denticulata*.

7. From *Moronobea coccinea*.

8. Hocket: 'The medieval term for a contrapuntal technique of manipulating silence as a precise mensural value in the 13th and 14th centuries. It occurs in a single voice or, most commonly, in two or more voices, which display the dovetailing of sounds and silences by means of the staggered arrangement of rests; a "mutual stop-and-go device"' (Sanders 2006).

9. Around 128 bpm.

10. The liana *ineku* (T) (of the genus *Lonchocharpus*) is beaten to a pulp and placed in a dammed section or pool in the river at low water during the dry season. The water turns milky as the juices of the liana mix with the water, dispersing rotenone that paralyses the breathing apparatus of the fish. This causes them to rise helplessly to the surface, to be speared or scooped up by the waiting fishermen and women.

11. Cf. Crevaux 1993: 322–23.

12. Of *maraka* (*Lagenaria siceraria*) gourd, wood, bound with cotton and sealed with *mani* resin (see footnote above), and decorated with feathers of *kïnolo*, scarlet macaw (*Ara macao*), mounted on a length of *pïreu* arrowcane (*Gynerium sagittatum*).

13. *Thevetia ahouai*, said to have alexiteric properties (i.e. to protect against contagion and serve as an antidote to poison) (DeFilipps, Maina and Crepin n.d.).

14. See Brightman 2008b for a comparison of Trio understandings of plant healing and those of an NGO specializing in plant medicine.

15. He told me that he had to undergo a very long apprenticeship to learn to do this. It must be done in the evening because there is a kind of bird that listens and copies the *ëlemi* if it is chanted during the day.

16. E.g. the melody of the deer played on the deer bone flute is difficult to categorize either as 'melancholy' or 'joyful', having elements of both; meanwhile, the *ruwe* pan-pipes are close to a B-flat major pentatonic scale, and this may help them to produce melodies that sound more obviously joyful to a Western ear, although it is important to note that 'sad' music can very well be produced in major keys.

17. See above (chapter 1). Bram had, of course, already 'converted' by this time and was acting as an indigenous 'missionary'.

18. Like Piro 'God's songs', this may be an imitation of the missionaries' midwestern US vocal style, as found in country and western music (Gow 2001: 239n. 17)

19. *Forro* is popular music from the Brazilian northeast region.

20. In which the female dancer bends forward, gyrating her hips, while her male partner, standing behind her, grinds his hips against her buttocks.

21. Cf. Aleman 2011.

22. Heterophony, the simultaneous production of different (in tone, rhythm or both) musical forms, is also found in celebrations among the Wayãpi (Beaudet 1997) and in other parts of Amazonia (S. Hugh-Jones pers. comm.). Salivas distinguishes between heterophony and 'polymusique': in the latter case each of the musical forms remains autonomous despite being brought together in one time and place with a single intentionality on the part of the participants (2002).

23. With the possible exception of the major pentatonic scale being adopted for the *ruwe*.

24. A boy was killed accidentally in the Trio village of Kwamalasamutu during my stay in Tëpu, when his brother played with a carelessly placed shotgun.
25. Ironically, some of the same *basjas* were themselves particularly liable to drunkenness and fighting.
26. In fact they are not; see chapter 3 and Menget 1993.
27. A term coined by Fock to describe the Waiwai's version of the same practice, the 'Oho chant'. He compares the *oho* to various forms of ceremonial dialogue from all over Amazonia, with the common characterization of 'a chanting dialogue with interspersed affirmatives' (1963: 216–30).
28. A further perspective linking ceremonial musical performance and ceremonial dialogue is suggested by Henley, who describes formal dialogues between dance owners and chanters, in which the former persuade the latter to take the maraka and lead the dance – thereby delegating their responsibility (2001: 213).
29. Urban (1986) draws attention to the musical nature of Kuna ceremonial dialogue.
30 As mentioned elsewhere, female leaders are rare. I do not know of an instance of a female leader organizing a dance festival of this kind.
31. It is for this reason that, although the simultaneous production of heterogeneous music is technically called 'cacophony' rather than 'heterophony' (H. Stobart pers. comm.), I prefer to retain the term 'heterophony', which seems more in keeping with the social dimensions of the overall phenomenon.

Chapter 5

OWNING PERSONS AND PLACES

There is much which can be translated as ownership.
—Marilyn Strathern, 'The Patent and the Malanggan'

The concept of the owner-controller permeates Suyá
society, even though there is relatively little property
in the material sense of the word ... it is a fallacy of
ethnocentrism to maintain that ownership and property are unimportant.
—Anthony Seeger, *Nature and Society in Central Brazil*

The typically Amazonian distinction between inside and outside has been
described as the very definition of a polity (Menget 1993: 60). Property is
classically thought of as the foundation of political power. The appropriation of natural resources is supposed to be the origin of moral and political
inequality (Locke 1988: 285–302, 350ff.; Rousseau 1992: 222). The idea
of the absence of political power in Amazonia rests on the assumption that
Amazonian societies are societies of nature in which property relations are
lacking. This has recently been challenged by authors who have placed native forms of ownership at the centre of analysis (Brightman 2010[1]; Brightman, Fausto and Grotti 2016; Costa 2007; Fausto 2008b). There is also
increasing pressure for indigenous norms and processes to be recognized
as legitimate ownership practices in jurisdictions embracing legal pluralism (Filoche 2011). This chapter outlines Trio ownership relations and

assesses their political implications. To do so it is not enough to examine the relations between persons with regard to things, as the anthropology of property has tended to do (Hann 1998). Amazonian ownership relations need to be translated without the bias deriving from Western ownership regimes: if Western ownership exists in a world measured by the objective universality of 'nature', then what kind of ownership must exist in a world measured by the subjective universality of 'society'?[2]

Ownership helps forge the distinction between 'our' 'consanguine' cultural domain and the chaos of the unknown and 'affinity'. In Trio and Wayana spatial terms, the difference between *itu*, the forest, and *pata*, place or village, is a basic cosmological distinction. *Itu* represents a category that cannot be owned as such. The artificial, the made and the social are, on the other hand, 'owned' in some way or another almost by definition. However, distinction between *itu* and *pata* is not absolute, but rather it depends on the social perspective of a given actor. *Itupon*, people/animals of the forest, have the same characteristics each from their own perspective. An armadillo or an agouti, for example, has its own *pata*. Even manioc has a *pata*, but in this case it is owned by its human 'parent', who may refer to his or her field as *wii pata*. Cultivated land becomes 'somebody's' garden; a basket becomes the property of its maker or a person to whom he[3] gives it, until it begins to rot or fall apart, and it is left to the *wiripëhtao* (T), the liminal fringe of the village where rubbish is thrown. The consanguinity : affinity opposition is therefore the key to understanding how ownership can be dependent on perspective: one person's affine is another's kin; ownership of land is a way of seeing the cultivation of land, which is the expression of the historical relationship of a person or group's relationship to that land.

The relative nature of relations of ownership in a perspectival universe makes it problematic to describe property in the customary way as 'thing'-centred, whether as 'things, as relations of persons to things, as person-person relations mediated through things, [or] as a bundle of abstract rights' (Verdery and Humphrey 2004: 1). Persons may themselves be regarded in a certain sense as owned, but when this is the case, it is expressed in the language of kinship, as we have seen is the case in the relationship between the Trio and the Akuriyo. The control of persons through kinship relations underlines that in this context kinship and ownership cannot be wholly separated. I argue that relationships of belonging between persons, especially when marked by the control or influence of one party over another, are an important part of the foundations of political organization in Guiana, as much as 'real' property is at the foundation of political organization in Western society.

The politics of property relations are frequently associated with a distinction between private and common property. In Guiana, in contrast to other regions, a sense of collectivity is the transient product of ritual, and is not represented in corporate groups or lineages, unlike other regions, or in age-sets or moieties. Although a leader ideally embodies the relations of the collectivity in his person, he only fleetingly succeeds in doing so in practice – during public speeches, feasts or when he is officially representing the village vis-à-vis external actors. But the collectivity must also be involved in property relations in order to exist – and narratives evoking the ownership of language, people, land and other things show that this is so. Indeed, it will become clear that the very thing that we describe as the group – a political entity or polity, in other words – is only recognizable as such because of its members' shared narratives of ownership of various types of wealth, both material and nonmaterial, including belonging (albeit temporarily, to place.

The Language of Possession

There are three different 'types of possession' in the Trio language. These are defined, not by alienability/inalienability (a distinction of importance in many languages), but rather along 'temporal parameters', which Carlin characterizes as: 'immediate possession' (as in, *karakuri nai jiweinje*, 'I have money on me'), 'temporary controlled possession' (as in, *maja entume wae*, 'I have a knife [that I can give away]') and 'permanent possession' (as in, *tïpapake nai*, 'he has a father') (2004: 459–76).

The first type, as it deals with immediate possession, may not seem to be relevant to the notion of property, because if, for example, one does not have money on one's person, but elsewhere, then it is used in the negative. This impression may be due merely to a narrower definition of property than any we are used to. Nonetheless, Adam Smith, while contributing to founding modern notions of property, conjectured that among hunters, because of their nomadic lifestyle, 'the notion of property seems ... to have been confined to what was about ones (*sic*) person' (1978: 485), and possession is indeed arguably the most basic form of ownership; there are many ways in which, in all kinds of societies, de facto possession can form the basis for de jure ownership. Whether or not it is universal among nomadic hunting societies for immediate possession to be the primary notion of property, the suggestion does carry some resonance in Guiana, and Akuriyo such as Sil do tend to carry their most treasured possessions on their persons.

As for temporary controlled possession: the word *entu* has no direct equivalent in English, but it carries the sense of both 'owner' and 'boss'. The Portuguese *dono* or Spanish *dueño* come reasonably close in this respect. *Entu* can also be translated as 'trunk of tree' and 'foot of mountain'. The leader or founder of a village is known as the *pata entu*, literally the 'place *entu*',[4] and persons in charge of particular tasks, such as running the generator or the radio, are known as the *montoru entu* and the *radio entu* respectively. This is despite the fact that the radio in Tëpu is officially the property of the telecommunications company, Telesur, and the generator belongs to the government Ministry of Social Affairs. The common factor uniting these examples of *entu* is the practical element of being in charge of, being responsible for and carrying out or delegating tasks related to the village, radio or generator.

The suffix *-me*, here meaning 'being in a state of', gives *entume*. *Entume wae* means 'I have it', usually with a sense of control; it can be used with objects that can be exchanged (*bateri entume wae*, 'I have batteries [to give away]'; *malaja entume manan?*, 'do you have a machete [for me]?'). Carlin does not comment on the fact that this expression may

Illustration 5.1. Bram plays the *ruwe* during New Year celebrations.

also be used to refer to features of one's own body: Bram, for example, once used it to point out to me that he had a pierced septum (see illustration 5.1), in contrast with another person who did not. Once again, this is because of the element of control – but also because of the transient nature of the body according to indigenous cosmology; although Bram cannot 'unpierce' his septum or give it away, and the piercing seems to be permanent, it is part of his body and therefore under his control (reminding us of Locke and the foundational emphasis he places on self-ownership). Moreover, the humanity of the body must be constantly maintained by artificial means. A possessor in this type of construction must be animate, and

X entume wae means 'I own/control X'. The question *karakuri entume manan?*, 'do you have money', implies a request for money, because it includes the suggestion, 'do you have enough money', or 'money to spare', or 'do you have control of the money [such that you can give me some]?' Exchange, or giving, and control are united in this linguistic feature, and this should be borne in mind as we discuss types of property. They are both transient, and subject to relationships, but imply the ability or power to change: a village leader's position is subject to his maintaining certain relationships with his *pëito* (subordinates/sons-in-law) or villagers, who may desert him at any time; yet he has control of the village and represents it (in ways discussed below and in other chapters).

Permanent possession may be inherent, or acquired, and the examples that Carlin gives are telling: "'I have a father [*tüpapake wae*], a sister", or "I have a house [*tüpakoroke wae*]'" (2004: 459). This type of construction describes a state, in these examples roughly corresponding to being 'be-fathered', 'be-sistered' or 'housed', and it does not imply any transaction. A permanent possessor does not have to be animate, and so features of objects or places can be described in this way. With regard to things as opposed to persons, whether they are described in terms of permanent or temporary possession depends upon context. In the case of 'hammock', the noun itself changes from *ëhke* (permanent) to *weitapi* (temporary) to emphasize this distinction: *tëhkeke manan?*, 'do you have a hammock' (lit. 'are you be-hammocked'); *weitapi entume manan?*, 'do you have a [spare] hammock [that I can use/ buy]?'

The animate or inanimate nature of the subject in possessive constructions is significant. Temporary controlled possession must have an animate subject. This supports my suggestion that it is action or practice – artifice, so to speak – that makes property. Some kind of action – either through exchange or through the manipulation of natural or cultivated materials – must be taken in order to have a temporary controlled possessed object, and this requires an animate subject. In more general terms, whereas temporary possession is concerned with the thing possessed, permanent possession is concerned with a status or an identity, although both modes concern relations of one kind or another. A village leader owes his position not to an innate status, but to his foundation of a village and his actions and speeches; it is these relationships and actions themselves that are described in terms of permanent possession.

What we can learn from these possessive constructions is that possession is described in a subjective way, depending upon context. The distinction between merely having an item and having it at one's disposal (and being ready and able to act upon it) is given considerable weight. The distinction between being in direct and indirect possession (having an item on one's person or at home) is also emphasized. This corresponds to the Trio's emphasis in their language upon distinguishing the seen from the unseen, and the certain from the uncertain. One may be the owner of an item, but this is not the same as having it in one's pocket. Experience, relationship and intention are all thus mobilized even in the most everyday possessive constructions. This makes it difficult and inappropriate to discuss ownership in absolute terms. As we shall see, types of space also have implications for ownership and possession – the transformation of space being one way in which ownership is created – and once again these types of space are constituted through their histories, the narratives surrounding them, as well as their visible features.

Moveable Wealth

Kapitein Silvijn finds himself giving vast quantities of goods to his father-in-law (Guus), and to other close relatives of his. He is also constantly in financial debt. As a village leader, he must be less resistant to the demands of others, in order to maintain his influence. Lévi-Strauss called the leader's need to give in response to the demands of his followers the 'first instrumental force' of the chief's power (1944a: 24). I would add that the leader must also acquire more wealth in order to sustain this generosity, necessitating and facilitating his greater social connectedness. The strong disapproval of meanness characterizes above all the attitude towards movable wealth. Possession and ownership amount almost to the same thing, however, and it is common for people who 'borrow' items to be slow to return them.[5] Having said this, the use of money and the increasing presence of long-lasting manufactured items are giving rise to an increasing tendency for people to lock their houses and secretly hoard objects. This is in contrast to the ostentatious way in which certain prestige items are displayed, such as comparatively expensive clothes, watches, jewellery, sunglasses and other paraphernalia. These appear not to be transferable, and may be regarded as 'permanent' extensions of the person who wears or carries them.

Some objects are clearly gendered, as everywhere in Amazonia: most obviously, hunting paraphernalia and fishing tackle belong to men and cooking utensils to women. More importantly, men vigorously maintain their monopoly on any items that involve interactions between nonkin. A good illustration of this is the case of the motorized manioc grater that was brought to Tëpu and first put into use while I was there. Manioc grating is women's work, but men (led by Jack, who had charge of the machine) maintained control of the machine, which was made easier for them by their ownership of the fuel. Whenever a group of women wanted to use the machine, they would ask Jack's permission, and he would set it in motion. The women who paid a small fee could then unload their backpack (*katari*) of manioc into its steel funnel.

Trio people tend to measure the value of objects by age and usefulness. They regard things that are visibly old as useless. Newness, beauty and desirability are expressed together in the word *kurano*. The vast majority of everyday objects are utilitarian: cooking utensils, manioc squeezers, hunting and fishing equipment. The newer they are, the better condition they are in, and therefore the more valuable they are. The same pattern partly applies to ritual and ornamental objects, whose value may also in a sense be regarded as utilitarian, in terms of their functions such as protection against spirit attacks, or invigoration of the body. The exceptions to this are bead necklaces, feather headdresses, elaborate *panti* beadwork waist adornments or belts (see illustration 5.2), *keweiju* bead aprons and flutes (or parts of flutes) made of bone or claw. These, although considered more beautiful when they are new, have greater value precisely because of their durability, and 'hardness' (*karime* [T]), highly prized qualities. Trio people attach no importance to the history or 'biography' of loose beads, and quality glass beads can be recycled when a particular ornament begins to become unstrung. They prefer glass beads to seeds not only because they are more difficult to procure (coming from further away), or because they

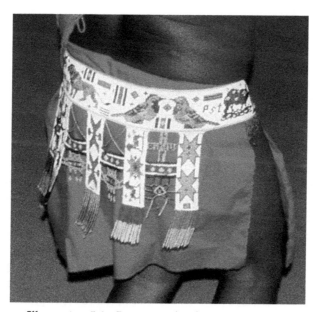

Illustration 5.2. *Panti* men's bead waist adornment.

require less work (seeds must be toasted, pierced and dyed), but above all because of their far greater durability and beauty, and because they come from the mysterious and powerful realm of the city. Value thus seems to be gendered: Trio people value objects that are hard and that come from the outside, both of which they consider to be masculine qualities.

The Value of Land

Trio people do not value land itself so much as the relationships that lead to its transformation in certain ways. In the Trio language, location must be expressed by suffix in one of five ways, distinguishing open space (*pata-po*, in the village), enclosed space (*itu-tao*, in the forest), in liquid (*tuna-hkao*, in the water/river), in fire (*mahto-renao*) or in contact (*itu-pë*, on the branch) (Carlin 2004: 172). The qualitative difference between types of space is most important between the village and the forest, space being subjectively experienced, either from within the forest or 'at' a place or village.

Akuriyo, Trio and Wayana give shared meaning to space or place through narration, and through situated narratives belonging of one sort or another is expressed. If 'place' corresponds to a network of histories, then *itu* is the holes in the net. *Itu* may be represented, much as the realm of myth and spirit is, whereas *pata* and *tëpitë* (the garden) are transformed. There is a subtle contrast to Melanesia, where what people value in the land is not so much its capacity for production, as its capacity for relationships (Strathern 2010). The radically differentiated spatial categories that define the Trio's relationship with the environment are such that the general concept of 'land' is almost meaningless (see below). The primary distinction for Amerindians remains that between the forest on the one hand, and the village and the garden on the other. The distinction is between cultivated and natural, consanguineal and affinal. In Melanesia, fields belong to lineages and are associated with particular ancestors. They can be left fallow, and they retain the 'name' (*eka*) of the group, clan or lineage. In Guiana, a garden, and even a village, only remains associated with its owner/creator until it is time to abandon it and create anew. Social space cannot be taken for granted. Places are historical, and people 'belong' to places only insofar as they belong to their creators through kinship. For this reason, it may seem impossible to say of Guiana what Strathern says of Melanesia – that territory produces people and social groups. Territory in Guiana, insofar as there is such a thing, is defined by the people that hunt, fish and cultivate on it. People produce territory, rather than the other way around.

Having said this, there is another level upon which places do produce people. As I showed in chapter 2, when houses and villages are created they reproduce an invisible ideal house, sometimes said to be situated in a stone archetype in the mountain. The mountain called Tukusipan can be regarded as an archetype of the Wayana house (*tukusipan*), and *paiman*, the Trio word for a large communal house, is also the name of a mountain. The Trio also associate their ancestry with the savannah area called Samuwaka. As with people, so with land: it is not so much continuity as the idea of continuity that leads to social reproduction. The idea or archetype of a house has its permanent manifestation in the landscape, and this hard, durable thing is fleetingly reproduced with the construction of each human habitation.

I suggest that the notion of creativity, which Strathern employs to show how land ownership can be similar to intellectual property, may be even more important in Guiana, because not even the group's relationship towards the land can be taken for granted. Social relationships are made first, and gardens themselves, which can belong to individuals, must be created out of them.

However, areas of the forest can loosely be said to belong to the spheres of influence of particular villages. Trio people prefer old and abandoned gardens to virgin forest as sites for cutting new gardens, not only because of the greater variety of useful plants that are to be found there, but also because of the vestigial humanity of such places, which makes it easier and safer to reappropriate them. Humanity and nonhumanity are sharply distinguished as ideal categories, but the humanity or nonhumanity of places is not always so clearly delineated. The significance of this is difficult to comprehend for outsiders, as Trio leaders have recognized through incipient negotiations with the government over land rights. Trio humanity is left in traces on the landscape, a network of histories, often only visible to Trio people themselves (cf. Viegas 2007).

A distinction can be made between the 'forest' as a category and situational relationships to locations in the forest, because paths and locations where a known event has taken place, such as cutting down a tree, killing an animal or gathering, are partially socialized by the human activity that has taken place there. Spirits belong to particular places (or the places belong to them), much as humans themselves own gardens and villages. Evangelical missionaries regarded this as a central problem when they were attempting to convince the Trio and Wayana of the superiority of their religion, and mounted expeditions to go to the 'big jaguar's village' or the 'big deer's village' to 'demonstrate' that there was no danger in going there. A place of historical and spiritual importance is one in which an important transformation has taken place, or in which a highly transformable being dwells, and part of the danger of such places is that further transformations, beyond the control of Trio and Wayana people, may take place there in the future.

There is no *terra nullius* in this context, then; the forest is not empty, but is the space of alterity – of encounters with nonhuman beings. What appears to be forest is in fact, from the point of view of *itupon* (forest dwellers or nonhuman agents such as spirits), their garden or a village. From the perspective of Trio and Wayana 'real people', the transformation that takes place when creating a village or garden is the transformation of alterity into kinship: clearing and burning send the spirits away, and they are replaced by manioc clones in the garden, which, nurtured as though they were kin, are truly domestic plants; this echoes the 'planting' of kin in the village, a creative appropriation of social space that takes place through the leadership of collective labour. Wealth, in both cases, is produced and reproduced through the expropriation and appropriation of persons, and the nurturing processes of kinship.

Names and Places

As I have mentioned, villages are named after, and 'belong' to, their founders or 'owners' (*entu*).[6] In more general terms, it may be said that *places* belong to, or are owned by, their *makers*; to create is to own and control. This is often reflected in naming practices, and the contrast between indigenous naming practices and those of external actors is informative. A man wishing to assert his independence and his leadership qualities founds a village or a section of a village today as in the past. This involves the organization of labour to clear and build, which creates a relationship of authority (where one does not already exist) between a founder and his followers. In most cases, village foundation involves the division of a previously existing local group, and therefore constitutes the creation of a new polity. For these reasons, it can be regarded as the consummate political act. As Lévi-Strauss wrote, 'the leader appears as the cause of the group's willingness to aggregate' (1944a: 22): the group comes together (in a particular place) around a leader (who chooses that place). Villages, like houses, are usually named after their builder/founders, and are inalienable from them. The village itself is a biographical entity.

It is worth making a brief comment on personal names. The resonance of a name must be understood in light of the fact that, among the Trio and Wayana, as among the Iatmul of Papua New Guinea, 'names contain relationships which people own' (Moutu 2003: 108). Names do not have the same exclusive value for the Trio and Wayana as for the Iatmul, and property does not tend to be disputed; such conflicts are preferably avoided. However, almost every individual has a unique name, and new names are enthusiastically adopted from outsiders. Although I was unable to obtain a clear explanation of this, it is coherent with the tendency to bring in persons and things from 'outside' to renew and nourish the 'inside'.

Names, *eka*, can be seen as performing the role of binding the body and soul together (Rivière 1997: 43). The name persists after death, although it is not uttered for a period, until body and soul are fully separated and the individual, corporeal elements of the individual person have been forgotten. At this point the name of a deceased person, often a grandparent, can be given to a baby. Names are important aspects of personhood, and the living cannot in principle share names. Moreover, each individual has several names, at least one of which is never uttered; the others are 'public' names that have less powerful associations with the soul.

The close association between names and personhood suggests that the appropriation of names from outside may be understood as a form of predation.[7] At the same time, each name reflects its source, and names are often adopted with the permission of their original holder: parents of a newborn child sometimes ask a non-Amerindian outsider if they can name the baby after them. The name thereafter contains the relationship. Naming a village thus leads to the encapsulation of the entire network of relationships comprising the future residents of the village in the name of its founder.

Villages in the past were smaller than they are now, and many contemporary villages, like Tëpu, were not founded by Amerindians; largely because of the attractions they present such as a school, health post and airstrip, they have lasted more than a generation and grown to unprecedented proportions. However, sections of the village in Tëpu (which are in some cases spatially quite distinct and separate) are themselves referred to as *pata*. They are named, as all villages were in the past, after people rather than features of the landscape, and as though they were separate villages: Douwe's *pata* and Silvijn's *pata* are at opposite ends of the village, and Jonathan's *pata* is on the other side of the river. Linguistically, there is a situational segmentary logic to the representation of space: when in Paramaribo, '*jipata*' refers to Tëpu as a whole, but when in Tëpu, '*jipata*' refers to the speaker's section of the village. But the pattern of abandonment and foundation of sections is the same as that of villages in the past. The larger 'village', such as Tëpu, taken as a whole, corresponds more closely to the cluster of villages that Rivière (1984) calls an 'agglomeration'.

Villages founded by missionaries tend to be named after features of localities, whereas villages founded by local people, and the small, shifting sections of large, missionary-founded villages (also known as *pata*), are referred to as 'so-and-so's village', after the local leader or founder.[8] Take, for example, the two principal villages in which I carried out fieldwork: Përëru Tëpu and Antecume Pata. Përëru Tëpu, 'frog rock' (usually known simply as 'Tëpu'), which the residents themselves often call a '*pananakiri* village', because it was founded by missionaries, was named after a frog-shaped rock forming part of the river bank, whereas Antecume Pata means 'Antecume's village', Antecume being André Cognat. Similarly, the founder of Twenke village was Twenke, and that of Pilima village was its current leader, Pilima.

This difference in naming practices reflects an important difference in relationships to land. Settlement solidarity revolves around the founder of a village or village section, and is based upon his authority over his daughters and sons-in-law. The practice of destroying the possessions and often the house of the deceased used to be extended to the entire settlement in the event of the death of its leader. This was the occasion for the migration of all the remaining residents – and often their simultaneous dispersal as rival new leaders founded separate new settlements. Today, numerous sites on riverbanks are spoken of as abandoned settlements where a *pata entu* died. Such places are said to be infested with spirits, and unsuitable for settlement or cultivation. They can be known as 'X's old place' or using toponyms. Today, within the larger, more permanent village, houses and even whole sections may be abandoned at times for the same reasons, but relocation may take place within the larger village.

The missionaries' naming of villages after features of the landscape represents part of a strategy to create permanent settlements. By giving neutral names, 'rock' (Tëpu) or Lawa (the name of a river), and installing a church, a medical centre, an airstrip and a school, they create a permanent centre of attraction, a nexus of spiritual and material resources, around which smaller, kin-based villages (founded in more or less the usual way) cluster.

In French Guiana, villages are smaller and more numerous, and named after their indigenous founders. The only factor ensuring the stability of village location is the permanent existence of schools and medical centres. Although this factor is a powerful one, it does not prevent relocation from occurring when desired by residents. In Antecume Pata, social tension and personal ambition as a potential leader led Erwan (Mimisiku's son) to found a new village on the French bank of the Maroni (Antecume Pata is located on an island). It is still within easy reach of the school and medical centre, but seems to be sufficiently far away to ease social tension. Although usually referred to as Erwan's 'place', it is also jokingly referred to as 'St. Laurent', after the main town on the French bank at the mouth of the Maroni. This joke has its roots in another strategic reason for the founding of the village by Erwan. A talented and intelligent young man, he manages to combine 'traditional' Wayana skills with an exceptionally high level of 'white peoples'' education. Highly literate by local standards, he has been employed on numerous occasions on governmental and nongovernmental projects. Conscious of his capacities, he claims to feel a sense of responsibility for the future of the village, and has different ideas from André Cognat (who is more conservative). His location of the new village firmly on French soil expresses his awareness and willingness to exploit the fact that state resources are more plentiful in France than in Suriname, and to make the point clearly, he flies a small tricolour over the frame of his house, which is under construction. Flying the tricolour, manifesting loyalty to the French state, stands in contrast to André Cognat's longstanding refusal to do the same, despite being put under considerable pressure by the French authorities. Erwan's use of French identity can be seen as a deliberate inversion of his ethnicity: he transforms himself into a Frenchman in order to seduce a French state that refuses to make cultural exceptions, such as providing special forms of schooling and healthcare. He hopes that this stance will help him to afford state patronage – his entrepreneurial efforts have already included applying for funding from the European Union to start a chicken farm.

Trio people often refer to the village of Tëpu as an 'urban people's village' (*Pananakiri ipata* [T]), because it was founded by American and Dutch missionaries. '*Pananakiri* villages' tend to grow bigger and last longer than traditionally founded ones. This is because of the wealth that the white people themselves bring, including metal goods at first, and later schools and clinics, but it also the result of the diminished need for relocation, deriving from the fact that the white founders are less likely to die in the village. There is a strong correlation between village permanence and its foundation by a *Pananakiri*. Most 'permanent' villages appear to have been founded by outsiders: Tëpu, Kwamalasamutu, Palumeu and Apalaí. Apart from the fact that outsiders often create attractions that outlast their own presence (health clinics, schools and churches) because they represent larger organizations, it is also significant that missionaries and other outsiders rarely die in the field, and that when they do their remains are quickly removed. The form of village leadership or ownership that they represent is different from that of the Amerindians themselves in many respects, but the spiritual danger that their death would bring to a village has never to my knowledge had to be considered. A large part of the danger of the spirits of the dead stems from their desire to rejoin the social world of their former kin; outsiders, however long they remain in a village, do not usually become socialized in the same way, and rarely marry local people. Missionaries in particular deliberately maintain a certain aloof distance. There is therefore no danger in living in Tëpu, for example, because Claude Leavitt, the main founder, left long ago.

Parc amazonien de Guyane

In practical terms, potentially the most significant Guianan case both testing and transforming different property practices at the present moment is that of the National Park project in French Guiana. Most of all, it affects the Wayana of the Lawa and Litani rivers. During the time of fieldwork, although the 'Mission' of the project sent delegations to consult Wayana villagers about how best to implement it, and designated local individuals as its representatives, who were to be informed of any progress, most Wayana to whom I spoke about the project told me that they knew little about it, and were sceptical partly for this reason. The two main debates were about how far hunting rights should extend around each village, and to what extent, if any, goldmining should be allowed in the park, by whom and using which methods. To the minds of those Wayana who had seen the draft maps of the proposed park, the defining effect of the project would not be to ensure that they had the clear right of use of an agreed territory, but to prohibit their use of land beyond the limits drawn. To quantify land in this way is a practice quite alien to them, as they experience land from the surface of the river and within the forest; it is their activity that makes land their own, and even then only temporarily. To reverse this relationship and make ownership – or, to be more precise, ownership of the right of use, which involves a further degree of abstraction – the prerequisite for activity is difficult to comprehend. Furthermore, because the gold industry lobby is so powerful that it had ensured that any national park would have some allowance for goldmining, the Wayana leaders saw the park as a threat, because it was likely to allow goldmining to take place upstream of the sections of river and creek where they fish, causing further mercury poisoning, as well as increasing the social problems that are brought by garimpeiros[9] such as prostitution, alcoholism, drug abuse, gambling, theft and violence. At the time of fieldwork, André Cognat told me that some parties (presumably mining lobbyists) are arguing for the Wayana to have a zone defined around each village, in which they would be allowed to hunt, but their hunting would be restricted to certain animals. He himself was arguing for the Wayana territory to extend to the source of all rivers and an equivalent distance downstream, although he had only proposed this orally, not in writing. The opaque, hierarchical structure of the 'Mission', and its mysterious objectives and procedures, contributed to giving Wayana people a feeling of powerlessness.

The *Parc amazonien de Guyane* was created on 27 February 2007,[10] and has confirmed the fears that I heard expressed. It retains zones of collective right of use for the Wayana, but Wayana territory is not included as part of the national natural reserve, which covers only the headwaters of the rivers affecting the Wayana, i.e. the Litani, the Marouini, the Tampok and the Waki. There is therefore no additional protection against gold prospecting, which continues to be an increasing cause of conflict.

With cases such as this, the redefinition of land as property, or the compartmentalization of the environment, slowly emerging from the process of political wrangling, inevitably further confirms and reinforces the Amerindians' position at the bottom of national society. Such is the way things appear to outsiders and to those Wayana, such as André Cognat and Erwan, who are able to adopt a white person's perspective. For those who are less skilled at doing so, who do not share an imaginary of the state and its hierarchical organization of social classes, these changes appear as the encroachment of the influence of white people's power, as manifested by the military, the police and other agents of the state, into Wayana territory.

Gender Asymmetry and Women as Property

Trio and Wayana ownership relations, as I have suggested, express primarily relations between persons *tout court*, rather than relations between persons with respect to things. The ownership of land is the product of relations of ownership and nurture between human and nonhuman persons. Relations of ownership are also produced between human persons, and especially between men and women. Although there is undoubtedly more equality of status between men and women in Guiana than in most parts of the world, the perspectivist principle of asymmetry whereby objectively equal men are each superior to the other according to their own point of view, does not seem to operate between the sexes. Guianan individual autonomy, such as it exists, is in fact to a degree a male privilege. Rivière argued that 'the concept of ownership is well developed' by the Trio with regard to women, because 'women are intrinsically valuable not only as vital economic partners but because they cannot be made or replaced' (1969: 41). This view of women as property, clearly expressing their inferiority in social status, raises the objection that such a statement is absolutely male-centred (Strathern 1988: 309–39). For my part, I am conscious that my point of view is biased by my own gender and limited by my analytical focus on masculinity and the male preserve of leadership. Even taking this into account, however, the evidence does seem to show that Trio men indeed own and exchange women in some privileged sense, although this does not mean that Trio society is characterized by hegemonic masculinity. It is also the case that from a feminine perspective women regard themselves as being subject to such exchanges – in their life histories, women described themselves as being 'given' by their fathers to their husbands – however this does not mean that women, or even young girls, lack agency. On the contrary, they chose their lovers and, to an extent, their husbands, but their agency is circumscribed by their parents' will. Later in life, they exercise greater autonomy.

Strathern herself previously observed that, among the Hageners, 'unlike a man, a woman has limited contacts; she serves men, and what prestige she has derives from her dependence on males. By herself she is nothing' (1972: ix). Only the first of these three statements could apply to Trio and Wayana women, who generally have far less access to people from outside the village and largely depend on men for obtaining trade goods.[11] Trio and Wayana women do not rely on men for prestige, as skill in making beer or cotton items such as *keweju* or hammocks is highly prized, as is the possession of prestige trade goods. A woman 'by herself' is a rare thing in Guiana, but there are exceptions, such as Julia, a divorced Wayana woman, who is one of the most influential and prosperous individuals in the village of Tëpu. Women do not assert their power or independence 'in between', unlike in Hagen, because it is precisely as sisters and daughters to be exchanged as wives that they are subordinate to men. However, mature women, such as Aniek, who no longer live with their parents, whose husbands have asserted their independence from their fathers-in-law by building their own house, have far greater autonomy and may display more initiative and a more public face. Julia's independence and autonomy is still greater, because she has been the head of her household since she divorced her husband. In this sense, it is above all by themselves that women are the equals of men, and regarded as such by the group, because by themselves they must at least partly assume a male role. As wives, sisters and daughters they are property, but it is possible for women to have political influence outside these roles. As Vanessa Grotti (2007) shows, this includes ritual nurturing strategies of women to 'suck in' male affines from outside, an important female dimension of the rituals discussed in chapter 4. Here it is worth distinguishing women and female agency: women such as Julia may enact male agency, but leaders may also enact female agency, such as when they theatrically feed the village.

Having said this, another important factor is knowledge, particularly white people's knowledge: Julia is exceptionally well educated, having shown a special affinity for learning since childhood, and this gives her an important advantage. She already had a job as a teacher in the village school when she divorced her husband, and her job seems to have made the process of initiating the separation much easier for her. She is now head of the school, which gives her great autonomy and earns her respect and prestige within the village, but when she went to live in Paramaribo after her divorce, she was constantly pestered by Douwe, the village Kapitein, to return to Tëpu; eventually she submitted. Julia's daughter, Lieke, is also an important woman, as a schoolteacher and excellent Dutch speaker, but also, perhaps, because she has no father. Education and literacy provide a new arena for personal abilities to allow women more independence and influence, as the case of Eefje also shows: she is the highly respected chief nurse at the clinic in Tëpu, and oversees most births and many other medical events that were previously the preserve of shamans (who are usually men). From this we can clearly see that education allows a change in the sexual division of labour that can allow greater equality and autonomy for women. However, it is important to recognize that Julia's autonomy only truly extends to the boundary of the village. When she left, the representative of the village exerted his influence to make her return. Women's influence is thus more locally restricted than that of men, whose travels are discussed in chapter 3.

There has been something of a reluctance on the part of anthropologists in recent years to discuss ways in which people, especially women, can be treated as property, despite their burgeoning interest in the idea of property in general. This is almost certainly because of the influence of critiques of functionalist kinship studies that emphasized the exchange of women (among others, Overing 1986; McCallum 2001: 7). Michael Asch, in an article defending Lévi-Strauss's *Elementary Structures of Kinship* as a classic text in political philosophy, strays from his central argument to accuse Lévi-Strauss of 'androcentrism … a mistake of fundamental proportions', though he excuses him by saying that it 'can be easily corrected by acknowledging that it is marriage partners of both genders and not solely women who are exchanged' (2005: 438).[12] In an ideal world, I certainly agree that marriage would be a gender-egalitarian form of exchange, but a distinction must be made between the normative and the descriptive, and to say that women are never exchanged as property is to close one's eyes to the weight of ethnographic evidence – among the Kali'na in the late sixteenth century, John Ley remarked upon the obedience of '"Common Indians to their Commannders (*sic*)" and of wives to their husbands' (Lorimer 1994: 209). Rivière notes that obtaining women was one of the prime motives for warfare: 'War is closely related to marriage and trade, and the object of raids on other villages is only conceivable as an attempt to capture women and dogs. Inversely, strangers who come to a village are regarded as a potential threat to the community's female resources' (1969: 42). Rivière qualifies the view of women as property, saying that the Trio do not refer to them as property; 'women belong to the society, but it is a male society' (ibid.: 42). Boasz's sister Nora was typical in describing herself as having been 'given' to her husband by her father, and I frequently found that when people, both men and women, talk about marriage, they do so in terms of 'giving' and 'taking' women. Rivière also noted that 'women own far less inheritable wealth' (ibid.) – this is to be expected in view of the fact that men have greater access to trade and travel. Overing describes Piaroa marriage in terms of the political machinations of men, and gives no place to the agency of women in politics (1975: 127–66)[13]; although here I would go less far, as women do frequently make demands on their husbands on political matters as well as others.

While women can only exert real influence when they are free of husbands and fathers, men present the opposite logic: they can only be influential through women, because they need a wife to produce beer and children, which are the keys to social influence and political action, as I have discussed already – this is precisely why women as 'property' are so important. Yet women are not owned absolutely or exclusively. Indeed, women's status as 'inalienable possessions' (Weiner 1992) enables them to manipulate the competing demands upon them as property to their advantage. A wife still remains partly the property of her father, and she can in turn make demands upon both husband and father, and have recourse to one in case of excessive demands from the other. The visibility of relations play a role here. A man will tolerate his wife having a lover, until he catches them in the act – and then, as occurred in the story of Sam and Luuk with which I began this book, the husband feels compelled to take action against the man who has been seen to have failed to respect his property.

Cecilia McCallum, discussing the analytical value of gender relations, asserts that 'in Amazonian societies capital is not accumulated and social inequality is not institutionalized in economic and political terms' (2001: 158). It is true that Trio people primarily use money to obtain things from the outside, and do not hoard or use it for profit in a capitalist sense. It is nevertheless also the case that social inequality is becoming institutionalized through the creation of official positions (Kapiteins are paid by the state, and maintain their position for life). This does not represent an entirely new phenomenon; indeed the discovery of pre-Columbian raised fields and mounds and other evidence of 'complexity' suggests that inequality, in the form of chiefdoms and large hierarchical societies, was far greater in the past (Versteeg 2003). The Trio, even in the 'atomized' state in which Rivière found them in the early 1960s, were no strangers to inequality. McCallum acknowledges that although 'I would say that the Cashinahua men and women I lived amongst enjoyed generally non-coercive and cooperative social relationship ... to make this expression explicit is not the same as stating that "male-female relations in Cashinahua society are egalitarian"' (ibid.: 158). I would say the same of Trio and Wayana male-female relations, although the evidence that I have seen of male domestic violence towards women (which is an accepted sanction against 'laziness') does suggest that there is an element of coercion.

Violence is not, however, at the root of the unequal relationship between the sexes. It is merely one expression of a conception of society whereby men are structurally superior to women. Another very obvious expression is the practice of women always to walk behind their husbands, or any other accompanying adult male.[14] Even my female field assistant, Emma, would automatically wait for me to walk in front of her, even when she was supposed to be my guide. Indeed, had I not been accompanied by my partner in the field, it would have been impossible for me (as a man) to have a female field assistant. For the first few weeks, she was too timid to raise her eyes to look at me, and she would not speak to me directly, but only through my partner. This is how she behaves with all men who are not consanguineal kin, with the exception of Akuriyo. This affinal avoidance does not properly apply to the Akuriyo because they are domesticated in a peculiar way that partially denies them 'real' humanity. But at the same time the exception of the Akuriyo also exposes the gendered nature of affinal avoidance: the inferior status of the Akuriyo makes avoidance unnecessary, whereas a woman, particularly an unmarried girl, must practise avoidance with a male affine of equal or superior status.

McCallum is correct in problematizing 'the idea that in Amazonian societies men dominate women or that an indigenous form of "masculine identity" is destined to find resonances with a global "hegemonic masculinity"' (2001: 158), because an excessively dualistic and insufficiently nuanced description of Amazonian male-female relations would be misleading. As Overing argued (1986: 148), women in Guiana do appear to be in control of their own fertility. Men and women also belong very much to each other, but women belong to men in a stronger sense than men belong to women. Men, as Overing showed (1975), arrange marriages for political purposes – political in the primary, overt sense, as opposed to the secondary, embedded sense. Yet it is through the latter that control takes place. Women control themselves in Guiana, but they are also controlled by men – although this is not to say that wives do not exercise a significant degree of control over their husbands, and their demands for objects from the city and game from the forest play a key economic role. The same nuanced gender inequality was observed in Jane Collier and Michelle Rosaldo's conclusions on sexual politics in 'brideservice societies': 'women … are not men's equals in terms of life possibilities or opportunities to enforce their wills upon others, but women are not dependent (sic) in the manner of unmarried bachelors nor do they appear to be "exploited" by husbands in ways that occur in certain more complex societies' (1981: 318).

Overing has denied that women play a politically subordinate role; she argues that Piaroa women are equal in daily life, but acknowledges that men, not women, are the 'great wizards': the shaman-leaders or *Ruwang*. She suggests, however, that it could be argued that the Piaroa have no 'political' institutions, but 'rather a religious structure only' (1986: 152). In fact, her argument that women are not *politically* subordinate seems to rest on such a view, but it is clear that politics is heavily bound up with religion in lowland South America; religion, there as elsewhere, is a reflection of political and social organization.

Claire Lorrain (2000) describes a gender hierarchy among the Kulina that may be 'soft and indirect', and which is partially enforced by actual or tacitly threatened violence. She argues that women's work is constrained by their dependence at all stages on previous male input, a structural dependency 'at the nexus of politics at large': women are almost completely dependent on men for game, for the creation of gardens and for trade goods, and this allows them to be manipulated – such goods are exchanged for sex, for example (ibid.: 298). Much of what Lorrain writes about the Kulina is also true of the Trio and Wayana, and I would agree with her that interdependence and complementarity between the sexes are not necessarily coterminous with equality. But the economic side of her argument is less convincing. Philippe Descola (2001) presents virtually the opposite perspective for the Jivaro, arguing that Jivaro women can survive without men (perhaps crucially, they can hunt), but men cannot survive without women because they cannot prepare food, garden or gather. One of the Akuriyo groups that were concentrated in Tëpu consisted of a woman and her young children, and the woman used to hunt. I think it is true that men are ideally superior to women in Trio and Wayana society because their roles encompass those of women, but this encompassment is to do with a certain view of cosmic order.

Overing has argued, 'the principle of "difference" can be just as much a mechanism for creating equality and complementarity as for creating hierarchy. Classifications are value-free in and of themselves: their meaning is arbitrary' (1986). It is true that difference can permit complementarity. However, only by removing difference can sameness be arrived at, as when kin are made out of Others (Vilaça 2002). Moreover, while it is true that the meaning of classifications is arbitrary, insofar as it is socially created rather than 'given' in some way, it does not follow that classifications are value-free. Classifications are very real to those who order their lives by them, and they are by definition value-laden. Classificatory value is relative and variable quality, rather than absolute and incommensurate quality as Overing seems to imply. Hierarchies of value are not the same as, and do not necessarily imply, relations of power or authority, or social stratification. They are merely a way of making sense of the world, or indeed of making the world. In the same way, it would be misleading to say that Trio or Wayana men dominate women. However, in Guiana men encompass women in the same way as affinity encompasses consanguinity, and there are many ways in which this manifests itself in daily life.

As Overing herself correctly states, 'the symbolism of gender or sexuality may be situated within a complicated network of meanings having to do with the material universe, forces beneath and above the earth, thus worlds beyond society, as well as with relationships between humans – with kin and affines, men and women' (1986: 142). Many myths are open to interpretation as parables serving to control women. The transformative 'ambiguous environment' is often presented as attractive but dangerous for women. A great deal of significance is attached to the caterpillar by Trio and Wayana, partly because, as I discussed above, the caterpillar is a symbol of transformation. It is also very obviously phallic, and in some myths it is presented as representing dangerous sexuality – sexual relations with the unknown, wild outsider. But the use of myth does not strike me as being one of social control. Instead, these myths are frequently transformations of one another, and manifest the same principles of social origin and meaning beyond questions of gender. Take for example the story of Caterpillar, referred to in chapter 2. To summarize, a women saw a beautiful caterpillar in the forest and said to herself that she would like it for a husband. A few days later, a beautiful man appeared in the village and said to her that he had come as she had requested, to be her husband. He lived for some time with her as an excellent husband, but eventually the villagers noticed that his beautiful body paintings were too perfect and did not fade away; the man then returned to the forest and became a caterpillar once more.

This myth can be seen as a feminine transformation of another myth, the story of *Kuluwayak*, according to which the caterpillar spirit gave men the cultural attributes of the Wayana: the perfect body paint of the caterpillar was 'seen', and therefore learned, by local people. The difference is that the metamorphosis within each myth takes place in the village when the protagonist is female, and in the forest when the protagonist is male.

Both men and women can therefore be protagonists in myths in which important events of social generation occur, but the social spheres of men and women, as outside and inside respectively, are taken for granted.

Challenges to the common-sense observation that men dominate women in various societies have tended to follow the formula: 'women do X to assert their independence despite their general subordination'. For example, Strathern's conclusion to her Hagen monograph: 'Women's challenge to male dominance lies elsewhere: in assertions of independence over marriage choices, sabotage of the exchange system through divorce; both in claims to be treated as quasi-transactors and manipulation of political subordination to their own advantage' (1972: 314). It is clear that in such a situation women are dominated, even controlled, by men; what is proven is merely that such domination or control is not absolute, although perhaps it is true that if women do not see themselves as victims then, from their own perspectives, they are not dominated (Strathern 1988).

Everyday relations between men and women among the Trio and Wayana, as among the Hageners, are generally relaxed, informal and uninhibited by the extreme awareness of difference in status that may be found in some other societies. Some Trio women display a somewhat proprietorial attitude towards their husbands, and make many demands on them to hunt certain game, to make things such as baskets and other woven objects. This relationship of control is frequently expressed in myths where a jaguar, an eagle or some other creature persuades a man to marry his daughter, and it is she who ultimately cajoles the man into doing her father's will (killing an enemy, for example). Women are thus often portrayed as persistent and nagging. However, the fact that, in practice, women are spoken of as given and received by men is simply due to the dynamics of power relations between the genders, and to marriage practice founded on men's influence over women. Moreover, the foundation of soceral authority is the influence of a man over his daughter, which, albeit characterized more by affection than by coercion, is based on his combined superiority in generation and gender. Overing gives an example of this: during pregnancy, a Piaroa husband must be present 'for the all-night chanting of the wizard, who includes in his chants the protection for pregnant women. If the father were not present, the mother would die in childbirth, a catastrophe for which the man if he is the cause pays heavily to the father of the woman' (1986: 146). She notes that 'such ethnographic detail makes one sceptical of Meillasoux's stance that kinship "is about" controlling women. What better way to keep a young father from wandering from his responsibilities than these ritual obligations which bind him to the house of the pregnant girl' (ibid.: 153n. 19). Like Overing, I do not accept Claude Meillasoux's argument that kinship is simply 'about' controlling women, and it is true that this example shows a way in which a man is controlled by his father-in-law. However, it also demonstrates that this control is founded upon the fact that a woman is understood to be the property of her father, for the damage of which he has a right to be compensated. Even if the ownership of women only exists from a male perspective, it has tangible and undeniable consequences.

To address the subject of women as property it is necessary to consider again the notion of value. As Katherine Verdery and Caroline Humphrey note, the economist's view of property is that it is a means of regulating access to scarce resources (2004: 3). In Guiana, as Rivière has argued, people, rather than land, have been the significant scarce resource since studies began, and many aspects of indigenous culture serve to counter the tendency for groups to disperse. The institution of marriage, with uxorilocality and brideservice, is the most important of these. Verdery and Humphrey criticize economists for the 'assumption that scarcity is a basis of property rights – a view presupposing that resources are "naturally" scarce a priori, rather than being *made* scarce only within a given system of values and power relations'; they therefore suggest that it is necessary to 'make the relation of property to scarcity a question' (2004: 9). I would be very surprised to find an economist arguing that resources are '"naturally" scarce a priori', since it is a central tenet of classical economics that values are constantly changing according to supply *and* demand – although the causal relationship between the two is still a matter of constant debate. Scarcity is, of course, the result of demand exceeding supply, and this may have political causes as well as consequences. An economic argument is therefore by no means inappropriate or inadequate as a contribution to the study of different types of property.

What, then, if any, is the relationship between people as property and people as a scarce resource in Guiana? The answer lies in the relations of consanguinity and affinity, to which we might add some subcategories such as 'family', 'potential kinship', 'potential affinity' (intended here in a narrower sense than that given to the term by Viveiros de Castro [2000]; I only mean the aspect of particular persons that makes them potential marriage partners) and 'potential enmity'. Briefly, kinship is a form of belonging, and in a certain sense this also gives it some of the features of property. This is less to do with having the power to make exclusive claims over objects or persons, and more to do with having a sense that these objects or persons are the elements of what one understands to be wealth, though there may also be elements of the former in certain cases, as we shall see.

Guianan Amerindians readily declare that one of their principal aims in life is to multiply their family and kin. This aim is set against certain entropic forces, sometimes mysterious or 'magical', which means that people constantly disperse and the kin group is constantly diminishing. In this context, therefore, the scarcity of people is not strictly the basis of their value; people are valued for their own sake, but because of a complex of causes including geography or village location, jealousy and disputes and the conjugal unit's ultimate self-sufficiency for subsistence, kin disperse; the desire and means to bring them together again can be regarded as political forces. Note that people are not merely valued as a labour force, and in this respect an approach restricted to considerations of political economy would indeed be inadequate, although the ideal situation of having many coresidents does of course result in more opportunities for cooperation in work and trade. As I have shown, even when a man musters a work force he does so by generating a congenial social atmosphere.

Clearly people can be valued as wealth as I have defined it, and women in particular are exchanged as property in a somewhat stronger sense.[15] By this I mean that women are valued by their fathers (and mothers) and husbands as both objects of affection and for their productive and reproductive capacities, and their father's prior claim to them results in the institution of brideservice: a prestation of services (which also involves the production of goods such as, in particular, canoes and basketry) in exchange for the gradual ceding of claims on the part of the husband. The process of social cohesion is gendered, as men hierarchically encompass women. This is expressed in the practice of uxorilocality, which is ultimately based upon the value of women, and the demands made upon them by their fathers and husbands. Women are not passive and disinterested in this matter: they obtain security from their position at the centre of the soceral relationship. It is also true that women are not necessarily coercively dominated, and they do have a great degree of autonomy in daily life, but the relatively overt and affinal character of male politics, as opposed to the relatively covert and consanguineal character of female politics, means that men exert greater control over women in overtly political terms.

Ownership, Wealth and Influence

As Daniel Miller (2005: 39n.) has pointed out, in societies in which objects are treated as persons, we should expect to find that persons are also treated as objects (cf. Hugh-Jones n.d.). I showed in chapter 3 that Trio and Wayana persons are not directly exchangeable for objects, although as I have suggested above, brideservice itself involves a prolonged exchange of services and goods for certain claims or rights over a person.

Broadly speaking, persons are nevertheless thought of as being exchanged on one plane (expressed clearly in the relationship terminology), and objects are exchanged on another; the difference is that the exchange of persons causes a proliferation of ties of property and belonging, because it creates kinship. Property relations cut and define social networks. In deciding to create or foster certain relationships, a person often breaks or neglects others, and the creation of new villages and new leaders through placemaking is often the result of a split in another village.

The relationship between gender, leadership, social relations and ownership highlights once again that it is asymmetry rather than equality that lies at the heart of Trio leadership and sociality. Overing claimed that the Piaroa's renunciation of property was at the foundation of their egalitarianism: 'In the Piaroa view, they have eradicated coercion as a social or political force within their society by refusing the possibility of the human ownership of material resources' (1986: 151). Trio people do own material resources. They also claim rights in human persons. Inequality is not necessarily founded upon coercion, and as the case of the Akuriyo outlined in previous chapters shows, both are present in Tëpu. Ownership practices in indigenous Amerindian society are founded upon historically contingent relationships unfolding over time, and the narratives that these create. They constantly change and do not necessarily imply permanence – with certain exceptions, especially lasting material objects such as bone flutes, feathers and beads. Because relationships are emphasized, rather than things themselves, social networks constitute things and places rather than the opposite. Leaders use their influence and reach to obtain and redistribute material wealth, responding to the demands of their kin. Their placemaking activities as housebuilders and village founders make them place owners, but places grow and expand to contain persons, whose relationships as kin constitute the wealth of the Trio as they truly value it.

Notes

1. I am grateful to the editors of the *Journal de la Société des Américanistes* for their permission to reprint certain passages from this article here.
2. In agreement with James Leach (pers. comm. 2011), I use the term 'ownership' rather than 'property' when possible, because the term is more suggestive of the processual nature of the relations that either term refers to (Strang and Busse 2011), but also of the agentivity implicit in appropriative processes.
3. Baskets are made by men.
4. Cf. Menget 1993: 71; Heckenberger 2005.

5. Cf. Strathern 2011, who shows how such concepts as borrowing, owning and stealing may elide.

6. 'Founder' is a very appropriate word to use, as another meaning of *entu* is the 'base [or foundation] of a mountain' (Carlin 2004: 461). As Rivière puts it, 'the term *entu* can be glossed as 'owner' but its semantic range is wider than that. It also has the sense of 'origin' or 'root', something from which a thing has sprung' (1995: 197).

7. This appears more likely in view of the fact that the Trio and Wayana share with the Jivaroans the tendency not to give the same name to more than one living Amerindian (non-Wïtoto [Amerindians] are not included), but dead Amerindian's names can be reused to name a newborn (cf. Taylor 1993: 659).

8. Schoepf (1998: 113) cites numerous toponyms, including names of villages, as 'place of [local geographical feature]': *Kulumulihpan* (*kulumuli* bamboo place), *Keyawokëh-pan* (place of the *keyawok* manioc ants), etc. He does not give precise details, however, and it is possible that these 'village' names are merely broadly used to refer to physical locations in which one *pata*, or more in a cluster, have been founded. All of the village names given by Hurault, with much more detail, correspond to the pattern I propose: Ilikwa, Elahé, Pileiké, Anapaiké, Touanké, Aloiké, Tiliwé, Tipiti, Malavat, Nanou, Yaloukana. Hurault gives an alternative 'lieu-dit' for each village, corresponding to geographical features, however (1968: 4), which seems to confirm the reason I have suggested for Schoepf's misleading assertion. Schoepf's villages may also be abandoned: old villages are often referred to using toponyms because of the dangers of pronouncing the names of the dead.

9. *Garimpeiros* are informal gold prospectors. Most are Brazilian (and come from the landless peasantry of the Northeast), but Maroons and Amerindians also now take part in gold mining, and some leaders (mostly Maroon but also Amerindian) accept rent from *garimpeiros* for allowing them to work on their territory.

10. Decree no. 2007-266 of the Ministry of Ecology and Sustainable Development.

11. Some doubt is cast on this view by the data presented by Mol and Mans (2013), whose social network analysis shows that women play important roles in the circulation of objects.

12. Cf. Lévi-Strauss: 'In human society, it is the men who exchange the women, and not vice versa' (1963: 47). This may not be universally true as he claims, but it is certainly true in Guiana.

13. Cf. Lorrain 2000.

14. Although in the city the urban practice of walking side by side is quickly adopted.

15. Akuriyo captive slaves are a still (much) stronger example of the overtly recognized ownership of individual persons.

CONCLUSION
Society Transcends the State

Each [big man or great man] seems an epitome, a concentration of characteristics, making visible what other men might be; he therefore stands out. At the same
time, in the sense in which all men might think of
themselves as big men, all men stand out.
—Marilyn Strathern, 'One Man and Many Men'

Amerindian leadership has held a special place in Western thought since
Europeans first encountered it, because it raised the questions of how order could exist without stratification, collective action without coercion,
solidarity without authority. Ever since Montaigne was inspired by minimalist Amazonian political organization to use it as a foil for political
reflections upon European society, the most influential authors on Amazonian politics have cast it in terms of noble or brutish savagery in the
absence of the State. Clastres's chief without power can be seen as the
concentration of these ideas into the impotent germ of the State, kept
in check by his vigilant band of wife-givers. In this book we have come
a long way from Clastres's canonical model of Amazonian leadership.
Far from being structurally opposed to the community, he represents and
embodies the social group and gives it form. Instead of a 'chief without
power', he is endowed with capacities and influence, the personification
of the internal relations of the collectivity, a magnified person who has
much in common with the Melanesian big man.

Running throughout this portrayal of Guianan leadership are the complementary images of networks and asymmetry. Leadership relies on net-

works of persons and things, but the leader's own person is also a network, concentrating in himself an array of heterogeneous elements, involving spirit power, multilingualism and hunting prowess, and neutralizing alterity itself as he mediates with the outside. A leader is thus a hybrid, whose hybridity is denied by his very success, for he uses foreign qualities and objects the better to identify himself with the collectivity. Asymmetry, epitomized in the atom of politics, the soceral relationship, is not of a static kind but constitutes the perpetual disequilibrium that gives society its dynamism.

This poses a challenge to the received image of Amazonian societies as egalitarian. Although native Amazonian societies are indeed egalitarian by Western standards, the idea of egalitaranism is absent from their ideologies. Indeed, it is striking that the most unequal societies that have ever existed in terms of economic wealth and coercive power (our own) have produced perhaps the most egalitarian ideologies ever known, while by contrast asymmetry, or inequality, is at the very heart of Amazonian societies, characterized as they are by an unusual degree of equality in terms of material wealth and coercive power.[1]

A leader's followers are structural sons-in-law (pëito), and the affinal nature of their relationship gives it its inherent instability, which is why the leader must constantly strive to maintain collective 'harmony'. Leadership is not only a relationship of affinal asymmetry, however. It is also a relationship of consanguineal asymmetry. As pata entu, the village owner, he is father and grandfather to the village, and the people are his adopted children. Grandfather, tamu, is the usual term of address for a leader, whether kapitein, hoofdkapitein or granman, and in this term the merging of consanguinity and affinity is implicit, because both cross and parallel cousins share the same grandparents. The leader's containment of all social relations is thus implicit in the relationship terminology as it expresses the position of the grandfather. This provides the structural potentiality for leadership to be realized through individual capacities and circumstances.

Leadership also operates on different levels or scales. In differing temporal and spatial dimensions (everyday life / ritual; the domestic house / the tukusipan / the forest), affinal or convivial relations are emphasized according to circumstances. The leader mediates between scales, and organizes the movement from ordinary time to ritual time. Meanwhile the house and household display the personal capacity of the builder-household head, just as the tukusipan and village display the capacity of the founder-village leader (cf. Strathern 1999). In showing the self-similar relationship between household and village, which can be extended inwards to the body and outwards to the cosmos (cf. Carsten and Hugh-Jones 1995; Viveiros de Castro 2001), I use the term 'scale' in a slightly different sense from Strathern,[2] but her 'display' function of scale measurement is also relevant here, and the two senses may not be entirely separable; indeed, the 'atom of politics', the unequal soceral relationship by which affinity is realized and consanguines produced, may well be the 'scale' by which society is measured on different levels.

Despite this attention to ideal structures, I have arrived at this conception of Amerindian leadership by refusing to see it merely as part of a structure or a system. Leadership is intrinsically historical; indeed, Guianan history is lived through leadership, as leadership is the motor of community formation. Insofar as structure or system exists 'out there', it is historically created through leadership. This in turn is represented in myth, as the historical action of leaders is mythologized, although the discernable patterns of leadership suggest that the action of leaders also follows a mythological template. This eternal reflection is further repeated in the relationship between the domestic unit and the larger local collectivity, the one not only being the microcosm of the other but also being its historical origin. This historicized view of leadership also shows that conviviality is a strategy; communities are neither given nor are they static ideals; instead they are contingent, ephemeral historical products of leadership and social disequilibrium.

The importance of this historicized view of leadership and community helps to resolve a problem in the interpretation of Guianan social formations in the way in which they have been defined in opposition to other areas of lowland South America. This has important implications for our understanding of indigenous political dynamics in the region as a whole. One of three 'analytical styles' in Amazonian indigenous ethnology, which Viveiros de Castro identifies in a well-known essay, is the 'political economy of control', which he associates with the work of Turner and Rivière. As Viveiros de Castro writes, these authors show 'the influence of the structural-functionalist distinction between the jural-political and the domestic "domains"' (1996: 189). Turner emphasizes the 'uxorilocal control of older over younger men through women, seeing the wife's father/daughter's husband relation as the structural axis of Central Brazilian social dynamics' (ibid.). The contribution of Rivière is that, based on Guiana material, he

> generalized the model by proposing (in opposition to [ecological] limiting factor theories) that the crucially scarce resource in Amazonia is human labor, which generates a political economy of people based on the distribution and control of women. From this he proceeded to explain the morphological variations present in tropical lowlands by examining the correlation between the ways of managing human resources and the presence or absence of supradomestic institutions. (ibid.)

Comparing Gê, and specifically Kayapó 'households', to Guiana 'settlements', Rivière had noted that

> the crucial difference is the social context in which the uxorilocal household is situated. Turner refers to Gê 'communities as agglomerations of multiple households' (1979: 165). What needs to be emphasized is that these households form a community because their members are also members of social formations (age-sets, moieties, etc.) that are community-wide and have an existence independent of any individual relationships. These social formations function to hold the households together to form a community. (ibid.).

Rivière argues that community is absent in Guiana, where households are 'dispersed, and this is consistent with the absence of any social formations to hold them together. It is this failure to combine individual sets of dyadic relationships into any higher and more enduring form of organization that gives the Guiana societies their particular stamp in the Lowland South American context' (1984: 97).

Rivière assumes that only 'higher and more enduring form of organization', by which he means the 'age-sets, moieties etc.' that Gê speaking peoples have and Trio lack, can create, constitute or sustain community. But I show in this book many other ways in which community is constituted. Historical events, including relations with powerful outsiders such as missionaries and state actors, bring people together and cause them to separate. Narratives about different identity groups, themselves historically constituted, regenerate and sustain collective identities that go beyond the household, though these should not be understood in terms of descent. Leaders themselves are magnified personifications of the community, and through their actions they constitute its identity and favour its cohesion. They do so through their privileged interaction with the outside, which today involves interacting especially with *pananakiri* of various kinds, and through their use of music, ritual and chiefly dialogue. These actions take place in spaces that represent the collectivity, such as the *tukusipan* collective house with its *maluwana* painted disc (which Rivière himself speculated was a representation of community [1995]), and the *anna* plaza.

Part of the interest in studying leadership in the 'minimalist' societies of Guiana lay in the fact that here, political structures (including clans, sibs, moieties or factions) are less obviously apparent than in northwest Amazonia or central Brazil.[3] Perhaps paradoxically, as I have shown, this actually increases the importance of leadership; here, society depends entirely upon the actions of leadership for their very existence. But the distinctions between these types of Amazonian society may have been overstated; as Cesar Gordon has also illustrated with respect to the Xikrin, the difference between 'dialectical' and 'minimalist' societies may not be so great after all (2006).[4] In Guiana, just as much as in these other lowland South American regions, the house clearly plays a role of 'structuring structure' in a much more concrete sense than in Viveiros de Castro's use of the phrase to refer to potential affinity (2002: 157). But the 'exteriority expressed as potential affinity' (ibid.) is also equally important, as it is in the Xingu (Menget 1993). In Guiana and the Xingu, neighbouring social groups cohabit peaceably without 'supra-communal institution or political apparatus', and unregulated by local or linguistic exogamy (ibid.: 62). Although territoriality is more pronounced and defined there, the Xinguano polity shares with the Guianan the features of 'moral community, association of solidary local groups in case of necessity but without automaticity, interconnected network of riverine villages' (ibid.: 64). Moreover, despite the existence of chiefly lineages (at least as an ideal) in the Xingu, leadership in practice is a matter of personal qualities there too (ibid.: 67–68). Here we find a more elaborate (but functionally similar) form of intertribal ceremonialism during the dry season that serves to periodically legitimate the integrity of the polity in the absence of supralocal institutions, and in which leaders play a fundamental organizational role (ibid.). The comparison even leads to the possibility that Guianan leaders have coercive power after all, for the argument that Patrick Menget uses to show how Xinguano leaders can use their influence and rhetorical skills obliquely to incite others to assassinate a rival could also be applied to this region (ibid.: 71).

The longer view of Xinguano cultures taken by Michael Heckenberger suggests that in their present form they are

> not merely a slightly complex variation on a generalized ('traditional') 'tropical forest' model … characterized by small-scale, egalitarian, and autonomous villages. Considered historically, it is clear that Xinguano society as we see it today is an egalitarian 'twist' of a fundamentally hierarchical model, the historical low (in demographic and political economic terms) of a genuinely Amazonian complex society. (2005: 337)

For this reason (among others) Heckenberger robustly rejects the Clastrean notion of 'strong internal (structural or ideological) or external (ecological) mechanisms against social hierarchy, regionality, or sedentism' as doing 'serious violence to Xinguano history' (ibid.). His analysis of the Xinguano *longue durée* also leads him to reject Menget's (1993) comparison of Xinguano chiefs to Melanesian big-men, '"aggrandizers", who achieve status through their personal skill and charisma' (Heckenberger 2005: 332) in favour of a comparison with Polynesian 'great-men' societies with hierarchy institutionalized above all by the 'exclusive control over critical elements of social and symbolic reproduction held by a hereditary "elite" group, the *kwaimatnie*-owners' (ibid.: 333). Just as Xinguano society today is the low historical ebb of a cultural formation that is hierarchical to the core, rather than being functionally opposed to social hierarchy, I would add that Guiana society lies similarly at one end of a continuum, characterized by quantitative variation over time and space in the level of social differentiation, and not by qualitative variation in the presence, nature or fundamental attitude towards differentiation itself. This observation extends and supports Heckenberger's critique of Anthony Giddens's (1984) distinction between existential and structural contradiction as too narrowly based on the rise of feudalism in Europe; as he writes, following Kwang-Chih Chang (1989), 'continuity as much as rupture defines the transition from *societas* to statehood' (Heckenberger 2005: 341–44).

Recognizing the asymmetrical foundations of politics in even the most apparently egalitarian societies makes it possible to see what these societies share with others in central Brazil, the Xingu and in northwest Amazonia that are still often described as more complex. It suggests that hierarchy is neither necessarily something that 'emerges', nor something that must come from outside like the stranger king, but that it is intrinsic to lowland South American societies and polities in nearly all their forms. This is an important caveat to claims such as that 'the peoples of Guiana have little or no social structure … defined by 1) structures of separation and opposition, and 2) structures of inequality, or the institutional elaboration of relations of dominance and subordination' (Overing 1993: 193); the problem hinges on the ambiguity between 'little or no', for there is indeed some and, however minimal it may be, it plays a fundamental role in ordering social relations.

Lévi-Strauss recognized that even the most 'minimalist' societies of Amazonia carry within them the potential for complexity when he wrote that, 'primitive institutions are not only capable of maintaining what is, or of temporarily keeping the vestiges of a past which is coming undone, but also of elaborating audacious innovations, even if the traditional structures must thereby find themselves profoundly transformed' (1943: 139). When they 'profoundly modify their structure', they do exactly this: the change is not radical or fundamental, but (to use a spatial analogy) the structure before and after transformation remains topologically equivalent (cf. Leach 1966). Dialectical and minimalist societies thus belong to the same 'transformational group' (Lévi-Strauss 1971: 604). Relationships of hierarchy, domination and power exist in even the most apparently egalitarian Amazonian societies, and their formal manifestations wax and wane through time – the fact that 'regressions and false archaisms' (Descola 1988: 819) are found to be ever more widespread as archaeological research progresses shows that the multiplication of social scales is not merely the result of missionization.

This carries implications for potential future developments among the Trio and Wayana and elsewhere. From their own perspective, Guianan Amerindians experience the changes wrought by national and transnational influence on their own terms, although from a more objective, economic perspective they are quite clearly disadvantaged. As Peter Gow has shown (2001), if they situate the initiative and motive force of change outside society, this constitutes a political stance consistent with their own indigenous cosmology. But more than this, it preserves the integrity of society itself, which remains a place in which external influence is transformed.

The study of leadership can contribute further still to our understanding of indigenous Amerindian history. Anne-Christine Taylor (2007) has described the complementary relationship between Jivaroan and Quichua historicities, whereby the difficulties of sustaining the Jivaroan self, which is based on an antagonistic relationship to the Other, can lead to illness, which must be cured by Quichua shamans whose power is based upon the ability to identify with alterity. The distinction between Jivaroan and Quichua identity is based upon differing views of history: Jivaroan history is narrated as the personal experience of a 'strong man', whereas Quichua history is presented as the collective experience of phases from 'times of wildness' through 'times of slavery' to 'times of civilization'. Trio and Wayana historicity echoes both those of the Jivaroans and the Quichua. The leader's acquisitive and transformative activities echo the Quichua shaman's songs which evoke a 'dream-like *bric-à-brac* mixing elements of different times, types of outsiders and ontological status' (ibid.: 23). But at the same time the forgetfulness of past identities, the focus on the leader's biography as constitutive of collective identity, and the leader's rhetorical maximization of shared ontology and collective selfhood, not to mention the predatory relationship to alterity that is characteristic of Guianan warfare and hunting, all recall Jivaroan historicity. If this antagonistic relationship with the Other is hard to sustain and is 'vulnerable to erosion' (ibid.) manifested as illness, and if Quichua-type historicity and shamanism are the cure, then it would seem that the Trio and Wayana have the best of both worlds: they balance their predatory and antagonistic ontology with an inclusive, identificational ontology capable of solving the problems of the former. The historical alternations between peace and war, between 'strong' and 'weak' forms of leadership, between inclusivity and exclusivity, and between fission and accretion, can be seen as corresponding to these two views of history, which are just as complementary and mutually dependent whether they coexist in one society or whether they are spread between two. For Amerindians, as Aparecida Vilaça has noted (2006: 501), following Lévi-Strauss (1991), 'difference is structural, and must be maintained'; this is tied to a paradoxical need to become the Other while remaining the same. In Guiana, leaders position themselves at this axis between identification and difference.

All of this may well raise as many questions as it answers. An understanding of leadership combined with an appreciation of the transitory and personalized nature of 'property' in Amazonia, for example, carries numerous implications for research on intellectual property and land rights: the exchange of plant knowledge needs to be seen in the context of a long history of trade in various forms with different kinds of people, and the difficulties of translating the intensely biographical relationships to space into collective titles, and vice versa, are but two subjects worthy of investigation. In the context of ever-increasing pressure and demand on lowland South American peoples for their land and their knowledge, there is urgent practical need for an Amazonian theory of property (cf. Brightman, Fausto and Grotti 2016).

Property is a basis for control, and a basis for a political economy, but has been neglected in Amazonia in large part due to the intellectual history of Amazonianist literature. According to this tradition, the State has been assumed to be absent in the region's primitive, apolitical indigenous societies, which lack property, for as readers of Locke and Rousseau know, property is one of the requisites for the development of the State or commonwealth. Property may be a defining attribute of the State, but it is also an attribute of Amerindian polities; in order to recognize this, property must be seen in a broader light; after all, if property is a condition for the State to exist, then it is prior to the State, and the State therefore does not define its form, although it may limit it.

Much as Andrew Moutu (2012) has proposed for Melanesian societies, the distinctive Amazonian ways of relating to place, object, technique and knowledge therefore need to be examined in terms of ownership and belonging. This has the added practical benefit of facilitating translations between Amerindian and State property regimes. Even the most sophisticated attempts to formulate theories of property tend to do so starting from Western categories and practices (e.g. Hirsch and Strathern 2004), because the final arbiter in property disputes is the law of the State. A convincing theory of Amazonian property has to be formulated on the basis of indigenous practices and indigenous perspectives. With this book I have tried to lay the groundwork for the development of such a theory.

I have focused on native politics as something autonomous from the State and even transcending it, rather than following Clastres in considering it as an active rejection of the State. However, Clastres's ideas have found most resonance outside Amazonian ethnology in reflections on relations between state and nonstate actors. Inspired by Clastres, James Scott has renewed interest in societies against the state, claiming that their anarchist struggle against the surrounding state formations defines their history (2009). He takes as his subject the 'nonstate periphery ... "the local mechanisms of bands, margins, minorities, which continue to affirm the rights of segmentary societies in opposition to the organs of state power". Such states themselves are, in fact, "inconceivable independent of that relationship"' (ibid.: 29, quoting Deleuze and Guattari 1987: 360). Gilles Deleuze and Félix Guattari themselves refined Clastres's famous argument into a logic of figure and ground: 'The same field circumscribes its interiority in States, but describes its exteriority in what escapes States or stands against States' (1987: 398).

It may be true that from a certain point of view native Amazonian societies are societies against the state in this sense, but these characterizations do not do justice to the way in which they remain autonomous from the state, or indeed to the way in which native Amazonians think about their own societies. The relationship is not really one of opposition or of resistance, but rather, as I have said above, of transcendence. To give an example: a process of land reform is slowly underway in Suriname, and a conference was organized by the government in October 2011. The Amerindian people's organization (VIDS) made a defiant statement at the beginning of the conference, which led to President Bouterse closing the conference in a fit of pique. During the ensuing public attempts to explain and pass blame for what was widely perceived as a failure, the Trio leaders took the trouble of apologizing in person to the president, thus apparently dissociating themselves from the other indigenous and tribal peoples. Now, it is true that Trio leaders have a more harmonious relationship with the government in Suriname than the Kali'na, who dominate VIDS, and the Maroons (and one should bear in mind that many Maroon tribes have their own representatives in government or in opposition). A superficial reading of these events might be that the Trio's relationship with government, less oppositional and aggressive, is a symptom of a tameness resulting from missionary success and continued influence. Hopefully the reader of this book will not have leapt to such a conclusion. Trio leaders are just as determined to prevent abuses from the government, whether in the form of encroachments to sack natural resources or of mooted road or dam projects, as their Kali'na or Maroon counterparts. I suggest that their less aggressive, more diplomatic relations with the state result instead from their greater sense of autonomy, thanks largely to the physical distance separating them from the city. The coastal Kali'na have suffered much more directly from expropriation and other abuses, and their leaders are also more forthright in their rhetoric in part because of their involvement in international indigenous political networks. It is therefore not surprising that they are more aggressive in their dealings with the state. The political attitude of all of the Amerindians of Suriname, Trio, Kali'na and others alike, contrasts, meanwhile, with that of the Saramaka, Ndjuka and other Maroons in one important way: they will not compromise on the fact that, as prior occupants of the territory, they are its only true owners; all others, both the state and the free Africans, are indebted to them for their very presence there. With this attitude, they escape the 'voluntary servitude' that so puzzled Étiene de La Boétie (Clastres 2010: 171ff.). But rather than this, it is the seeming ease with which they give in, the very amenability to missionaries and officials – together with the persistence of a form of political organization that runs through society like the fibres of a plant or the grain of a piece of timber – that constitutes the secret of native Amazonian resilience. This, then, is perhaps the sense in which native Amazonian society stands against the state today. Like the myrtle, which finds its own form again after the topiarist has sculpted it, and unlike the marble, which keeps its sculpted form (Viveiros de Castro 2002), inconstant Amerindian society does not so much stand 'against' the state, as transcend it, as though it were made of a different substance that the latter's crude, coercive and, above all, bureaucratic means could not bend to its will.

To end with some more general conclusions: there are many implications for political anthropology in the fact that leadership is not only ingrained in the fabric of the everyday, and in gender relations, but also articulates the transitions from ordinary life to extraordinary event, whether ritual ceremony or political gathering. Without any need for reliance on the introduction of crude distinctions such as between 'tradition' and 'modernity', music and objects can be seen as politically charged modes of communication and appropriation. There is no need for political anthropology to take the State as given or universal; on the contrary, it should be open to different types of power relations, whether overtly political or embedded in daily practice. Nor are politics necessarily only about power relations. Mauss described politics as the 'conscious direction' of society (1990: 247), which sums up well how Amerindian leadership can take many forms and requires many types of quality, without the need for coercion. It can also take place on the smallest of scales: what is meant by 'society' in this phrase clearly has important implications for the nature of politics.

The multiple scales of social action are most clearly illustrated by the Guianan distinction between the domestic and the ceremonial house, and this distinction also highlights that the dynamics of kinship relations can provide an 'atom of politics' that radiates a minimal template for the disequilibrium on which all political relations are predicated. These scale relations show the interrelatedness of kinship, ritual and space, and how these should be understood alongside the personal qualities of leadership, and indigenous notions of property.

Lack of attention to leadership in Amazonianist scholarship has led to focus on the 'individualism', personal autonomy and disaggregation said to be typical of Guiana, and to attempts to subvert such an image. The study of leadership shows that such a polarization of perspectives is misplaced. It reveals the existence and the value of a notion of collectivity, which has been ignored largely because of its ephemerality and because it is expressed in an idiom of kinship and social harmony rather than in formal institutions. Understanding the role of leadership in making and, indeed, embodying the collectivity, shows both why the study of leadership has for so long been dominated by exchange models, and why these models miss the mark. As I showed in chapter 4, the leader does give things, such as words, objects and food, to coresidents. But, vitally, his very act of giving – a feminine, homogenizing act – dissolves the difference between giver and receiver, obviating the requirement for reciprocity. Previous authors following Clastres and Lévi-Strauss have seen the leader's prestation and assumed a relationship of exchange (or its negation), ignoring the fact that the transaction transformed the very opposition between giver and receiver into mutual identification.

I have drawn attention to the importance of dual or multiple perspectives and their use by leaders, and it is this capacity of proliferation of identity and assimilation of the powers associated with difference that lies behind Amerindian leadership: leaders identify with alterity, creating solidarity among their coresidents; but they simultaneously identify with their coresidents, and share in their solidarity. Illustration 6.1 is an illustration of this process: Silvijn, dressed in a shirt and trousers, distributes white bread from the city in the *tukusipan*. He wears the clothes of the Other (a *pananakiri*), and feeds villagers the food of the Other; but he does so in the collective house that he himself sponsored, and the act of feeding is the quintessential process of kinship – a feminine, nurturing act. This makes visible the dual nature of Guianan leadership. Clothing and substance here represent one facet (alterity and masculinity); place and act represent the other (identification and femininity). If the transformation of alterity is the principal condition for the reproduction of society, leadership makes this happen by encompassing sameness and difference.

Illustration 6.1. Silvijn distributes *pananakiri* bread to the revelers.

Notes

1. This is true not only of Amazonian societies: as Lévi-Strauss was the first to note (1956), asymmetry is 'almost invariably encountered' in moiety systems (Turner 1984: 336).
2. Strathern uses the term in the sense of 'standardised computable or quantifiable dimensions' (1999: n. 33).
3. Hugh-Jones 1979; Maybury-Lewis 1967; Turner 1979.
4. See preface to Gordon 2006 by Fausto. Minimalist societies *are* dialectical in their relationship to alterity (Taylor 1993: 654; cf. Viveiros de Castro and Fausto 1993, who describe a continuum between Amazonian and Central Brazilian societies; see also Fausto 1995: 62).

GLOSSARY

Trio

anna	– plaza
ëire	– fierce
eka	– name
ëremi	– spirit songs, spells
enpa	– teacher
entu	– owner, creator, source
ikopija	– spirit helpers, familiars
-imuku	– son
-ipawana	– trading partner, friend
itïpï	≈ continuity
itu	– forest
itupon	– forest people
jahko	≈ friend, comrade (term of address)
jana	≈ subgroup, Amerindian collectivity with shared identity
Jesu	– Jesus
-jomi	– language
Kan	– God
kanawa	– canoe
kanawaimë	– aeroplane
karakuri	– money
karaiwa	– Brazilian

karime	– strong, hard, healthy
kawai	– seed rattle, *Thevetia ahouai*
keweju	– bead apron
kororo	– stool
kurairu	– chicken
kurano	– beautiful, good, sympathetic
kure(-ta)	– good (bad)
kuri	– spirit stones
maraka	– rattle
okoropagë	– roundhouse
omore	– eye-soul, image-soul
paiman	– house (lozenge shaped)
pata	– village, place
patapon	– village people
pakoro	– house
panti	– beadwork belt
pëito	– subordinate/son-in-law, junior
piana	– harpy eagle, *Harpia harpyja*
pito	≈ brother-in-law
ruwe	– flute, aerophone; friction drum with panpipes
sawaru	– tortoise
sasame	– content, happy, collective harmony, euphoria
tamu	– old man, leader (see appendix)
tarëno	– Trio / 'the people here'
tënisen	– manioc beer
tëpitë	– garden
tuna	– water, river
mahto	– fire
mekoro	– Maroons
-moitï	– family, kin
mono	– big
mono eka	– inclusive group, set of *janas* with shared identity
pananakiri	– urban people (Whites, Creoles, Javanese, Hindustani, etc.)
pena	– long ago
wajiarikure	– wild people

wïtoto	– people, Amerindians
wïrïpë	– spirit
wïrïpëhtao	– edge of the village

Wayana

ëlemi	– spirit songs, spells
ëlukë	– caterpillar
kunana	– woven mat for stinging rituals during *marake*
luwe	– flute, aerophone
maluwana	– disc-shaped painted ornament
marake	– rite of passage for both sexes
peito	– subordinate/son-in-law
piana	– harpy eagle, *Harpia harpyja*
tëpamnehe	– taming, domestication
tukusipan	– collective house, roundhouse
yepe	≈ friend, comrade (cf. *jahko* [T])

Akuriyo

| *kare* | – subgroup, collectivity with shared identity (cf. *jana* [T]) |
| *kule* | – good |

Sranan

granman	– paramount chief
krutu	– meeting of leaders
poku	– music

Dutch

basja	– minor official, overseer
bestuursopzichter	– minor official, government supervisor
hoofdkapitein	– head captain
kapitein	– captain

APPENDIX
Trio Relationship Terminology

Generation	Parallel			Cross	
	Male	Female		Male	Female
Grandparent	Tamo, tamusinpë	Noosi, noosinpë, kuku		Tamu, tamusinpë	Nosi, noosinpë, kuku
Parent	Papa, pa, pahko	Mama, ma, manko	(=)	(J)ee, (Jee)tï, Tamu, tamusinpë; jau (W/HF)	Jaupï (W/HM)
Ego/e	Piipi, pii, pihko	Wëi, wëiko		Konoka, Pito (m. ego)	kori, koko (f. ego)
Ego/y	(j)akëmi, (ji)kïri, kami, jarï	(Ji)wëri		Enmerïnpë (f. ego; addressed as jeetï) (j)injo (H) mi, minko, ae, aenpë (H)	Enmerïnpë (m. ego; addressed as jiwëri or address avoided) (ji)pï (W) mi, minko, ae, aenpë (W)
Child	(j)inmuku	(j)eemi		(j)inmuku Jipamï (DH, BDH, ZDH, SDH)	(j)eemi Jipaeje (SW, BSW, ZSW, MBW)
Grandchild	(j)ipa			(j)ipa	

(After Dumont 1983: 10; based on Rivière 1969: 284ff. and Carlin 2003: 139–40, and checked against my own data.)

Names given in italics, including the possessive suffix (given in brackets) when applied, are also terms of address. All others are simply terms of reference for a third person.

Terms not necessarily expressing specific relationships:

- *kïrinmuku*: boy
- *wërinmuku*: girl
- *tamutupë*: old man
- *notipë*: old woman
- *Musere, mupiro, kunme, kïrï-pisi*: little boy
- *Papoï, tato, wëri-pisi*: little girl
- *(j)emu*: baby boy (lit. 'testicle')
- *(j)epa*: baby girl (lit. 'vagina') (Carlin glosses these last four sets as 'grandson' and granddaughter')
- *jako*: friend, comrade

Carlin glosses *jako* as 'of the same (age) status (male ego)'. In today's usage, unrelated women of the same age status frequently address each other as *kori* – *jako* and *kori* are the terms that were used by most people of our own age to address me and my partner in the field. In Tëpu, Trio, Wayana and Akuriyo men address each other as *jako* in most cases (e.g. Boasz: Sil, Jonathan: Mike). Carlin also gives the Wayana *yepe* as a rough equivalent of *jako* now also used by the Trio. Rivière states that *kori* and *koko* were not used as address terms, and the reason for this is undoubtedly because relationships between affines used to be more reserved.

According to Carlin, *jarï* is a Pïropï word (see chapter 1). She appears to claim (although her meaning is not quite clear to me) that *jarï* and *kami* are mutual address terms for men sharing a grandfather. But the conflation of affines and kin in the grandparents' generation means that if this were so then everyone would call everyone else of the same generation *kami* or *jarï*, which is clearly not the case.

A development that seems to have occurred between the time of Rivière's fieldwork and that of Carlin is that men and women can now address their potential wives and husbands as *jiwëri* and *jeetï* respectively. In the past, and in my own experience, there was no direct address form for such a relationship. Again, like the use of *kori* and *jako*, this is a reflection of the recent relaxation of the relationship between affines. However, I never witnessed this usage, and it is therefore possible that it is restricted to Kwamalasamutu, where Carlin conducted her research. Note that cross and parallel grandparents and grandchildren are not distinguished in the relationship terminology, a fact that greatly reduces the likelihood of the existence of descent groups or lineages, and which corresponds to the canonical dravidianate (cf. Henley 1996).

My data correspond with those of Rivière with the following exceptions and additions:

1. *Piipi* does not refer to MH.
2. *Akëmi* does not refer to SW..
3. *Jenmërinpë*, according to one (male) interlocutor, can be used to address a potential spouse, although it would be 'funny' – suggesting a relationship of joking or flirtation, rather than avoidance.[1] However, another (female) interlocutor said that there was no appropriate term of address for MBS or ZH. *Jaupï* still has no direct address term.
4. *Inmuku* does not refer to ZH.
5. *Eemi* does not refer to BW.
6. *Tamusimpë* is also used of someone long dead.
7. *Jau* and *jaupï* can both be used for both mother- and father-in-law, and the former appears to be less common.
8. *Jipamï* can also refer to SDH (Boasz addressed Ronaldo in this way).
9. *Tamo* is also used of spirits (as in the past, although this was not included as part of the relationship terminology by Rivière), and now it is additionally used of 'our Lord'.
10. *Pahko* is similarly used to translate 'Our Father'.

In one case (Pepijn of Nora and Boasz), *wëiko* and *pïhko* ('elder sister', 'elder brother') were used to address W(d)M and W(d)MB respectively. The speaker, Pepijn, lives with his W(d)M, and next door to his W(d)MB; this case shows that the institution of ZD marriage can also operate in reverse: marriage to a woman can make her mother and mother's siblings into brothers and sisters.

In sum, the principal changes in terminology appear to reflect a weakening or softening of the reserved nature of relationships between affines (*jau, jaupï, jenmërinpë*), and an increased familiarity between genealogical nonrelatives. The cause of this may be the increased frequency of marriage between individuals more distantly related than cross-cousins, and the more regular and sustained company of genealogical nonrelatives, both of which are due to increased village size and travel between villages.

According to my data, in Akuriyo relationship terminology, as in Trio, there is one word for parents-in-law of both sexes: *kutune:ton* (cf. *jaupï*). Akuriyo has an additional noteworthy feature: *kutune:ton* is also the equivalent of the Trio word *pito*. The Akuriyo term thus captures the essence of the nature of the affinal relationships of parents- and brother-in-law: it can be suitably glossed as 'wife-giver' – although Akuriyo does have other terms for affines, such as *wëtinana* (T. *konoka*, WB, etc.), *ye:na:no* (T. *enmërinpë*, FZD, etc.), *pahtje* (T. *jipaeje*, SW, etc.), *jitanana* (if 'near') or *wïtinananme* (if 'far') (T. *ipamï*, DH, etc.) (this distinction seems to refer to an uxorilocal and an autonomous son-in-law respectively), *tʃe:empë* (T. *jeetï*, MB, etc. – direct address).

Notes

1. Cf. Radcliffe-Brown 1940.

REFERENCES

Ahlbrinck, W. 1956. *Op Zoek naar de Indianen: Verslag van een Expeditie naar de Zuidgrens van Suriname ter Opsporing en Bestudering van Twee Onbekende Indianenstammen: de Wama's en de Wajarikoele's*. Mededeling No. CXVIII, Amsterdam: Koninklijk Instituut voor de Tropen.

Aleman, S. 2011. 'From Flutes to Boom Boxes: Musical Symbolism and Change among the Waiwai of Southern Guyana.' In J. Hill and J.-P. Chaumeil (eds), *Burst of Breath: Indigenous Ritual Wind Instruments in Lowland South America*. Lincoln: University of Nebraska Press, pp. 219–38.

Amazon Conservation Team. 2010. 'Support to the Traditional Authority Structure of Indigenous Peoples and Maroons in Suriname.' Final Draft Report.

Arvelo Jiménez, N. 1973. *The Dynamics of the Ye'cuana (Maquiritare) Political System: Stability and Crises*. Copenhagen: IWGIA.

Asch, M. 2005. 'Lévi-Strauss and the Political: The Elementary Structures of Kinship and the Resolution of Relations between Indigenous Peoples and Settler States.' *Journal of the Royal Anthropological Institute* 11(3): 425–44.

Barbosa, G. 2002. 'Formas de Intercâmbio, Circulação de Bens e a (Re)Produção das Redes de Relações Apalai e Wayana.' Masters dissertation, University of São Paolo.

Beaudet, J.-M. 1997. *Souffles d'Amazonie: Les Orchestres Tule des Wayãpi*. Paris: Société d'Ethnologie.

Beier, C., L. Michael and J. Scherzer. 2002. 'Discourse Forms and Processes in Indigenous Lowland South America: An Areal-Typological Perspective.' *Annual Review of Anthropology* 31: 121–45.

Blacking, J. 1974. *How Musical is Man*. Seattle: University of Washington Press.

Bloch, M. 1989. 'Symbols, Song, Dance and Features of Articulation: Is Religion an Extreme Form of Religious Authority?' In *Ritual, History and Power: Selected Papers in Anthropology*. London: Athlone, pp. 19–45.

———. 1995. 'The Resurrection of the House amongst the Zafimaniry of Madagascar.' In J. Carsten and S. Hugh-Jones (eds), *About the House: Lévi-Strauss and Beyond*. Cambridge: Cambridge University Press, pp. 69–83.

Boyer, P. 2001. *Et l'Homme créa les Dieux. Comment Expliquer la Religion*. Paris: Robert Laffont.

Brightman, M. 2008a. 'Strategic Ethnicity on the Global Stage: Perspectives on the Indigenous Peoples Movement from the Central Guianas to the United Nations.' *Bulletin de la Société Suisse des Américanistes* 70: 21–29.

———. 2008b. 'Plants, Property and Trade among the Trio and Wayana of Southern Suriname.' In M. Lenaerts and A.-M. Spadafora (eds), *Pueblos Indigenas, Plantas y Mercados, Amazonia y Gran Chaco*. Bucharest: Zeta, pp. 153–68.

———. 2010. 'Creativity and Control: Property in Guianese Amazonia.' *Journal de la Société des Américanistes* 96(1): 135–67.

———. 2011. 'Archetypal Agents of Affinity: "Sacred" Flutes in the Guianas.' In J.-P. Chaumeil and J. Hill (eds), *Burst of Breath: Indigenous Ritual Wind Instruments in Lowland South America*. Lincoln: University of Nebraska Press.

———. 2012. 'Maps and Clocks in Amazonia: The Things of Conversion and Conservation.' *Journal of the Royal Anthropological Institute* 18(3): 554–71.

Brightman, M., and V. Grotti 2010. 'The Other's Other: Nurturing the Bodies of "Wild" People Among the Trio of Southern Suriname.' *Etnofoor* 22(2): 51–70.

———. 2012. 'Humanity, Personhood and Transformability.' In M. Brightman, V. Grotti and O. Ulturgasheva (eds), *Animism in Rainforest and Tundra: Personhood, Animals and Non-Humans in Contemporary Amazonia and Siberia*. New York and Oxford: Berghahn Books, pp. 162–74.

———. 2016. 'First Contacts, Slavery and Kinship in Native Amazonia.' In M. Brightman, C. Fausto and V. Grotti (eds), *Ownership and Nurture: Studies in Native Amazonian Property Relations*. New York and Oxford: Berghahn Books, pp. 63–80.

Brightman, M., V. Grotti and O. Ulturgasheva (eds). 2006/7 *Cambridge Anthropology* 26(2), Special Issue, *Rethinking the 'Frontier' in Amazonia and Siberia: Extractive Economies, Indigenous Politics and Social Transformations*.

———. 2012. 'Introduction: Shamanism, Ecology and Invisible Worlds: the Place of Non-Humans in Indigenous Ontologies.' In M. Brightman, V. Grotti and O. Ulturgasheva (eds), *Animism in Rainforest and Tundra: Personhood, Animals and Non-Humans in Contemporary Amazonia and Siberia*. New York and Oxford: Berghahn Books, pp. 1–27.

Brightman, M, C. Fausto and V. Grotti (eds). 2016. *Ownership and Nurture: Studies in Native Amazonian Property Relations*. New York and Oxford: Berghahn Books.

Butt, A. 1965. 'The Shaman's Legal Role.' *Revista do Museu Paulista* N.S. 16: 151–86.

Butt Colson, A. 1973. 'Inter-Tribal Trade in the Guiana Highlands.' *Antropológica* 34: 5–70.

———. 1985. 'Routes of Knowledge: An Aspect of Regional Integration in the Circum-Roraima Area of the Guiana Highlands.' *Antropológica* 63–64: 103–49.

Campbell, A. 1989. *To Square with Genesis: Causal Statements and Shamanic Ideas in Wayãpi*. Edinburgh: Edinburgh University Press.

Carlin, E. 2004. *A Grammar of Trio: A Cariban Language of Suriname*. Frankfurt: Peter Lang.

Carsten, J. 1995. 'Houses in Langkawi: Stable Structures or Mobile Homes?' In J. Carsten and S. Hugh-Jones (eds), *About the House: Lévi-Strauss and Beyond*. Cambridge: Cambridge University Press, pp. 105–28.

Chagnon, N. 1974. *Studying the Yanomamö*. New York: Holt, Rinehart & Winston.

Chang, K. 1989. 'Ancient China and its Anthropological Significance.' In C. Lamberg-Karlovsky (ed.), *Archaeological Thoughts in America*. Cambridge: Cambridge University Press, pp. 155–66.

Chapuis, J. 1998. 'La Personne Wayana entre Sang et Ciel.' PhD dissertation, University of Aix-Marseille.

Chapuis, J., and H. Rivière. 2003. *Wayana Eitoponpë: (Une) Histoire (Orale) des Indiens Wayana*. Paris: Ibis Rouge.

Chaumeil, J.-P. 1983. *Voir, Savoir, Pouvoir*. Paris: Éditions de l'Ecole des Hautes Études en Sciences Sociales.

———. 2001. 'The Blowpipe Indians: Variations on the Theme of Blowpipe and Tube among the Yagua Indians of the Peruvian Amazon.' In L. Rival and N. Whitehead (eds), *Beyond the Visible and the Material: The Amerindianization of Society in the work of Peter Rivière*. Oxford: Oxford University Press, pp. 81–100.

Chernela, J. 2001. 'Piercing Distinctions: Making and Remaking the Social Contract in the North-West Amazon.' In L. Rival and N. Whitehead (eds), *Beyond the Visible and the Material: The Amerindianization of Society in the work of Peter Rivière*. Oxford: Oxford University Press, pp. 177–96.

Clastres, P. 1974. *La Société Contre l'État*. Paris: Les Éditions de Minuit.

———. 1997 [1977]. *Archaeologie de la Violence: La Guerre dans les Sociétés Primitives*. La Tour d'Aigues: Éditions de l'Aube.

———. 2010. *Archaeology of Violence*, trans. J. Herman. Cambridge: Semiotext(e).

Cleary, D. 1990. *Anatomy of the Amazon Gold Rush*. Iowa City: University of Iowa Press.

Cognat, A., and C. Massot. 1977. *Antécume ou Une Autre Vie*. Paris: Laffont.

Collier, J., and M. Rosaldo. 1981. 'Politics and Gender in Simple Societies.' In S. Ortner and H. Whitehead (eds), *Sexual Meanings*. Cambridge: Cambridge University Press, pp. 275–329.

Conley, J. F. 2000. *Drumbeats that Changed the World: A History of the Regions Beyond Missionary Union and the West Indies Mission*. Pasadena: William Carey Library.

Cortez, R. 1977. '"Diaconato" Indígena: Articulação Étnica no Reconcavo do Tumucumaque Brasileiro.' Masters dissertation, Museu Nacional, Universidade Federal.

Costa, L. 2000. 'Modelos do Presente, Narrativa do Passado: Por uma antropologia histórica na Guianas.' Masters dissertation, Museu Nacional, Universidade Federal.

Coudreau, H. 1887a. *La France Equinoxiale*. Paris: Challamel.

———. 1887b. 'Guyane Française' (map). In *La France Equinoxiale*. Paris: Challamel.

———. 1887c. 'Carte des Sources des Rivières Takutu, Mapouerre, Trombetta, Essequibo, etc. Levée par H.A. Coudreau 1884–85' (map). In *La France Equinoxiale*. Paris: Challamel.

Crevaux, J. 1993. *Le Mendiant de l'Eldorado: De Cayenne aux Andes (1876–1879)*. Paris: Payot.

Darbois, D. 1956. *Yanamale, Village of the Amazon*. London: Collins.

DeFilipps, R., S. Maina and J. Crepin. N.d. *Medicinal Plants of Guiana (Guyana, Surinam, French Guiana)*. http:// www.mnh.si.edu/ biodiversity/ bdg/ medicinal/ (accessed 20 March 2006).

Descola, P. 1988. 'La Chefferie Amérindienne Dans l'Anthropologie Politique.' *Revue Française de Science Politique* 38(5): 818–27.

———. 1993. *Les Lances du Crépuscule: Relations Jivaros, Haute Amazonie*. Paris: Plon.

———. 2001. 'The Genres of Gender: Local Models and Global Paradigms in the Comparison of Amazonia and Melanesia.' In T. Gregor and D. Tuzin (eds), *Gender in Amazonia and Melanesia: An Exploration of the Comparative Method*. Berkeley: University of California Press.

———. 2005. *Par-Delà Nature et Culture*. Paris: Gallimard.

Détienne, M., and J. Vernant. 1974. *Les Ruses de l'Intelligence: La Mètis des Grecs*. Paris: Flammarion.

Dowdy, H. E. 1963. *Christ's Witchdoctor: From Savage Sorcerer to Jungle Missionary*. New York: Harper & Row.

Dreyfus, S. 1980. 'Notes sur la Chefferie Taino d'Aiti: Capacités Productrices, Resources Alimentaires, Pouvoirs dans une Société Précolombienne de la Forêt Tropicale.' *Journal de la Société des Américanistes* 67: 229–48.

———. 1982. 'The Relationships between Political Systems, History, Linguistic Affiliation and Ethnic Identity, as Exemplified by XVIth to XVIIIth Centuries Social Organisation of the So-Called "Island Caribs" (Arawak-speaking) and "True-speaking Caribs" of the Mainland Coast.' Paper presented at the 44th International Congress of Americanists, Manchester.

———. 1992. 'Les Réseaux Politiques Indigènes en Guyane Occidentale et leurs Transformations aux XVIIe et XVIIIe Siècles.' *L'Homme* 122–24: 75–98.

Drucker-Brown, S. 2001. 'House and Hierarchy: Politics and Domestic Space in Northern Ghana.' *Journal of the Royal Anthropological Institute* 7: 669–85.

Dumont, L. 1980. *Homo Hierarchicus: The Caste System and Its Implications*. Chicago: University of Chicago.

———. 1983. *Affinity as a Value*. Chicago: University of Chicago.

Durkheim, E. 2001 [1912]. *The Elementary Forms of Religious Life*. Oxford: Oxford University Press.

Durkheim, E., and M. Mauss. 1968 [1903]. 'De Quelques Formes Primitives de Classification: Contribution à l'Étude des Représentations Collectives.' In M. Mauss, *Oeuvres 2: Représentations Collectives et Diversité des Civilisations*. Paris: Les Éditions de Minuit, pp. 13–89.

Erikson, P. 2000. 'Dialogues à Vif ... Notes sur les Salutations en Amazonie.' In A. Monod Becquelin and P. Erikson (eds), *Les Rituels du Dialogue: Promenades Ethnolinguistiques en Terres Amérindiennes*. Paris: Nanterre, Société d'Ethnologie, pp. 115–38.

———. 2001. 'Myth and Material Culture: Matis Blowguns, Palm Trees, and Ancestor Spirits.' In L. Rival and N. Whitehead (eds), *Beyond the Visible and the Material: The Amerindianization of Society in the Work of Peter Rivière*. Oxford: Oxford University Press, pp. 101–21.

Erikson, P., and F. Santos Granero. 1988. "Politics in Amazonia. Correspondence." *Man* (N.S.) 23: 164–67.

Farabee, W. C. 1924. *The Central Caribs*. Philadelphia: University of Pennsylvania Museum.

Fardon, R. 1985. *Power and Knowledge: Anthropological and Sociological Approaches*. Edinburgh: Scottish Academic Press.

Fausto, C. 1991. 'Os Parakanã: Casamento Avuncular e Dravidianato na Amazônia.' Masters dissertation, Museu Nacional, Universidade Federal.

———. 1995. 'De Primos e Sobrinhas: Terminologia e Aliança entre os Parakanã (Tupi) do Pará.' In E. Viveiros de Castro (ed.), *Antropologia do Parentesco: Estudos Ameríndios*. Rio de Janeiro: Editora UFRJ.

———. 1999. 'Of Enemies and Pets: Warfare and Shamanism in Amazonia.' *American Ethnologist* 26(4): 933–56.

———. 2001. *Inimigos Fiéis. História, Guerra e Xamanismo na Amazônia*. São Paulo: Editora da Universidade de São Paulo.

———. 2007. 'Feasting on People: Eating Animals and Humans in Amazonia.' *Current Anthropology* 48(4): 497–530.

———. 2008. 'Donos Demais: Maestria e Domínio na Amazônia.' *Mana* 14(2): pp. 329–66.

———. 2012. 'Too Many Owners: Mastery and Ownership in Amazonia.' In M. Brightman, V. Grotti and O. Ulturgasheva (eds), *Animism in Rainforest and Tundra: Personhood, Animals and Non-Humans in Contemporary Amazonia and Siberia*. New York and Oxford: Berghahn Books, pp. 29–47.

Filoche, G. 2011. 'Formaliser l'Informel, Capter l'Évanescent? Juridicisation des Normes Indigenes et Gestion de l'Environnement en Amerique du Sud.' In C. Gros and D. Dumoulin (eds), *Le Multiculturalisme 'Au Concret'. Un Modèle Latino-Américain?* Paris: Presses Sorbonne Nouvelle, pp. 199-211.

Fock, Niels 1963. *Waiwai: Religion and Society of an Amazonian Tribe*. Copenhagen: National Museum.

Foucault, M. 1975. *Surveiller et Punir: Naissance de la Prison*. Paris: Gallimard.

Freire, G. 2002. 'The Piaroa: Environment and Society in Transition.' DPhil dissertation, Oxford University.

Frikel, P. 1960. 'Os Tiriyó (Notas Preliminares).' In *Boletim do Museu Paraense Emilio Goeldi (N.S.) Antropologia*, no. 9, pp. 1–19.

———. 1964. 'Das Problem der Pianakoto-Tiriyó.' In *Beiträge zur Völkerkunde Südamerikas. Festgabe für Herbert Baldus. Völkerkundliche Abhandlungen*, pp. 97–104.

———. 1971. *Dez Anos de Aculturação Tiriyó, 1960–70. Mudanças e Problemas*. Belém: Publicações Avulsas do Museu Goeldi, no. 16.

———. 1973. *Os Tiriyó: Seu Sistema Adaptativo*. Hannover: Völkerkunde-Abteilung des Niedersächsischen Landesmuseums.

Frikel, P., and R. Cortez. 1972. *Elementos Demográficos do Alto Paru de Oeste, Tumucumque Brasileiro: Índios Ewarhoyána, Kaxúyana e Tiriyó*. Belém: Museu Paraense Emílio Goeldi (Publicações Avulsas, no. 19).

Gell, A. 1986. 'Style and meaning in Umeda dance.' In P. Spencer (ed.), *Society and the Dance*. Cambridge: Cambridge University Press, pp. 183–205.

Giddens, A. 1984. *The Constitution of Society*. Berkeley: University of California Press.

Gillespie, S. 2000. 'Beyond Kinship: An Introduction.' In R. Joyce and S. Gillespie (eds), *Beyond Kinship: Social and Material Reproduction in House Societies*. Philadelphia: University of Pennsylvania, pp. 1–21.

Goldman, I. 1963. *The Cubeo: Indians of the Northwest Amazon*. Urbana: University of Illinois Press.

Goody, J. (ed.). 1958. *The Developmental Cycle in Domestic Groups*. Cambridge: Cambridge University Press.

Gordon, C. 2006. *Economia Selvagem: Ritual e Mercadoria entre os Índios Xikrin-Mebêngôkre*. São Paolo: UNESP.

Grotti, V. 2007. 'Nurturing the Other: Well-being, Social Body and Transformation in Northeastern Amazonia.' PhD dissertation, Cambridge University.

———. 2009a. 'Un Corps en Mouvement: Parenté, Diffusion de l'Influence et Transformations Corporelles dans les Fêtes de Bière Tirio, Amazonie du nord-est.' *Journal de la Société des Américanistes* 95(1): 73–96.

———. 2009b. 'Protestant Evangelism and the Transformability of Amerindian Bodies in Northern Amazonia.' In A. Vilaça and R. Wright (eds), *Native Christians: Modes and Effects of Christianity among Indigenous Peoples of the Americas*. London: Ashgate, pp. 109–25.

———. 2010. 'Incorporating the Akuriyo: Contact Expeditions and Interethnic Relations in Southern Suriname.' *Tijdschrift voor Surinamistiek en het Caraïbisch Gebied* 29(2): 284–99.

Grupioni, D. Fajardo. N.d. 'Espaço e Tempo no Sistema de Relações Tarëno.' Manuscript for contribution to *Sociedades Indígenas e suas Fronteiras na região Sudeste das Guianas*.

———. 2002. 'Sistema e mundo da vida Tarëno: um 'jardim de veredas que se bifurcam' na paisagem Guianesa.' PhD dissertation, Universidade de São Paolo.

———. 2005. 'Tempo e espaço na Guiana indígena.' In D. Gallois (ed.), *Redes de relações nas Guianas*. São Paolo: Humanitas, pp. 23–58.

Gow, P. 2001. *An Amazonian Myth and its History*. Oxford: Oxford University Press.

Guss, D. 1989. *To Weave and Sing: Art, Symbol and Narrative in the South American Rainforest*. Berkeley: University of California Press.

Habermas, J. 1989[1962]. *The Structural Transformation of the Public Sphere: An Inquiry into a Category of Bourgeois Society*. (trans. T. Burger). Cambridge: MIT Press.

Hann, C. 1998. *Property Relations: Renewing the Anthropological Tradition*. Cambridge: Cambridge University Press.

Harcourt, R. 1928. *A Relation of a Voyage to Guiana by Robert Harcourt 1613. With Purchas's Transcript of a Report made at Harcourt's instance on the Marrawini District*, C. A. Harris (ed.). London: Hakluyt Society.

Heckenberger, M. 2005. *The Ecology of Power: Culture, Place and Personhood in the Southern Amazon, A.D. 1000–2000*. Abingdon: Routledge.

Heemskerk, M. 2001. 'Maroon gold miners and mining risks in the Suriname Amazon.' *Cultural Survival* 25(1): 25–29.

Helms, M. 1988. *Ulysses' Sail: An Ethnographic Odyssey of Power, Knowledge, and Geographical Distance*. Princeton, NJ: Princeton University Press.

———. 1993. *Craft and the Kingly Ideal: Art, Trade and Power*. Austin: University of Texas.

———. 1998. *Access to Origins: Affines, Ancestors and Aristocrats*. Austin: University of Texas.

Hemming, J. 2003. *Die If You Must: Brazilian Indians in the Twentieth Century*. London: Macmillan.

Henley, P. 1982. *The Panare: Tradition and Change on the Amazonian Frontier*. London: Yale University Press.

———. 1996. *South Indian Models in the Amazonian Lowlands*. Manchester Papers in Social Anthropology 1. Manchester: University of Manchester Press.

———. 2001. 'Inside and Out: Alterity and the Ceremonial Construction of the Person in Guiana.' In L. Rival and N. Whitehead (eds), *Beyond the Visible and the Material: The Amerindianization of Society in the work of Peter Rivière*. Oxford: Oxford University Press, pp. 197–220.

High, C. 2010. 'Warriors, Hunters, and Bruce Lee: Gendered Agency and the Transformation of Amazonian Masculinity.' *American Ethnologist* 37(4): 753–70.

Hill, J. (ed.). 1996. *History, Power and Identity: Ethnogenesis in the Americas, 1492–1992*. Iowa City: University of Iowa Press.

———. 2001. 'The Variety of Fertility Cultism in Amazonia: A Closer Look at Gender Symbolism in Northwestern Amazonia.' In T. Gregor and D. Tuzin (eds), *Gender in Amazonia and Melanesia: An Exploration of the Comparative Method*. Berkeley: University of California Press, pp. 45–68.

———. 2011. 'Soundscaping the World: The Cultural Poetics of Power and Meaning in Wakuénai Flute Music.' In J. Hill and J.-P. Chaumeil (eds), *Burst of Breath: Indigenous Ritual Wind Instruments in Lowland South America*. Lincoln: University of Nebraska Press, pp. 93–122.

Hill, J., and J.-P. Chaumeil. 2011. *Burst of Breath: Indigenous Ritual Wind Instruments in Lowland South America*. Lincoln: University of Nebraska Press.

Hirsch, E., and M. Strathern (eds). 2004. *Transactions and Creations: Property Debates and the Stimulus of Melanesia*. Oxford: Berg.

Hobbes, T. 1996 [1651]. *Leviathan*. Cambridge: Cambridge University Press.

Holbraad, M. 2005. 'Expending Multiplicity: Money in Cuban Ifá cults.' *Journal of the Royal Anthropological Institute* 11(2): 231–54.

Hoskins, J. 1998. *Biographical Objects: How Things Tell the Stories of Peoples' Lives*. London: Routledge.

Howard, C. 2001. 'Wrought Identities: The Waiwai Expeditions in Search of the "Unseen Tribes".' PhD dissertation, University of Chicago.

Howell, S. 'The Lio House: Building, Category, Idea, Value.' In J. Carsten and S. Hugh-Jones (eds), *About the House: Lévi-Strauss and Beyond*. Cambridge: Cambridge University Press, pp. 149–69.

Hugh-Jones, S. 1979. *The Palm and the Pleiades: Initiation and Cosmology in Northwest Amazonia*. Cambridge: Cambridge University Press.

———. 1992. 'Yesterday's Luxuries, Tomorrow's Necessities: Business and Barter in Northwest Amazonia.' In C. Humphrey and S. Hugh-Jones (eds), *Barter, Exchange and Value: An Anthropological Approach*. Cambridge: Cambridge University Press.

———. 1994. 'Shamans, Prophets, Priests and Pastors.' In C. Humphrey and N. Thomas (eds), *Shamanism, History and the State*. Ann Arbor: University of Michigan Press.

———. 1995. 'Inside-Out and Back-to-Front: The Androgynous House in Northwest Amazonia.' In J. Carsten and S. Hugh-Jones (eds), *About the House: Lévi-Strauss and Beyond*. Cambridge: Cambridge University Press, pp. 226–52.

———. 2001. 'The Gender of Some Amazonian Gifts: An Experiment with an Experiment.' In T. Gregor and D. Tuzin (eds), *Gender in Amazonia and Melanesia: An Exploration of the Comparative Method*. Berkeley: University of California Press, pp. 245–78.

———. 2003. 'Brideservice and the Absent Gift: Questioning Received Truths in Amazonia.' Paper presented at Manchester University, 28 April.

Hurault, J. 1968. *Les Wayana de la Guyane Française. Structure Sociale et Coutume Familiale*. Paris: ORSTOM.

———. 1972. *Français et Indiens en Guyane*. Paris: Union Générale d'Editions.

Ibsen, H. 1936. *Peer Gynt: A Dramatic Poem*, trans. R. Farquharson Sharp. Edinburgh: J. M. Dent.

Ingold, T. 2000. 'Building, Dwelling, Living: How Animals and People Make Themselves at Home in the World.' In *The Perception of the Environment: Essays in Livelihood, Dwelling and Skill*. London: Routledge.

Jara, F. 1990. *El Camino del Kumu. Ecología y Rituál entre los Akuriyó de Surinam*. Utrecht: ISOR.

Kaeppler, A. 1986. 'Structured Movement Systems in Tonga.' In P. Spencer (ed.), *Society and the Dance*. Cambridge: Cambridge University Press, pp. 92–118.

———. 2000. 'Dance Ethnology and the Anthropology of Dance.' In *Dance Research Journal* 32(1): 116–25.

Kambel, E.-R., and F. MacKay. 1999. *The Rights of Indigenous Peoples and Maroons in Suriname*. Copenhagen: IWGIA Document No. 96.

Keifenheim, B. 1997. 'Futurs Beaux-Frères ou Esclaves? Les Kashinawa Découvrent des Indiens Non Contactés.' *Journal de la Société des Américanistes* 83: 141–58.

Kelly, J. A. 2003. 'Relations within the Health System among the Yanomami in the Upper Orinoco, Venezuela.' PhD dissertation, Cambridge University.

Koelewijn, C. (ed.). 1984. *Tarëno Tamu Inponopï Panpira* (2 vols). Leusden: Algemeen Diakonaal Bureau.

Koelewijn, C., and P. Rivière. 1987. *Oral Literature of the Trio Indians of Surinam*. Dordrecht: Foris.

Kracke, W. 1978. *Force and Persuasion: Leadership in an Amazonian Society*. Chicago: University of Chicago.

——— (ed.). 1993. *Leadership in Lowland South America*. Special edition of *South American Indian Studies* 1.

Kuper, A. 1982. 'Lineage Theory: A Critical Retrospect.' *Annual Review of Anthropology* 11: 71–95.

Lapointe, J. 1971. 'Residence Patterns and Wayana Social Organization.' PhD dissertation, Columbia University.

Latour, B. 1997. Nous N'Avons Jamais Été Modernes: Essai d'Anthropologie Symétrique. Paris: La Découverte.

Lavie, S., K. Narayan and R. Rosaldo. 1993. 'Introduction: Creativity in Anthropology.' In S. Lavie, K. Narayan and R. Rosaldo (eds), Creativity/Anthropology. Ithaca, NY: Cornell University Press, pp. 1–8.

Lea, V. 1995. 'The Houses of the Mebengokre (Kayapó) of Central Brazil – a New Door to their Social Organization.' In J. Carsten and S. Hugh-Jones (eds), About the House: Lévi-Strauss and Beyond. Cambridge: Cambridge University Press, pp. 206–25.

Leach, E. 1966. 'Rethinking Anthropology.' In Rethinking Anthropology. New York: Athlone, pp. 1–27.

Leach, J. 2004. 'Modes of Creativity.' In E. Hirsch and M. Strathern (eds), Transactions and Creations: Property Debates and the Stimulus of Melanesia. Oxford: Berg, pp. 151–75.

Leavitt, C. 2004 [1979]. Kan Panpira Kainan Ehtëto Awënton: The New Testament for the Trio Indians of Suriname and Brazil, South America. Bala Cynwyd, PA: UFM International.

Lepri, I. 2005. 'The Meanings of Kinship among the Ese Ejja of Northern Bolivia.' Journal of the Royal Anthropological Institute 11: 703–24.

Lévi-Strauss, C. 1943. 'Guerre et Commerce chez les Indiens de l'Amérique du Sud.' Renaissance 1: 122–39.

———. 1944a. 'The Social and Psychological Aspect of Chieftainship in a Primitive Tribe: the Nambikuara of Northwestern Mato Grosso.' Transactions of the New York Academy of Science 7: 16–32.

———. 1944b. 'Reciprocity and Hierarchy.' American Anthropologist 46: 266–68.

———. 1956. 'Les Organisations Dualistes, Existent-Elles?' Bijdragen tot de Taal-, Land-, en Volkenkunde 112: 99–128.

———. 1958. 'L'Analyse Structurale en Linguistique et en Anthropologie.' In Anthropologie Structurale. Paris: Plon, pp. 43–69.

———. 1964. Le Cru et le Cuit. Paris: Plon.

———. 1971. L'Homme Nu. Paris: Plon.

———. 1983. The Way of the Masks, trans. S. Modelski. London: Jonathan Cape.

———. 1985. La Potière Jalouse. Paris: Plon.

———. 1987. Anthropology and Myth: Lectures 1951–1982, trans. R. Willis. Oxford: Blackwell.

———. 1991. Histoire de Lynx. Paris: Plon.

Lizot, J. 2000. 'De l'Interprétation des Dialogues.' In A. Monod Becquelin and P. Erikson (eds), Les Rituels du Dialogue: Promenades Ethnolinguistiques en Terres Amérindiennes. Paris: Nanterre, Société d'ethnologie, pp. 165–82.

Lima, T. Stulze, and M. Goldman. 2001. 'Pierre Clastres, Etnólogo da América.' Sexta-Feira 6: 291–309.

Locke, J. 1988 [1698]. Two Treatises of Government. Cambridge: Cambridge University Press.

Lorimer, J. 1994. 'The Reluctant Go-Between: John Ley's Survey of Aboriginal Settlement on the Guiana Coastline.' In C. Clough and P. Hair (eds), The European Outthrust and Encounter. Liverpool: Liverpool University Press, pp. 191–223.

Lorrain, C. 2000. 'Cosmic Reproduction, Economics and Politics among the Kulina of Southwest Amazonia.' Journal of the Royal Anthropological Institute 6: 293–310.

Machiavelli, N. 1994. Il Principe. Milan: Mondadori.

MacMillan, G. 1995. *At the End of the Rainbow? Gold, Land and People in the Brazilian Amazon.* New York: Columbia University Press.

Maybury-Lewis, D. 1967. *Akwë-Shavante Society.* Oxford: Oxford University Press.

Mauss, M. 2001 [1922]. *The Gift: The Form and Reason of Exchange in Archaic Societies,* trans. W. Halls. London: Routledge.

McCallum, C. 2001. *Gender and Sociality in Amazonia: How Real People are Made.* Oxford: Berg.

Meira, S. 1999. 'A Grammar of Tiriyó.' PhD dissertation, Rice University.

McEwan, C. 2001. 'Seats of Power: Axiality and Access to Invisible Worlds.' In C. McEwan, C. Barreto and E. Neves (eds), *Unknown Amazon: Nature and Culture in Ancient Brazil.* London: British Museum Press, pp. 176–95.

Menget, P. 1993. 'Les Frontières de la Chefferie.' *L'Homme* 126–28: 59–76.

Menezes Bastos, R. 1978. *A Musicológica Kamayurá: Para uma Antropologia da Communicação no Alto Xingu.* Brasília: FUNAI.

Mentore, G. 1993.'Tempering the Social Self: Body Adornment, Vital Substance, and Knowledge among the Waiwai.' *Archaeology and Anthropology* 9: 22–34.

Meunier, F. (ed.). 2004. *Piranhas Enivrés: des Poissons et des Hommes en Guyane.* Paris: SFI/RMN.

Miller, D. 2005. 'Materiality: An Introduction.' In *Materiality.* Durham, NC: Duke.

Mithen, S. 2006. *The Singing Neanderthals: The Origins of Music, Language, Mind and Body.* London: Phoenix.

Mol, A., and J. Mans. 2013. 'Old-Boy Networks in the Indigenous Caribbean.' In C. Knappett (ed.), *Network Analysis in Archaeology: New Approaches to Regional Interaction.* Oxford: Oxford University Press.

Monod Becquelin, A., and P. Erikson (eds). 2000. *Les Rituels du Dialogue: Promenades Ethnolinguistiques en Terres Amérindiennes.* Paris: Nanterre, Société d'Ethnologie.

Montaigne, M. de 1969 [1580]. 'Des Cannibales.' *Essais,* vol. I. Paris: Gallimard, pp. 251–64.

Moore, H. 2013. *Feminism and Anthropology.* Cambridge: Polity.

Moutu, A. 2004. 'Names are Thicker than Blood: Concepts of Ownership and Person amongst the Iatmul.' PhD dissertation, Cambridge University.

———. 2012. *Names are Thicker than Blood: Kinship and Ownership amongst the Iatmul.* Oxford: Oxford University Press.

Nettl, B. 2005. *The Study of Ethnomusicology: Thirty-One Issues and Concepts.* Urbana: University of Illinois.

Overing, J. 1975. *The Piaroa: A People of the Orinoco Basin – A Study in Kinship and Marriage.* Oxford: Clarendon.

———. 1981. 'Review Article: Amazonian Anthropology.' *Journal of Latin American Studies* 13(1): 151–64.

———. 1986. 'Men Control Women? The Catch 22 in the Analysis of Gender.' *International Journal of Moral and Social Studies* 1(2): 135–56.

———. 1993a. 'I Saw the Sound of the Waterfall: Shamans, Gods and Leadership in Piaroa Society.' In W. Kracke (ed.), *Leadership in Lowland South America.* Special edition of *South American Indian Studies* 1, pp. 23–39.

———. 1993. 'Death and the Loss of Civilized Predation among the Piaroa.' *L'Homme* 126–28: 191–211.

Overing, J., and A. Passes. 2000. 'Introduction.' In J. Overing and A. Passes (eds), *The Anthropology of Love and Anger: The Aesthetics of Conviviality in Native Amazonia.* London: Routledge, pp. 1–30.

Pakosie, A. 1996. 'Maroon Leadership and the Surinamese State (1760–1990).' *Journal of Legal Pluralism* 37–38: 263–78.

Parry, J., and M. Bloch. 1989. *Money and the Morality of Exchange*. Cambridge: Cambridge University Press.

Perrone-Moisés, B. 2006. 'Notas Sobre uma Certa Confederação Guianense.' Paper delivered at Colóquio Guiana Ameríndia Historia e Etnologia Indígena, Belém, 31 October.

Perrone-Moisés, B., and R. Sztutman. 2010. 'Notícias de uma Certa Confederação Tamoio.' *Mana* 16(2): 401–33.

Plumwood, V. 2006. 'Feminism.' In A. Dobson and R. Eckersley (eds), *Political Theory and the Ecological Challenge*. Cambridge: Cambridge University Press, pp. 51–74.

Price, R. 1976. *The Guiana Maroons: A Historical and Bibliographical Introduction*. Baltimore, MD: Johns Hopkins University Press.

Rivière, H. 1994. 'Les Instruments de Musique des Indiens Wayana du Litani (Surinam, Guyane française).' *Anthropos* 89: 51–60.

Rivière, P. 1969. *Marriage Among the Trio*. Oxford: Clarendon.

———. 1970. 'Factions and Exclusions in Two South American Village Systems.' In M. Douglas (ed.), *Witchcraft Confessions and Accusations*. London: Tavistock, pp. 245–55.

———. 1971. 'The Political Structure of the Trio Indians as Manifested in a System of Ceremonial Dialogue.' In T. O. Beidelman (ed.), *The Translation of Culture*. London: Tavistock, pp. 293–311.

———. 1977. 'Some problems in the Comparative Study of Carib Societies.' In E. Basso (ed.), *Carib-Speaking Indians: Culture, Society and Language*. Anthropological Papers of the University of Arizona No. 28. Tucson: Arizona University Press, pp. 39–41.

———. 1981. '"The Wages of Sin is Death": Some Aspects of Evangelisation among the Trio Indians.' *Journal of the Anthropological Society of Oxford* 12: 1–13.

———. 1983–84. 'Aspects of Carib political economy.' *Antropológica* 59–62: 349–58.

———. 1984. *Individual and Society in Guiana*. Cambridge: Cambridge University Press.

———. 1994. 'WYSINWYG in Amazonia.' *Journal of the Anthropological Society of Oxford* 25: 255–62.

———. 1995. 'Houses, Places and People: Community and Continuity in Guiana.' In J. Carsten and S. Hugh-Jones (eds), *About the House: Lévi-Strauss and Beyond*. Cambridge: University Press, pp. 189–205.

———. 1997. 'Carib Soul Matters – Since Fock.' *Journal of the Anthropological Society of Oxford* 28: 139–48.

———. 2000. 'The More We Are Together. …' In J. Overing and A. Passes (eds), *The Anthropology of Love and Anger: The Aesthetics of Conviviality in Native Amazonia*. London: Routledge, pp. 252–67.

———. 2001. 'A Predação, a Reciprocidade e o Caso das Guianas.' *Mana* 7(1): 31–53.

Roosevelt, A. 1993. 'The Rise and Fall of the Amazonian Chiefdoms.' *L'Homme* 126–28, XXXIII(2–4): 255–83.

Rousseau, J.-J. 1992 [1754]. *Discours sur l'Origine et les Fondements de l'Inégalité Parmi les Hommes*. Paris: Flammarion.

Russell, B. 2004 [1938]. *Power: A New Social Analysis*. London: Routledge.

Sahlins, M. 1985. *Islands of History*. Chicago: Chicago University Press.

Salivas, P. 2010. *Musiques Jivaro. Une Esthétique de l'Hétérogène*. Sarrebrücken: Editions Universitaires Européenes.

Sanders, E. 2006. 'Hocket', ed. L. Macy. *Grove Music Online*, http://www.grovemusic.com (accessed 11 April 2006).

Santos Granero, F. 1986. 'Power, Ideology, and the Ritual of Production in Lowland South America.' *Man, n.s.* 21: 657–79.

———. 1991. *The Power of Love*. London: Athlone.

———. 1993. 'From Prisoner of the Group to Darling of the Gods: An Approach to the Issue of Power in Lowland South America.' *L'Homme 126–28*.

———. 2007. 'Of Fear and Friendship: Amazonian Sociality Beyond Kinship and Affinity.' *Journal of the Royal Anthropological Institute* 13: 1–18.

———. 2009. *Vital Enemies: Slavery, Predation and the Amerindian Political Economy of Life*. Austin: University of Texas Press.

Schoen, I. N. d. 'Report on the Second Contact with the Akurio (Wama) Stone Axe Tribe, Surinam, September 1968.' Unpublished manuscript.

———. 1971. 'Report of the Emergency Trip Made by the West Indies Mission to the Akoerio Indians June 1971.' Smithsonian Institution Center for Short-Lived Phenomena.

Schoen, I., and W. H. Crocke. N.d. 'Notes from Two Telephone Conversations between Ivan L. Schoen and William H. Crocker.' Unpublished manuscript.

Schoepf, D. 1998. 'Le domaine des Colibris: Accueil et Hospitalité chez les Wayana (Region des Guyanes).' *Journal de la Société des Américanistes* 84(1): 99–120.

Schomburgk, R. H. 1845. 'Journal of an Expedition from Pirara to the Upper Corentyne, and from thence to Demarara.' *Journal of the Royal Geographical Society of London* 15: 1–104.

Schopenhauer, A. 1966 [1818]. *The World as Will and Representation*, vol. I, trans. E. Payne. New York: Dover.

Schultz-Kampfhenkel, O. 1940. *Riddle of Hell's Jungle: Expedition to Unexplored Primeval Forests of the River Amazon*. London: Hurst & Blackett.

Seeger, A. 1981. *Nature and Society in Central Brazil: The Suya Indians of Central Brazil*. Cambridge, MA: Harvard University Press.

———. 1987. *Why Suyà Sing? A Musical Anthropology of an Amazonian People*. Cambridge: Cambridge University Press.

Seeger, A., R. Da Matta and E. Viveiros de Castro. 1979. 'A construção da Pessoa nas sociedades indígenas brasileiras.' *Boletim do Museu Nacional* 32: 2–19.

Silverwood-Cope, P. 1972. 'A Contribution to the Ethnography of the Colombian Maku.' PhD dissertation, Cambridge University.

Smith, A. 1978. *Lectures on Jurisprudence*, eds R. Meek, D. Raphael and P. Stein. Oxford: Clarendon Press.

Stedman, J. 1988 [1790]. *Narrative of a Five Years' Expedition against the Revolted Negroes of Surinam in Guiana*. Baltimore, MD: Johns Hopkins University Press.

Strang, V., and M. Busse (eds). 2011. *Ownership and Appropriation*. Oxford: Berg.

Strathern, M. 1972. *Women in Between: Female Roles in a Male World: Mount Hagen, New Guinea*. London: Seminar Press.

———. 1985. 'Kinship and economy: Constitutive Orders of a Provisional Kind.' *American Ethnologist* 12(2): 191–209.

———. 1991a. 'Introduction.' In M. Godelier and M. Strathern (eds), *Big Men and Great Men: Personifications of Power in Melanesia*. Cambridge: Cambridge University Press, pp. 1–4.

———. 1991b. 'One Man and Many Men.' In M. Godelier and M. Strathern (eds), *Big Men and Great Men: Personifications of Power in Melanesia*. Cambridge: Cambridge University Press, pp. 197–214.

———. 1996. 'Cutting the Network.' *Journal of the Royal Anthropological Institute* 2: 517–35.

———. 1999. 'Puzzles of Scale.' In *Property, Substance and Effect: Anthropological Essays on Persons and Things*. London: Athlone, pp. 204–28.

———. 2000. 'Environments Within: An Ethnographic Commentary on Scale.' In K. Flint and H. Morphy (eds), *Culture, Landscape, and the Environment: The Linacre Lectures 1997*. Oxford: Oxford University Press, pp. 44–71.

———. 2001a. 'Same-Sex and Cross-Sex Relations: Some Internal Comparisons.' In T. Gregor and D. Tuzin (eds), *Gender in Amazonia and Melanesia: An Exploration of the Comparative Method*. Berkeley: University of California Press, pp. 221–44.

———. 2001b. 'The Patent and the Malanggan.' *Theory, Culture & Society* 18(4): 1–26.

———. 2010. 'The Tangible and the Intangible: a Holistic Analysis.' In A. Iteanu (ed.), *La cohérence des sociétés: Mélanges en hommage à Daniel de Coppet*. Paris: Editions de la Maison des sciences de l'homme, pp. 53–82.

———. 2011. 'Sharing, Stealing and Borrowing Simultaneously.' In V. Strang and M. Busse (eds), *Ownership and Appropriation*. Oxford: Berg, pp. 23–42.

Sztutman, R. 2005. 'O Profeta e o Principal: A ação política ameríndia e seus personagens.' PhD dissertation, University of São Paolo.

Sullivan, L. 1988. *Icanchu's Drum: An Orientation to Meaning in South American Religions*. London: Macmillan.

Taylor, A.-C. 2000. 'Le sexe de la proie: Représentations jivaro du lien de parenté.' *L'Homme* 145–55: 309–34.

———. 2007. 'Sick of History: Contrasting Regimes of Historicity in the Upper Amazon.' Unpublished manuscript, for C. Fausto and M. Heckenberger (eds), *Time Matters: History, Memory and Identity in Amazonia*. Gainesville: University of Florida Press, pp. 133–68.

Thomas, D. 1982. *Order Without Government: The Society of the Pemon Indians of Venezuela*. Urbana: University of Illinois.

Turner, T. 1979. 'The Gê and Bororo Societies as Dialectical Systems.' In D. Maybury-Lewis (ed.), *Dialectical Societies: The Gê and Bororo of Central Brazil*. Cambridge: Harvard University Press.

———. 1984. 'Dual Opposition, Hierarchy and Value: Moiety Structure and Symbolic Polarity in Central Brazil and Elsewhere.' In J.-C. Galey (ed.), *Différences, valeurs, hiérarchie: Textes offerts à Louis Dumont*. Paris: Éditions de l'EHESS, pp. 335–70.

Urban, G. 1986. 'Ceremonial Dialogues in Native South America.' *American Anthropologist* 88: 371–86.

Van Velthem, L. 2001. 'The Woven Universe: Carib Basketry.' In C. McEwan, C. Barreto and E. Neves (eds), *Unknown Amazon: Culture and Nature in Ancient Brazil*. London: British Museum, pp. 198–213.

———. 2003. *O Belo é a Fera: A estética da produção e da predação entre os Wayana*. Lisbon: Museu Nacional de Etnologia.

Veiga, M. 1997. *Artisanal Gold Mining Activities in Suriname*. Vienna: UNIDO.

Verdery, K., and C. Humphrey (eds). 2004. *Property in Question: Value Transformation in the Global Economy*. Oxford: Berg.

Versteeg, A. 2003. *Suriname Voor Colombus*. Paramaribo: Stichting Surinaams Museum.

Verswijver, G. 1992. *The Club-Fighters of the Amazon: Warfare among the Kaiapo Indians of Central Brazil*. Gent: Rijksuniversiteit Gent.

Viegas, S. de Matos. 2007. *Terra Calada: Os Tupinambá na Mata Atlântica do Sul de Bahia*. Rio de Janeiro: 7Letras.

Vilaça, A. 2002. 'Making Kin out of Others in Amazonia.' *Journal of the Royal Anthropological Institute* 8: 347–65.

————. 2006. *Quem Somos Nós: os Wari' Encontram os Brancos*. Rio de Janeiro: Editora Universidade Federal.

————. 2010. *Strange Enemies: Indigenous Agency and Scenes of Encounters in Amazonia*. Durham, NC: Duke University Press.

Viveiros de Castro, E. 1993. 'Alguns Aspectos da Afinidade no Dravidianato Amazônico.' In E. Viveiros de Castro and M. Carneiro da Cunha (eds), *Amazônia: Etnologia e História Indígena*. São Paulo: Núcleo de História Indígena e do Indigenismo da USP: FAPESP.

————. 1996. 'Images of Nature and Society in Amazonian Ethnology.' *Annual Review of Anthropology* 25: 179–200.

————. 1998. 'Cosmological Deixis and Amerindian Perspectivism.' *Journal of the Royal Anthropological Institute* 4(3): 469–88.

————. 2001. 'GUT Feelings about Amazonia: Potential Affinity and the Construction of Sociality.' In L. Rival and N. Whitehead (eds), *Beyond the Visible and the Material: The Amerindianization of Society in the Work of Peter Rivière*. Oxford: Oxford University Press, pp. 19–44.

————. 2002. 'O Problema da Afinidade na Amazonia.' In *A Inconstância da Alma Selvagem*. São Paolo: Cosac & Naify, pp. 87–180.

————. 2010. 'Introduction: The Untimely, Again.' In Pierre Clastres, *The Anthropology of Violence*. Cambridge: Semiotext(e), pp. 9–51.

Viveiros de Castro, E., and C. Fausto. 1993. 'La Puissance et l'Acte: la Parenté dans les Basses Terres de l'Amérique du Sud.' *L'Homme* 126–28: 141–70.

Wagner, R. 1991. 'The Fractal Person.' In M. Godelier and M. Strathern (eds), *Big Men and Great Men: Personifications of Power in Melanesia*. Cambridge: Cambridge University Press, pp. 159–73.

Waterson, R. 'Houses and Hierarchies in Island Southeast Asia.' In J. Carsten and S. Hugh-Jones (eds), *About the House: Lévi-Strauss and Beyond*. Cambridge: Cambridge University Press, pp. 47–68.

Weiner, A. 1992. *Inalienable Possessions: The Paradox of Keeping-While-Giving*. Berkeley: University of California Press.

Whitehead, N. 1988. *Lords of the Tiger Spirit*. Dordrecht: Foris.

————. 1996. 'Ethnogenesis and Ethnocide in the European Occupation of Native Surinam, 1499–1681.' In J. Hill (ed.) *History, Power and Identity: Ethnogenesis in the Americas, 1492–1992*. Iowa City: University of Iowa Press, pp. 20–35.

Whitehead, N., and S. Alemán (eds). 2009. *Anthropologies of Guayana: Cultural Spaces in Northeastern Amazonia*. Tucson: University of Arizona Press.

Williams, D. 2003. *Prehistoric Guiana*. Kingston: Ian Randle.

Yde, J. 1965. *Material Culture of the Waiwái*. Copenhagen: National Museum.

Yohner, A. 1970a. 'Contact with a New Group of Akurijo Indians of Suriname.' Smithsonian Institution Center for Short-Lived Phenomena.

————. 1970b. 'Akurijo Indian Tribe Discovery (Wama Stone Axe Tribe Discovery).' Event 6-69, Index 910, Event information report: 6, Smithsonian Institution Center for Short-Lived Phenomena.

————. 1970c. 'Akurijo Indian Tribe Discovery.' Event 6-69, Index 910, Event information report: 7,8, Smithsonian Institution Center for Short-Lived Phenomena.

INDEX

Lightning Source UK Ltd.
Milton Keynes UK
UKHW021819290120
357801UK00016B/401